Personal Growth for Entrepreneurs

Your Time, Your Way

Roger Best

Copyright © 2024 by Roger Best

All rights reserved.

The content contained within this book may not be reproduced, duplicated, or transmitted without direct written permission from the author or the publisher.

Under no circumstances will any blame or legal responsibility be held against the publisher or author for any damages, reparation, or monetary loss due to the information contained within this book, either directly or indirectly.

Legal Notice: This book is copyright protected. It is only for personal use. You cannot amend, distribute, sell, use, quote or paraphrase any part, or the content within this book, without the consent of the author or publisher.

Disclaimer Notice: Please note the information contained within this document is for educational and entertainment purposes only. All effort has been executed to present accurate, up-to-date, reliable, complete information. No warranties of any kind are declared or implied. Readers acknowledge that the author is not engaged in the rendering of legal, financial, medical or professional advice. The content within this book has been derived from various sources. Please consult a licensed professional before attempting any techniques outline in this book.

By reading this document, the reader agrees that under no circumstances is the author responsible for any director or indirect losses incurred as a result of the use of the information contained within this document, including, but not limited to, errors, omissions, or inaccuracies.

Contents

Introduction	1
1. Breaking Free	3
2. Vision of Freedom	23
3. Uncovering the Myths of Hard Work and Burnout	51
4. Purpose-Driven Goals	91
5. Simplification Strategies	117
6. The Art of Saying No	147
7. Mindfulness and Meditation	169
8. Beyond Boundaries	199
9. Continuous Improvement	225
10. Sustaining Freedom	241
11. Embracing the Journey	267
12. About the Author	279

Introduction

IMAGINE THIS: YOU'RE A spirited entrepreneur bursting with energy, dreams, and big plans. You spot this shiny, intriguing wheel — what I once called *The Entrepreneurial Wheel*, but now we all know it as "The Hamster Wheel." With great enthusiasm, you jump on, full of excitement, thinking this is the path to achieving everything you've ever wanted.

At first, it feels like you're flying. The wheel spins faster, matching the rhythm of your heartbeat, and for a while, you believe you're making real progress. But soon, the thrill begins to fade. Days blur into nights, nights blur into days, and yet, no matter how fast you run, the scenery never changes.

You find yourself running harder, pushing faster, but you're still in the same place. Exhaustion creeps in, your legs ache, and stopping doesn't feel like an option. The fear of what might happen to your business if you slow down keeps you moving, even though each step feels heavier than the last. But what if I told you there's a way to slow down and still reach your goals? What if it didn't have to be this hard?

Meanwhile, life outside that wheel is moving on without you. The world is vibrant and full of opportunities, and freedom is just beyond the bars of that metaphorical cage. But you? You're stuck in the loop — powering your business with everything you have, as those initial dreams of flexibility, family time, fulfillment, pursuing personal passions, creative projects, traveling, or even just having a peaceful night's sleep slip further away.

The longer you stay on the wheel, the more those dreams drift out of reach. Every day you keep running, another opportunity passes you by, and the life you've always envisioned feels a little further away — but it doesn't have to be that way. Today is your chance to make a different choice: step off the wheel and reclaim what you've lost. And that's what this book is about.

In *From Hamster Wheel to Hammock: A Guide to Taking Back Your Day*, we talked about recognizing the wheel as the first step toward breaking free. Now, in *Personal Growth for Entrepreneurs: Your Time, Your Way*, we're going deeper. This book is part of the *Getting Your Day Back for Entrepreneurs* series, designed to help you not only step off the wheel but reclaim the time and lifestyle you've been chasing all along. This freedom isn't just about having more time; it's about rediscovering joy in your business, reconnecting with your vision, and building a life that energizes you every single day.

The key to your freedom has been in your pocket all along. Let's take it out together and unlock the life you truly deserve. It's time to step off the wheel and create a life on *your* terms, one that runs on *your* time, *your* way.

Chapter One

Breaking Free

Understanding the Hamster Wheel Trap

ENTREPRENEURSHIP, IN ITS RAWEST form, often mirrors the hamster wheel phenomenon. I've lived it, studied it, and consulted with countless entrepreneurs over the years, and the patterns are unmistakable.

You, the ambitious entrepreneur, are drawn to the allure of the "Entrepreneurial Wheel." It promises progress, innovation, and success. In the beginning, every rotation feels exhilarating, each spin a step closer to your dreams. But then, a deceptive monotony sets in.

You're running faster, pushing harder, but the horizon never changes. The wheel, once a symbol of your drive and ambition, becomes a cage, trapping you in a relentless cycle. Fatigue sets in, and your once-vivid vision begins to blur.

Here's the profound irony: while you're caught in this exhausting loop, the world of entrepreneurship keeps evolving. Opportunities arise, innovations emerge, and the landscape shifts. But in the frenzy of keeping pace, even the most brilliant minds can miss these chances.

Over the years, through my own experiences and conversations with fellow entrepreneurs, I've seen this trap ensnare many. The ambition that should propel you forward instead keeps you spinning in place. The very essence of entrepreneurship—innovation, freedom, and flexibility—seems to slip through your fingers, and with it, the personal growth that's necessary to truly thrive.

Feel that weight? It's not just fatigue; it's the burden of unmet potential and deferred dreams. But here's the good news: recognizing the trap is the first step to breaking free.

It's time to harness that entrepreneurial spirit not just to run faster, but to grow smarter. To step off the wheel and reclaim your time, your energy, and your personal growth.

And the longer you stay on the wheel, the more those dreams slip away. Every moment spent running in place is a moment lost to the opportunities, growth, and fulfillment waiting just beyond the wheel. The time to step off is now.

In this chapter, we'll delve into the frustrations of being caught on the Hamster Wheel—those days when you're busy from dawn to dusk but never feel like you've truly accomplished anything. We'll explore the distractions that steal your time and energy, from endless emails to unexpected client calls, and the emotional toll of consistently falling short of your dreams.

Take a moment to reflect on those days when busyness overshadowed productivity, when the pursuit of your big dreams felt like a distant memory. There's a world of difference between being busy and making real progress toward your goals, especially those BIG dreams. I've lived through those days—days where the list of tasks seemed endless, yet nothing of significance was achieved. I speak not from theory, but from personal experience.

Progress, as elusive as it may seem, is within reach. I've made strides, and while I'm not perfect, I'm closer today than I was yesterday. Each step brings me nearer to my dreams, and more importantly, it's expanding those dreams into something greater. That's the essence of personal growth—continuously evolving as your vision for your life grows.

When my wife and I first got married, we started with modest dreams—a single-wide mobile home, the occasional Sunday drive to look at new cars. Over time, those dreams grew, evolving with us. The life of an entrepreneur isn't about winning every battle; it's about always reaching for your best life and growing into the person you need to be to achieve it.

Looking back, those early dreams seem small now, but they were huge at the time. It's essential to keep revisiting your current state and where you want to go, based on the growth you've experienced. It can be hard to dream bigger when you feel like you're constantly missing the mark, but staying focused on your destination is key. As Robin Sharma says, "What you focus on grows, what you think about expands, and what you dwell upon determines your destiny."

Stepping off the wheel gives you space not only to achieve your goals but to evolve and redefine what true success means for you as you grow. As we journey through this chapter, I'll encourage you to identify the distractions that keep you from your goals and dreams. Recognizing these obstacles is the first step in finding the solutions that work for you. Let's start this journey together, breaking free from the hamster wheel and moving toward a life where your time, your energy, and your growth are fully in your hands. True freedom and fulfillment are within reach—your time, your way.

The Tale of Sarah: A Journey from Hamster Wheel to Personal Growth

You may recall Sarah from my first book, *From Hamster Wheel to Hammock: A Guide to Taking Back Your Day*. She was the kind of entrepreneur who believed in the power of hard work. She had big dreams and a fire in her belly that pushed her to give everything to her business. Every morning, she'd wake up before dawn, ready to tackle the day with the enthusiasm of someone who knew that success was just one more sprint away.

Sarah had started her own graphic design business from the ground up, pouring her creativity, energy, and countless hours into it. At first, it was exhilarating. Every new client and completed project felt like a step toward her dream life—freedom, flexibility, and more time with her family.

But as the months turned into years, something began to change. The business that was supposed to bring her freedom was slowly becoming her cage. Her days were packed from start to finish with client meetings, urgent emails, and design revisions that seemed to never end. No matter how hard she worked, her to-do list grew longer, and the time she had once imagined spending with her family dwindled to a few exhausted hours at the end of each day.

One Friday evening, after yet another 12-hour workday, Sarah sat down on the couch with her laptop, planning to catch up on emails while her family watched a movie. Seeing the tired lines on her face, her husband gently took the laptop from her lap and closed it. "Sarah, you're always working. When was the last time you just...stopped?"

His words hit her harder than she expected. When *was* the last time she had stopped and really stopped? She couldn't remember. She had been so focused on moving forward, on making progress, that she hadn't realized she was running in place.

That night, as she lay in bed, Sarah had a moment of clarity. She was stuck in the hamster wheel—running endlessly but getting nowhere. Her business was thriving, but at what cost? The dreams of freedom and flexibility had faded, replaced by a relentless grind that left her exhausted and unfulfilled.

The next morning, Sarah did something she hadn't done in years: she took the day off. No work, no emails, just a day spent with her family. They went to the beach, laughed, played in the sand, and for the first time in a long time, Sarah felt something she hadn't felt in years—joy. Real, unfiltered joy.

That day marked the beginning of a transformation for Sarah. She realized that the business she had built didn't have to trap her. It was time to reclaim her time and her life by making intentional choices that aligned with the life she truly wanted.

Sarah started setting boundaries, saying no to projects that didn't fit her vision, and delegating tasks that were draining her energy. It wasn't easy at first, but with each step, she began to reclaim her time and her sense of purpose. The more she focused on what truly mattered, the more her business flourished in a way that was both sustainable and fulfilling.

Today, Sarah still runs her graphic design business, but she does it on her terms. She's found a balance that allows her to thrive both professionally and personally. And every now and then, when she feels the pull of the hamster wheel, she remembers that Friday night and the moment she decided to stop running and start living.

In this chapter, we're diving deep into the concept of the Hamster Wheel—a metaphor for the relentless, often fruitless cycle that many entrepreneurs find themselves trapped in. We'll start by defining what exactly the Hamster Wheel is, breaking down how it manifests in your day-to-day life and business.

Next, we'll explore why we get stuck in this trap in the first place. It's not just about working hard; it's about the mindset and societal pressures that push us to keep running even when we're not getting anywhere. Understanding these underlying causes is crucial because it helps us recognize when we're spinning our wheels and, more importantly, why.

We'll then take a closer look at the impact of being stuck in this cycle. It's more than just physical exhaustion—it also takes an emotional toll, including missed opportunities and deferred dreams that come with constantly being in motion but never really moving forward.

To make this personal, we'll guide you through identifying your own Hamster Wheel. This isn't a one-size-fits-all concept; your version of the Hamster Wheel might look different from someone else's. By examining real-life examples, we'll help you see how this plays out in your life and business.

Finally, we'll touch on the initial steps you can take to break free. It's one thing to know you're stuck; it's another to start the journey toward getting off the wheel. These first steps are about reclaiming your time, refocusing your energy, and setting the stage for real progress toward your dreams.

Understanding the Hamster Wheel trap is crucial because it's the first step in breaking free. If you don't recognize the cycle you're in, you'll never escape it. This chapter lays the groundwork for everything that follows, helping you see where you're stuck so that you can begin the journey toward true freedom and fulfillment—your time, your way.

Defining the Hamster Wheel

Most of you probably have a pretty good idea of what I mean when I talk about the Hamster Wheel, but let's make sure we're all on the same page. The Hamster Wheel is a metaphor for any repetitive, unproductive, and often exhausting cycle of activity that leaves you feeling like you're working hard but not really getting anywhere. Picture that little hamster running with all its might on a wheel that spins endlessly but takes it nowhere—no matter how fast or hard it runs, the scenery never changes.

Now, think about areas of your life or business that feel the same. You might be putting in countless hours, tackling a never-ending to-do list, or spinning your wheels trying to meet every demand thrown your way. Despite all the effort, you're left with the nagging feeling that you're stuck in place, missing out on the progress, growth, and success you set out to achieve. That's the Hamster Wheel, and it's a trap that's all too easy to fall into, especially for driven, ambitious people like you.

Understanding the Hamster Wheel Trap

I'm confident I'm not alone in feeling trapped on the Hamster Wheel. You know the drill: working from early morning until late night yet seeing no real progress. You start your day with a list of important tasks, fully intending to check them off, only to find most, if not all, of them still staring back at you the next morning. An occasional day like this isn't a big deal—we all have them—but when it becomes the norm, it's a serious problem.

It's more than just frustrating; it's like getting the wind kicked out of your sails day after day. And it's not because you're slacking off. You've been working HARD all day, but despite all the effort, you've made little to no headway on the things that truly matter. Sure, you might have a long list of things you did accomplish, but they're not the tasks that move the needle. That's a BIG "just," and it's what keeps you spinning in place.

Let's be clear: getting a lot done is not the same as making meaningful progress. We start the day with the best intentions, ready to tackle those priority items the moment we walk into the office. But first, there's the coffee to brew and, of course, the inevitable bathroom break after that first cup (or two) from home. Then it's onto the list, right? Not so fast.

Before you can even start, your inbox pings with new messages, and you think, "I'll just clear these out so I can focus." Next thing you know, you've handled 25 emails, replied to 12, and spent 20 minutes hunting down answers for three of them. And oh, look, there are another 20 from yesterday that you never got to. Damn that inbox!

Then your staff starts trickling in—yes, this is all before official business hours—with greetings and questions that need addressing. And because you value your team, you spend some extra time chatting, making sure everyone feels heard. Before you know it, a client calls, which reminds you of the voicemails waiting from yesterday. By the time you finish those, it's lunch, and you still haven't touched the first item on your list.

The afternoon unfolds much like the morning, a whirlwind of tasks that, while necessary, weren't part of your plan. As the day wraps up, you can barely bring yourself to look at your list because you know it's untouched. Sure, you've been productive—you took care of clients, supported your team, and dealt with the day's alligators (you know, those things that pop up out of nowhere to bite you in the ass)—but none of it was what you intended to do when the day started.

And that's the trap of the Hamster Wheel: getting caught up in the busyness, justifying it as productivity, while your real priorities gather dust. It's easy to get stuck in this cycle, but recognizing it is the first step toward reclaiming your time and energy.

Breaking Free from the Hamster Wheel

After years—yes, years—of frustration and a nearly stagnant business, I began to realize something had to change. That realization was the first step in breaking free from the Hamster Wheel trap. The key wasn't just about working harder or finding better productivity hacks; it was about shifting my focus to the things that truly mattered—both in my business and my personal growth.

Breaking free from the Hamster Wheel is about more than time management. It's about making intentional choices that align with your bigger vision for your life and business. It's about growth, not just in terms of professional success, but in creating a life where your time and energy are spent in ways that fulfill you.

Common Signs and Symptoms of the Hamster Wheel Trap

Here are some common signs and symptoms that indicate you might be caught in the hamster wheel trap—working hard but not making the kind of intentional progress that truly moves you forward:

1. **Constant Busyness Without Progress:** You're always busy, with a packed schedule and a never-ending to-do list, but at the end of the day, it feels like you haven't made any meaningful progress toward your long-term goals.

2. **Overwhelming Fatigue:** Despite working hard every day, you feel physically and mentally drained, with little energy left for anything outside of work. This constant exhaustion leaves no room for personal growth or recharging.

3. **Unfulfilled Goals:** The goals you set at the beginning of the day, week, or even year consistently go unmet. You find yourself repeatedly pushing important tasks and growth opportunities to the next day or week, never quite catching up.

4. **High Stress Levels:** You're constantly stressed, feeling like you're always racing against the clock but never gaining control over your time or your life.

5. **Lack of Work-Life Balance:** Your work consumes most of your time, leaving little room for personal interests, family, or the relaxation that fuels personal growth.

6. **Diminished Creativity and Innovation:** The daily grind leaves little time or energy for creative thinking or innovation, which are essential for growth both personally and professionally.

7. **Frustration and Disillusionment:** You feel a growing sense of frustration and disillusionment, questioning why you're putting in so much effort without seeing the progress or fulfillment you imagined.

8. **Reactive Rather Than Proactive:** Your days are spent reacting to immedi-

ate demands—emails, calls, meetings—rather than intentionally focusing on long-term strategies or projects that align with your personal and business goals.

9. **Neglecting Personal Health:** Exercise, healthy eating, and other self-care practices often get sidelined because work always seems to take priority, leaving little space for personal well-being.

10. **Feeling Stuck:** Despite all your hard work, you feel stuck in place, unable to move forward in your business or personal life. It's as if you're running in circles, without any real progress toward the life you want.

These signs are red flags that you might be caught in the hamster wheel trap. Recognizing them is the first step toward reclaiming your time, refocusing your energy, and breaking free to pursue meaningful growth—on your own terms, your time, your way.

Why Do We Get Stuck?

As entrepreneurs, getting trapped in the hamster wheel isn't just about working hard—it's often the result of a mix of internal and external factors that keep us spinning in place. The first and perhaps most deceptive cause is the illusion of productivity. Many of us equate busyness with making progress, but just because you're checking off tasks doesn't mean you're moving closer to your long-term goals. The hamster wheel keeps spinning because we believe that as long as we're doing something, we must be getting somewhere. But real progress isn't about how much you do—it's about making intentional choices that align with your vision.

Another common trap is the fear of failure, coupled with perfectionism. The fear of falling short can drive us to overcompensate by working longer hours, even on tasks that won't move the needle. Perfectionism only makes this worse, as we obsess over details that don't truly matter, believing everything must be flawless to avoid criticism or failure.

Then there's the pressure from outside forces. Society glorifies "hustle culture," making long hours and constant busyness seem like badges of honor. Add to that the expectations of clients, colleagues, or even family, and it becomes incredibly hard to step back and focus on what really matters—both for your business and your personal growth.

And let's not forget how easy it is to lose sight of priorities. Without a clear sense of what's important, we tend to respond to whatever is urgent, even if it doesn't align with our long-term goals. The inability to say no only compounds this, as we take on too many responsibilities, stretching ourselves thin and leaving little room to focus on what truly matters.

Another factor is the lack of effective systems or delegation. Many of us fall into the trap of believing we have to do everything ourselves. This not only overloads us with day-to-day tasks but also prevents us from focusing on strategic growth and our own personal development.

Ingrained habits also play a significant role. Over time, constant busyness becomes second nature. We become so used to the fast pace that slowing down or stepping back feels uncomfortable, even when it's necessary. Breaking free from these habits requires conscious effort and the willingness to redefine what success looks like.

Understanding why we get stuck is crucial because it allows us to address the root causes. By identifying these factors in your own life, you can begin to take intentional steps toward breaking free from the hamster wheel and reclaiming your time for what matters most—your growth, your life, your way.

The Impact of Being Stuck

Imagine waking up each morning with a sense of urgency, your mind already racing through the endless tasks demanding your attention. You pour yourself a cup of coffee, telling yourself that today will be the day you finally catch up, the day you'll make real progress. But as the hours pass, you find yourself running in place—drowning in emails, meetings, and urgent requests. By the time the sun sets, you're exhausted—physically, mentally, emotionally—but when you look back on the day, it's hard to point to anything meaningful that you've truly accomplished. This is the hamster wheel trap, and it's one that many of us fall into.

The impact of being stuck in this cycle is profound. It starts with the relentless stress that never seems to let up. You're constantly on edge, pushing yourself to the limit day after day, with no real break in sight. This stress begins to wear you down, leading to burnout. Tasks that once excited you now feel like heavy burdens, and the passion that used to fuel your work begins to fade.

It's not just your work that suffers. Your creativity and innovation—the very qualities that helped define your entrepreneurial spirit—start to wane. You become so focused on just keeping up with the daily grind that you lose the mental space to think outside the box or dream up new ideas. The grind becomes all-consuming, leaving no room for the fresh thinking that could propel you or your business forward.

Meanwhile, your relationships with the people who matter most—your family, your friends—begin to suffer. You're always working, always busy, and time with loved ones becomes a rare luxury. They start to notice that you're not fully present, that your mind is always elsewhere. The relationships that once brought you joy now feel strained under the weight of constant busyness, and the disconnect grows.

Opportunities also start to slip through your fingers. While you're buried in the day-to-day tasks, chances for personal growth, strategic decisions, and new ventures pass by unnoticed. You're so focused on immediate demands that you miss the bigger picture—the very opportunities that could help you reach your goals in more meaningful ways.

Even the quality of your work takes a hit. You're rushing through tasks, trying to keep up with the demands of the day, and the attention to detail that once set you apart begins to falter. Mistakes happen more often, and the high standards you've always prided yourself on start to slip.

But perhaps the most insidious impact is the growing sense of unfulfillment, or simply dissatisfaction. Despite all your hard work, you can't shake the feeling that something's missing. The joy and satisfaction you once felt are replaced by a gnawing emptiness. You begin to wonder if all the effort is even worth it, as the gap between where you are and where you want to be seems to widen.

Your health starts to suffer as well. The stress, long hours, and lack of balance take their toll. You're not eating as well as you should, not exercising, and not getting enough sleep. These sacrifices may seem small at first, but over time, they add up, and suddenly you're dealing with health issues that could have been avoided by taking better care of yourself.

The most tragic part of this hamster wheel trap is how it jeopardizes your long-term success. You might think you're working hard to secure your future, but in reality, you're just spinning your wheels. Without stepping back to reflect, plan strategically, and align your actions with your long-term goals, you may find that your business or career growth stalls. The potential for future success slowly slips away, buried under the demands of the day-to-day grind.

And through all of this, you lose sight of your original vision. The dreams that once inspired you now feel distant and unattainable, overshadowed by the never-ending demands of each day. The work that once felt purposeful now feels meaningless, leaving you with a deep sense of disillusionment. You start to wonder how it all went wrong, and whether it's too late to find your way back to the path you once dreamed of.

This is the true cost of being stuck in the hamster wheel—a life where stress, missed opportunities, and a loss of purpose become the norm. But recognizing this trap is the first step toward breaking free, reclaiming your time, and refocusing on the life and work you've always envisioned—on your terms, your way.

Identifying Your Own Hamster Wheel

Recognizing whether you're stuck in the hamster wheel is a crucial first step toward breaking free and reclaiming your time. This reflective exercise is designed to help you step back, assess your current lifestyle, and identify areas where you may feel stagnant or unfulfilled. By exploring your daily routines, habits, and feelings, you can gain valuable insights into where you might be spinning your wheels without making real progress.

Take some time for yourself—grab a journal, find a quiet space, and work through the following prompts. Be honest and open with yourself. This is your opportunity to reflect deeply on where you are today and where you truly want to go. These reflections will help you begin to make intentional choices that align with your personal and professional goals. Go to and download the workbook.

Uncovering Patterns and Behaviors that Contribute to the Hamster Wheel

Our daily routines and habits play a significant role in keeping us stuck in the hamster wheel. Often, these patterns become so ingrained that we hardly notice them, even as they consume our time and energy without moving us closer to what truly matters. This exercise is designed to help you identify and analyze the routines and habits that may be contributing to your sense of stagnation.

By bringing these behaviors to light, you can begin to make conscious changes that lead to greater progress, balance, and fulfillment.

Take some time to reflect on the following prompts, using a journal to jot down your thoughts and observations. The goal is to uncover the routines and behaviors that might be keeping you trapped in the hamster wheel, so you can start making intentional choices that align with your long-term vision and personal growth.

I Love Examples

Here are some examples of other notable individuals who successfully escaped the hamster wheel.

1. Sheryl Sandberg:

Sheryl Sandberg, COO of Facebook and author of *Lean In*, faced her own version of the hamster wheel during her early years in the tech industry. Sandberg found herself working long hours and struggling to balance her demanding job with her personal life. After a particularly stressful period, she realized she needed to take control of her time and energy. Sandberg became an advocate for setting boundaries, such as leaving the office at a reasonable hour and prioritizing time with her family. She's since spoken extensively about the importance of work-life balance and has implemented policies at Facebook to help others avoid burnout and achieve greater balance.

Set Boundaries for Work-Life Balance

- Sandberg's experience emphasizes the necessity of setting clear boundaries to maintain a healthy work-life balance. By prioritizing personal time and leaving work at a reasonable hour, you can protect your well-being and avoid burnout, leading to greater long-term success.

2. Elizabeth Gilbert:

Elizabeth Gilbert, the best-selling author of *Eat, Pray, Love*, experienced her own hamster wheel moment after the massive success of her book. The pressure to continue producing hit after hit left her feeling creatively drained and disconnected from her true passions. Gilbert decided to step back and reassess her approach to writing and life. She chose to focus on projects that genuinely inspired her, rather than chasing commercial success. Gilbert's journey led her to write *Big Magic*, a book about creative living beyond fear, where she encourages others to follow their curiosity and break free from the pressures that can stifle creativity.

Follow Your Curiosity

- Gilbert's journey teaches us that chasing external validation and commercial success can lead to creative stagnation. Instead, focusing on projects that genuinely inspire and fulfill you can reignite your passion and lead to a more satisfying and meaningful career.

3. David Allen:

David Allen, productivity consultant and author of *Getting Things Done* (GTD), spent years in the hamster wheel of overwhelming workloads and stress before developing his famous GTD system. Allen realized that traditional methods of time management weren't enough to handle the constant influx of tasks and information in modern life. To escape the cycle of busyness without progress, he created a system that helps people manage their tasks and commitments more effectively, freeing up mental space for more meaningful work. Allen's approach has helped millions of people worldwide regain control over their lives and work more intentionally.

Implement Effective Systems

- Allen's development of the GTD system demonstrates the power of organizing tasks and commitments effectively. By implementing a system that helps you manage your workload, you can free up mental space and focus on what truly matters, breaking free from the hamster wheel

4. Jessica Jackley:

Jessica Jackley, co-founder of Kiva, the micro-lending platform, faced the hamster wheel in her early career working in the nonprofit sector. Jackley found herself bogged down by the administrative and fundraising demands of traditional nonprofit work, which often left her feeling disconnected from the real impact she wanted to make. To break free, she co-founded Kiva, a platform that allows individuals to lend money directly to entrepreneurs in developing countries, cutting through the red tape and bringing her closer to her mission of empowering others. Jackley's decision to innovate and simplify her approach allowed her to create a more impactful and fulfilling career.

Innovate and Simplify for Impact

- Jackley's creation of Kiva shows that cutting through bureaucracy and simplifying processes can lead to greater impact and fulfillment. By aligning your work with your core mission and finding innovative solutions, you can escape the hamster wheel and make a more meaningful difference.

These takeaways illustrate that escaping the hamster wheel often involves a combination of setting boundaries, focusing on meaningful work, aligning with your values, and implementing effective systems. By taking these lessons to heart, you can create a more balanced, fulfilling, and impactful life and career.

Initial Steps to Break Free from the Hamster Wheel

Breaking free from the hamster wheel doesn't happen overnight, but it starts with small, intentional steps that gradually lead to greater freedom, fulfillment, and personal growth. Imagine standing at the edge of a familiar path, one you've walked countless times before—long days filled with busyness, exhaustion, and a sense of spinning your wheels without moving forward. You know this path well, but deep down, you sense there's another path that leads not just to more work but to meaningful progress and a life that truly feels like your own.

The first step to breaking free is simple yet profound: awareness. It's about recognizing the patterns that have kept you stuck in this cycle. You start by stepping back from the daily grind to reflect on your life and work. You begin to notice how much of your time is spent reacting to immediate demands—emails, meetings, endless tasks—rather than focusing on what truly matters to you. This awareness isn't just about identifying the problem; it's about acknowledging that change is not only necessary but possible.

Once you're aware of the trap, the next step is to reclaim control of your time and energy. This begins with setting clear boundaries—both with others and with yourself. It might mean turning off email notifications during specific hours to protect your focus. It could involve blocking time in your calendar each day for deep, uninterrupted work on projects that align with your long-term goals. And it certainly means learning to say no, recognizing that not every request or opportunity deserves your attention.

As you start to set these boundaries, something begins to shift. You feel a space opening up in your life—a space where you can breathe, think, and reflect. This is where the real transformation begins. You use this time to reconnect with your core values and your personal and professional goals. What truly matters to you? What dreams and ambitions have gotten lost in the daily grind? You start to refocus your energy on these priorities, letting go of tasks and commitments that no longer serve them.

Breaking free from the hamster wheel also involves simplifying your life and work. You start identifying low-impact activities that consume your time but don't move you forward. Maybe it's replacing endless meetings with a quick email update or delegating tasks others could handle. You begin streamlining your processes, cutting out the noise so you can focus on what truly drives progress and fulfillment.

This journey isn't about radically overhauling your life all at once. It's about making small, consistent changes that gradually lead to significant results. Each day, as you take these steps, you'll notice a difference. You're no longer just busy, you're productive, moving steadily toward your goals. You feel less stressed, more energized, and increasingly fulfilled. The hamster wheel may still turn, but you're no longer running in place. You're moving forward—with purpose and intention.

Over time, these initial steps build momentum. What started as small changes evolve into new habits, and those habits transform your life. You've stepped off the hamster wheel and onto a path that feels uniquely yours—a path where your work aligns with your values, your time is spent on what truly matters, and you're not just surviving, but thriving.

Mindset Shift

If you read my first book, you'll recall my emphasis on mindset, and I don't want to overlook that here so let's cover this before we move from this first chapter. I'm going to ask you to stop and think about the way you may be living right now. Running from task to task, constantly putting out fires, and never feeling like you're making real progress—isn't how it has to be. For so long, you've been caught in a cycle, convinced that this relentless pace is just the price of success. But what if it isn't? What if the key to breaking free lies not in working harder but in shifting your mindset?

This is the moment of awakening, the moment you realize that you are not a victim of circumstance but the architect of your life. The first step in this mindset shift is to recognize that you are in control. It's a powerful realization that shakes the foundation of everything you've believed about success and productivity. You've spent years thinking that the harder you worked, the closer you'd get to your goals. But now, you start to see that real progress isn't just about effort—it's about direction, intention, and clarity.

This shift in mindset is transformative. It begins with understanding that you have the power to choose how you spend your time, where you focus your energy, and what you allow into your life. No longer do you have to say yes to every request; no longer do you have to fill every minute of your day with activity. You start to see that it's okay—necessary, even—to slow down, reflect, and be deliberate about where you're going.

As you embrace this new mindset, you begin to recognize the difference between being busy and being effective. You've been caught in the hamster wheel, thinking that constant motion was the same as making progress. But now, you see that the real power lies in knowing when to step back, when to say no, and when to focus deeply on what truly matters.

This mindset shift also involves letting go of the guilt that comes with taking time for yourself. You've been conditioned to believe that every moment not spent working is a moment wasted. But now, you start to see that rest, reflection, and personal time are not luxuries—they are essential components of a fulfilling, balanced life. You are in control, and that means making space for the things that nourish you, not just the things that move you forward.

The most profound part of this shift is the realization that your worth is not tied to how much you do or how busy you are. For so long, you've equated productivity with value, thinking that if you weren't constantly producing, you weren't enough. But now, you begin to see that your value comes from who you are, not just what you accomplish. This understanding frees you from the relentless pressure to always be doing, allowing you to focus on being—being present, being intentional, being true to yourself.

As this new mindset takes root, you start to experience life differently. You approach your work with a sense of calm and clarity, knowing that you are in control of your choices. You prioritize your well-being, knowing that taking care of yourself is the foundation for everything else. You become more discerning with your time, saying yes only to the things that truly matter and align with your goals.

In the end, this mindset shift isn't just about changing how you work—it's about changing how you live. It's about reclaiming your power, recognizing that you are the author of your story, and choosing to write a narrative that reflects your true values and desires. You are in control, and with this realization comes the freedom to create a life that is not just successful, but deeply fulfilling.

Practical Tips

Breaking free from the hamster wheel starts with small, intentional changes that can make a big difference over time. Here are some practical tips to help you begin this journey toward a more balanced and fulfilling life:

1. **Set Clear Boundaries:**
   - **Define Your Work Hours:** Establish specific start and end times for your workday, and stick to them. This helps you create a clear separation between

work and personal time, preventing work from spilling over into every part of your life.

- **Learn to Say No:** Practice saying no to tasks or commitments that don't align with your priorities or values. Not every opportunity is worth your time, and protecting your energy for what truly matters is key to breaking free.

- **Limit Accessibility:** Turn off email notifications outside of work hours or set specific times during the day when you check your inbox. This reduces the constant pull of emails and helps you stay focused on more important tasks.

2. **Reduce Unnecessary Tasks:**
   - **Identify Low-Impact Activities:** Take a close look at your daily tasks and identify which ones are consuming your time without adding significant value. These might include routine meetings, excessive email communication, or tasks that could be automated or delegated.

   - **Delegate Wisely:** If you're doing everything yourself, it's time to start delegating. Trust your team or hire help to handle routine tasks so you can focus on high-impact activities that require your expertise and attention.

   - **Simplify Processes:** Streamline workflows by eliminating steps that don't add value. Whether it's simplifying your reporting process or reducing the number of approvals needed for decisions, small adjustments can free up considerable time.

3. **Prioritize Deep Work:**
   - **Block Out Focus Time:** Schedule uninterrupted blocks of time each day for deep work—tasks that require concentration and creativity. During these periods, eliminate distractions by turning off notifications and finding a quiet space to work.

   - **Work on High-Impact Tasks First:** Start your day with the most important and challenging tasks when your energy and focus are at their peak. This ensures that your most critical work gets done before the demands of the day take over.

4. **Create Daily Rituals:**

- **Morning Routine for Clarity:** Begin your day with a morning routine that sets a positive tone. This could include meditation, journaling, or a brief review of your goals for the day. A consistent routine helps you start each day with intention and focus.

- **Evening Wind-Down:** End your day with a routine that helps you disconnect from work and transition into relaxation. This might involve reviewing what you accomplished, setting priorities for the next day, and engaging in activities that help you unwind.

5. Practice Mindful Decision-Making:

- **Ask 'Is This Essential?':** Before taking on a new task or commitment, ask yourself if it's truly essential to your goals. If it's not, consider whether it can be postponed, delegated, or removed altogether.

- **Focus on Progress, Not Perfection:** Aim for progress in your work rather than getting caught up in perfectionism. Small, consistent improvements over time lead to significant results, without the stress of trying to make everything perfect.

6. Regularly Reflect and Adjust:

- **Weekly Check-In:** Set aside time each week to reflect on what's working and what's not. Are there tasks or activities that consistently drain your energy without yielding results? Adjust your approach as needed to keep your focus on what truly matters.

- **Celebrate Small Wins:** Acknowledge and celebrate the small steps you're taking toward breaking free from the hamster wheel. Recognizing your progress, no matter how incremental, can boost your motivation and reinforce positive change.

These small changes may seem simple, but they can have a powerful impact on your life over time. We will cover each of these in more depth as we work through the processes throughout the book. But, by setting boundaries, reducing unnecessary tasks, and prioritizing what truly matters, you'll begin to free yourself from the endless cycle of busyness and move toward a more intentional, balanced, and fulfilling life.

Conclusion

As we wrap up this first chapter, take a moment to reflect on what we've covered. We've explored the concept of the hamster wheel—how it traps you in a cycle of endless busyness, leaving you exhausted and unfulfilled. We've delved into the reasons why you get stuck, from the illusion of productivity to external pressures and ingrained habits. We've also discussed the profound impact this trap can have on your life, from chronic stress and burnout to strained relationships and a loss of purpose.

Perhaps the most important takeaway from this chapter is the realization that you are not powerless in this situation. You can reclaim your time, energy, and sense of fulfillment. It all starts with awareness—recognizing the patterns and behaviors that have kept you stuck—and continues with small, intentional steps that lead to meaningful change.

Now, it's time to take action. The journey toward a more balanced and fulfilling life begins with a single step, and that step is within your reach today. Start by setting boundaries that protect your time and energy. Eliminate unnecessary tasks that drain you without adding value and prioritize deep work that aligns with your true goals and makes a real impact. Most importantly, shift your mindset to recognize that you are the architect of your own life and growth.

Remember, breaking free from the hamster wheel doesn't require drastic changes overnight, that seldom works. It requires consistent, deliberate actions that gradually shift your life in the direction you want to go. You've already taken the first step by reading this chapter; now it's time to put what you've learned into practice.

Your future isn't something you have to chase relentlessly; it's something you can create one step at a time, with intention and purpose. So, take that first step today and start building a life that reflects your deepest values, ambitions, and desires. You have the power to change your story, and it begins right now.

Chapter Two
Vision of Freedom
Defining our Ultimate Lifestyle

IMAGINE A LIFE WHERE every day reflects your deepest values and desires—where you wake up with a sense of purpose and go to bed each night feeling fulfilled. This is the essence of true freedom—not just the absence of constraints, but the presence of a life you've consciously designed to align with your unique vision.

Consider the story of a young entrepreneur who, after years of relentless hustle, reached a turning point. Despite achieving financial success, they found themselves exhausted and unfulfilled, trapped in a cycle of constant busyness. It wasn't until they paused and asked, "What does freedom truly mean to me?" that they began to transform their life. They realized that freedom wasn't just about more money or time; it was about aligning their life with their passions, purpose, and vision of a fulfilling lifestyle.

In this chapter, we'll explore what it means to live freely by defining your ultimate lifestyle. Having a clear vision of freedom is essential because it serves as your guiding star, helping you make intentional choices that bring you closer to the life you truly want. Without this vision, it's easy to get caught up in the hamster wheel—endlessly working without feeling like you're moving forward.

We'll start by diving into the concept of freedom itself—what does it mean to you personally? Freedom is a deeply individual experience that can take many forms, whether it's the freedom to spend quality time with loved ones, pursue your passions, or achieve financial independence that brings peace of mind. We'll explore how aligning this vision with your purpose and passions can make the pursuit of freedom not just possible but deeply fulfilling.

Next, we'll guide you through the process of visualizing your ideal lifestyle. Visualization is a powerful tool that brings your dreams into focus. Whether through creating a vision board or engaging in descriptive visualization exercises, you'll start to see your ultimate lifestyle take shape, making it easier to turn that vision into reality.

We'll also discuss the key components of an ultimate lifestyle—work-life balance, health and well-being, and meaningful relationships. These elements are crucial to living a life of true freedom, and we'll help you define what they mean for you personally.

Finally, we'll cover the importance of setting clear, achievable goals and overcoming the limiting beliefs that can hold you back. It's not enough to have a vision; you need a plan to bring it to life. By the end of this chapter, you'll be equipped with the tools to start building your ultimate lifestyle and the confidence to overcome any obstacles that come your way.

This chapter is your invitation to step off the hamster wheel and begin creating a life that's not just busy but truly fulfilling. It's about taking control of your future, defining what freedom means to you, and setting the stage for the life you've always dreamed of. Let's dive in and start building your vision of freedom, one step at a time.

> *"Freedom is not the absence of commitments, but the ability to choose—and commit myself to—what is best for me."*
> *– Paulo Coelho*

Having a clear vision of freedom is essential because it serves as the foundation for the life you truly want to create. Without a defined sense of what freedom means to you, it's easy to get caught up in the daily grind, chasing goals that don't align with your deepest values and desires. This chapter is all about helping you define that vision—what does freedom look like for you, and how can you build a lifestyle that reflects your idea of freedom?

We'll begin by exploring the concept of freedom from a personal perspective, understanding that it means different things to different people. Whether it's financial independence, control over your time, emotional peace, or the ability to pursue your passions, your vision of freedom is uniquely yours.

Next, we'll guide you through visualization techniques to bring your ideal lifestyle into focus. This includes creating a vision board and engaging in exercises that vividly imagine your ultimate day-to-day life. By the end of this process, you'll have a clear picture of the life you're working toward and the steps needed to get there.

We'll also delve into the key components of an ultimate lifestyle—work-life balance, health and well-being, and meaningful relationships. Each of these elements plays a crucial role in your vision of freedom, and we'll help you define what they mean for you personally.

Finally, we'll discuss how to set clear, achievable goals that will guide you toward your vision, and we'll address the limiting beliefs that might be holding you back. This chapter is designed to empower you to take control of your life, define your own version of freedom, and start making it a reality—your time, your way.

Reimagining What Freedom Really Means (Hint: It's More Than Just Skipping Mondays)

My Personal Definition of Freedom

To me, freedom is the ability to design my days around what truly matters, both in my business and personal life. As an entrepreneur, it means having the autonomy to steer my company in a direction that aligns with my vision without getting bogged down by the minutiae that often consume time and energy. It's about delegating effectively so I can focus on what excites me—innovation, strategic growth, and mentoring my team—activities that push the business forward and bring me fulfillment.

On a personal level, freedom is the assurance that I can step away from work when needed, whether to spend quality time with my family, seek inspiration through travel, or enjoy a leisurely afternoon without the weight of unfinished tasks hanging over me. It's about achieving the balance of being fully engaged in my business when needed, while also being completely present in my personal life, all with a sense of control and intention over my own path.

What's Your Definition of Freedom:

I'm not here to hand you *my* definition of freedom or tell you that the examples I'm about to share are the right ones for you. Instead, I want to offer a starting point—examples to spark your imagination and help you deeply explore what freedom means to you. So, grab a pen and some paper (I'm personally a fan of composition notebooks). Find a quiet place where you won't be disturbed and start writing.

Don't worry about getting it perfect on the first try. In fact, you probably won't. Whenever I do this kind of exercise, I usually end up with several drafts before landing on something that feels right—at least for that moment. And that's the point: your definition of freedom will evolve over time, just as you do. The version of my personal definition I shared earlier went through more than a dozen iterations, and that's after years of refining it.

So, take your time with this. Write, reflect, rewrite, and let your thoughts flow freely. This isn't just another task on your to-do list—it's an investment in understanding what you truly want out of life. I promise, the time you spend on this will be worth it.

Here are a few examples to inspire your vision of freedom:

1. **The Freedom to Travel the World on Your Terms**: Imagine having the freedom to pack your bags and travel anywhere, whenever the mood strikes. You're not bound by vacation days or rigid schedules—your business runs smoothly even in your absence. Whether it's a month in a beach villa in Bali, a spontaneous road trip through the Italian countryside, or exploring the vibrant markets of Marrakech, you have the flexibility to immerse yourself in new experiences whenever you choose.

2. **The Freedom to Create and Innovate Without Limits**: Picture a life where you have the time and mental space to dive into your wildest creative ideas. You're no longer bogged down by day-to-day operations because you've built a team that handles the details. This gives you the freedom to launch passion projects, explore new ventures, or develop groundbreaking products without the constraints of time or the fear of failure.

3. **The Freedom to Design Your Ideal Day, Every Day**: Imagine waking up each morning with the ability to design your day exactly how you want it. Perhaps you start with a yoga session, enjoy breakfast with family, dive into a few hours of focused work, and spend your afternoon hiking or volunteering. You end your day with a dinner party or quiet time under the stars. Every day is crafted around your passions, relationships, and well-being, with work seamlessly integrated into a life you love.

4. **The Freedom to Spend Quality Time with Loved Ones**: Envision having the freedom to be fully present with family and friends, without work distractions pulling you away. You have the flexibility to take long weekends, attend important events, or simply enjoy spontaneous adventures with your loved ones. Your work fits around your life—not the other way around—allowing you to create lasting memories with the people who matter most.

5. **The Freedom to Invest in Your Personal Growth and Well-Being**: Picture dedicating time every day to your personal growth and well-being. You have the freedom to meditate, read, exercise, or learn new skills without feeling guilty. Whether it's attending workshops or mastering new hobbies, you're continuously growing as a person, knowing that investing in yourself is just as valuable as investing in your business.

6. **The Freedom to Give Back on a Large Scale**: Visualize having the freedom to make a significant impact on causes you care about. You're financially secure and have the time to devote to philanthropy, whether that's funding scholarships, building schools, or mentoring young entrepreneurs. Your business success enables you to leave a legacy that extends beyond personal achievements.

These examples aren't meant to be your personal vision statement, nor are they written as such. They're simply prompts designed to help you craft your unique vision of freedom. Take the time to dive into this exercise—your future self will thank you for it.

Aligning Freedom with Personal Passion and Purpose

When it comes to defining your vision of freedom, purpose, and passion, serve as your guiding stars. Freedom isn't just about having endless time or financial resources—it's about aligning your life with what truly matters to you. It's about waking up each day with a sense of direction and fulfillment, knowing that the choices you make and the paths you follow are deeply connected to your core values and the things that ignite your spirit.

Think of your passions as the fuel that drives your journey and your purpose as the compass that guides you in the right direction. When your vision of freedom aligns with these two powerful forces, you're not just free to do anything, you're free to do what you love and what you're meant to do. This alignment transforms freedom from a vague concept into a life rich with meaning and excitement.

For example, if you're passionate about creating art, your vision of freedom might include having the time and space to pursue your creative projects without the constraints of a traditional job. If your purpose is to help others, your freedom might be defined by the ability to work on projects that positively impact the world—whether through entrepreneurship, volunteering, or advocacy.

When your vision of freedom aligns with your passions, every day becomes an opportunity to do what you love. And when it aligns with your purpose, every action you take moves you closer to living a life that feels authentic and fulfilling—one that is truly yours.

Understanding How Purpose Influences Your Vision of Freedom

Your purpose isn't just a vague notion or lofty ideal; it's the driving force behind everything you do. It's what gives your life direction and meaning. Understanding your purpose is essential because it influences every aspect of your vision of freedom, guiding your choices and helping you prioritize what truly matters.

When you're clear on your purpose, your vision of freedom becomes more than just an escape from obligations—it transforms into a path toward fulfilling your deepest desires and making a meaningful impact. For example, if your purpose is to educate and inspire others, your vision of freedom might include creating a lifestyle where you have the time and resources to write, teach, or mentor—without the burden of financial stress.

Your purpose also acts as a compass, helping you prioritize in a world filled with distractions and competing demands. When you know what drives you, it becomes easier to make decisions that align with your long-term goals and values. This clarity can prevent you from falling into the hamster wheel trap, where busyness takes over, but real progress toward meaningful goals feels elusive.

As you reflect on your personal passions and purpose, think about how they shape your vision of freedom. What does life look like when you're free to fully express your passions and live your purpose? How does this influence your goals, daily activities, and the way you define success?

Aligning your vision of freedom with your purpose and passions isn't just a luxury—it's a necessity for living a life that feels whole and satisfying. Grounding your idea of freedom in what you love and what you're here to do ensures that you're not just creating a vision—you're building a life that is deeply meaningful and uniquely yours.

Visualizing Your Ideal Lifestyle

Now that you've explored what freedom means to you and how it aligns with your purpose and passions, it's time to take the next step: visualizing your ideal lifestyle. This is where your dreams begin to take shape, transforming from abstract ideas into a vivid picture of the life you truly want to live.

Visualization is a powerful tool that helps bridge the gap between your current reality and your ultimate goals. It allows you to see, feel, and experience your ideal lifestyle in your mind's eye, making it more tangible and achievable. By clearly envisioning what your days would look like if you were living your version of true freedom, you create a roadmap for your journey ahead—one that's aligned with your values and designed *your way*.

In this section, we'll guide you through exercises that will help you craft a detailed vision of your ideal lifestyle. Whether it's creating a vision board that captures the essence of your dreams or engaging in visualization exercises that bring your ideal day to life, these practices will help you clarify what you're working toward.

This is your opportunity to dream big, imagine without limits, and begin designing a life that reflects your deepest values, desires, and aspirations. So, let's dive in and start visualizing the lifestyle that truly embodies your vision of freedom and personal growth.

Vision Board Exercise: Crafting Your Ideal Lifestyle

A vision board is a powerful tool that helps you visualize and manifest your ideal lifestyle. It serves as a tangible representation of your goals, dreams, and the life you're working to create. By regularly seeing these images and words, you reinforce your intentions and stay motivated to pursue your unique vision of freedom. In this exercise, we'll guide you through the process of creating a vision board that captures the essence of your ideal lifestyle.

Before we dive in, I want to share a real-life example that's personal to me—or, rather, to my wife. Nearly a decade ago, after countless evenings of talking and dreaming about the life we wanted to build together, she decided to capture that vision on a vision board. One of the images she included was a breathtaking view from a high-rise balcony overlooking a pristine beach—people lounging under umbrellas, others strolling along the shore. It encapsulated the lifestyle we envisioned.

Fast-forward to today, and we're living in a beachfront condo that matches her vision almost exactly. While the picture on her vision board wasn't an exact replica, the essence of it—the feeling, the lifestyle—was spot on.

Another powerful example involves a friend who once created a vision board featuring a stunning beachfront home he found online. At the time, it was just a dream. Years later, after achieving financial success, he purchased his dream home. It wasn't until after he moved in that he realized something extraordinary: the house he now owned was the exact one from his vision board. He had unknowingly manifested the very home he had admired years before.

These stories aren't just coincidences, they're examples of how visualizing your goals and dreams can help turn them into reality. As you begin creating your own vision board, remember that the images you choose and the intentions you set can profoundly impact your future. Take this process seriously, and don't be afraid to dream big. You never know where those dreams might lead.

Exercise 1: Creating Your Vision Board: If you do only one exercise from this book—or any other—for the rest of the year, let it be this one! The power of visualizing your dreams and creating your vision board can, and likely will, change your life. Visit [www.RogerGBbest.com/workbooks] to access everything you need to turn your vision into reality!

Final Thoughts

If you haven't done the exercise, please do it now. Creating a vision board is more than just a fun craft project; it's a powerful tool for manifesting your ideal lifestyle. By visualizing your goals and dreams daily, you keep them at the forefront of your mind, which helps you stay focused and motivated to achieve them. So, take your time with this exercise, let your creativity flow, and enjoy the process of designing the life you truly want to live. The book will still be here when you finish the vision board.

The Importance of Visual Representation

Visual representation of your goals and dreams is more than just a creative exercise; it's a powerful tool that brings clarity, focus, and motivation to your journey. When you translate your aspirations into images, you make them tangible and real, turning abstract ideas into something you can see and touch. This visual connection deepens your commitment to achieving those goals, serving as a constant reminder of what you're working toward.

One of the most significant benefits of visual representation is its ability to keep you motivated. Life is full of distractions and challenges that can easily pull you off course. But when you have a vision board or other visual reminders of your goals, they act like a compass, guiding you back to your path. Every time you see these images, you're reminded of the life you're striving to create, which can reignite your passion and determination, even on tough days.

Visual representation also engages your subconscious mind. The brain responds powerfully to imagery—often more than to words alone. By regularly exposing yourself to images that represent your dreams, you start to internalize these visions, making them feel more achievable. This internalization can influence your thoughts, decisions, and actions, often in subtle but powerful ways, leading you closer to your goals.

In addition, visual representation helps you maintain focus. It's easy to get bogged down in the day-to-day tasks and lose sight of the bigger picture. But when your goals are visually represented, they stay front and center in your mind. This constant visibility helps you prioritize your actions and make decisions aligned with your long-term vision.

In essence, visual representation transforms your goals from mere ideas into a reality you can see and believe in. It bridges the gap between where you are and where you want to be, making your dreams feel more attainable and your journey more purposeful.

Descriptive Visualization Exercise: Imagine Your Ideal Day

Visualization is a powerful tool that allows you to vividly imagine your ideal life, helping you connect deeply with your goals and make them feel tangible and within reach. This exercise will guide you through the process of envisioning your perfect day—one where your life aligns seamlessly with your values, passions, and personal vision of freedom.

Find a quiet space, get comfortable, and allow yourself to fully immerse in the experience. As you visualize, picture every detail of how your ideal day would unfold, from the moment you wake up to the time you go to bed. Let this exercise be your roadmap, connecting you to the life you truly want to live.

Don't wait—visit www.RogerGBbest.com/workbooks now to download the workbook and start your journey toward the life you truly want to live.

Key Components of an Ultimate Lifestyle

In the pursuit of freedom, one of the most essential elements to consider is work-life balance. True freedom isn't just measured by financial success or career milestones—it's about creating a life where your professional and personal worlds coexist harmoniously. Work-life balance is the foundation that allows you to thrive in both areas, ensuring that neither is sacrificed at the expense of the other.

When you achieve this balance, you create space for your passions, relationships, health, and well-being, all while moving forward in your career or business. It's the key to building a life that feels both productive and fulfilling.

Work-Life Balance: The Foundation of a Life that Works!

While I'm going to transition from Work-life balance to Work-life integration later on, I'm going to start with a concept that you have mostly likely heard before. If you're opposed to the whole idea, just stick with me for a while and play along for now. I think you'll like the transition later in the book. And, this section won't hurt you in the mean-time.

So, work-life balance doesn't have a one-size-fits-all definition. It's a deeply personal concept that varies depending on your values, goals, and life circumstances. For some, balance might mean setting clear boundaries between work hours and personal time, ensuring that evenings and weekends are dedicated to family, hobbies, or simply unwinding. For others, it might mean integrating work and life in a way that offers flexibility, taking breaks throughout the day to attend to personal matters or working remotely to better accommodate family needs.

At its core, work-life balance is about feeling in control of your time and energy so that you can give your best to both your work and personal life without feeling overwhelmed or stretched too thin. It's about making intentional choices that align with your priorities rather than constantly reacting to external demands and pressures.

Practical Examples of Balanced Lives

1. **The Structured Entrepreneur:** Meet Jane, a successful entrepreneur who runs her own consulting firm. For Jane, work-life balance means maintaining a strict schedule that separates work from personal time. She starts her day early, dedicating the first few hours to deep, focused work before her team arrives. By setting clear boundaries, Jane ensures that her workday ends by 5 PM, leaving her evenings free for family dinners, exercise, and unwinding with a good book. On weekends, she disconnects from work entirely, using the time to recharge and pursue her hobbies like painting and hiking.

2. **The Flexible Freelancer:** Then there's Jake, a freelance graphic designer who values flexibility above all else. Jake's work-life balance is about blending work with life in a way that feels natural and unforced. He structures his work around his personal life, often working in the evenings or early mornings so he can spend afternoons surfing or meeting up with friends. For Jake, balance isn't about rigid schedules but about having the freedom to work when he's most inspired and enjoy life's moments as they come.

3. **The Remote Worker and Parent:** Emily is a remote software developer and a mother of two young children. For Emily, work-life balance involves integrating her work into her daily life in a way that supports her family. She structures her workday around her children's school schedule, working during the hours they're in class and taking breaks when they're home. Emily also takes advantage of her remote work setup by occasionally working from a café or a park, blending work with her love of the outdoors. Through flexibility and setting clear priorities, she's able to be present for her kids while advancing her career.

4. **The CEO with a Passion for Wellness:** Finally, there's Michael, the CEO of a growing tech startup. For Michael, balance means prioritizing his physical and mental health alongside his demanding job. He starts each day with a morning workout and meditation session, which helps him stay focused and energized throughout the day. Michael also makes time for regular therapy sessions

and personal development courses, seeing these as crucial investments in his long-term success. He leads by example, encouraging his team to prioritize their well-being as well, which has fostered a culture of balance within his company.

Why Work-Life Balance Matters

These examples show that work-life balance can take many forms, and it's up to you to define what balance looks like in your own life. Whether it's setting firm boundaries, embracing flexibility, or integrating your work with your personal passions, finding the right balance is key to maintaining your energy, creativity, and overall well-being.

Achieving work-life balance allows you to fully enjoy your personal life while also being productive and effective in your work. It prevents burnout, reduces stress, and gives you a sense of control over your time and priorities. Ultimately, a balanced life is one where you can pursue your professional goals without sacrificing the things that make life meaningful—your health, your relationships, and your passions.

As you consider your own vision of freedom, reflect on what work-life balance means to you. How can you structure your life to honor both your work and personal life? What changes can you make today to start moving toward a more balanced, fulfilling lifestyle? These questions will guide you in creating a life that supports both your well-being and your success.

Health and Well-being: The Cornerstones of Your Vision of Freedom

As you craft your vision of freedom, it's crucial to remember that true freedom isn't just about financial independence or professional success—it's about taking care of your physical and mental health. Without a strong foundation of well-being, even the most exciting achievements can feel hollow, and the ability to fully enjoy your life can slip away.

Health and well-being are not just components of a balanced life; they are the pillars that support it. When you prioritize your well-being, you create a solid foundation that allows you to sustain the energy, focus, and resilience needed to pursue your goals and live your life with intention. Whether it's through regular exercise, mindfulness practices, or simply taking time to rest, investing in your health ensures that you have the capacity to show up fully in both your work and personal life.

Incorporating Physical and Mental Health into Your Vision

When you envision your ideal lifestyle, consider how your physical and mental health plays a pivotal role in that picture. Imagine waking up each day feeling energized and ready to tackle whatever comes your way—not because of sheer willpower, but because you've consistently taken care of your body and mind. Think about the activities that make you feel truly alive, whether it's a morning jog along the beach, practicing yoga to center yourself, or cooking a nutritious meal that nourishes you from the inside out.

Physical health is more than just exercise; it's about creating a sustainable routine that includes movement, nutrition, and rest. It's about finding activities you genuinely enjoy so that staying active becomes a natural part of your day, rather than a chore. Whether you're drawn to high-energy workouts or prefer gentler activities like walking or swimming, consistency is the key to building a strong foundation for your well-being.

But physical health alone isn't enough. Mental and emotional well-being are equally essential. Your vision of freedom should include practices that support your mental health, helping you cultivate resilience and manage stress. This could mean incorporating daily mindfulness exercises, dedicating time to hobbies that bring you joy, or ensuring regular moments of quiet reflection. It's about designing a life where stress doesn't dominate, and you have the tools to handle challenges with grace and ease.

Sustainable Habits for Long-Term Wellbeing

Imagine waking up each day, feeling energized and ready to tackle whatever comes your way—not because you forced yourself into a grueling routine, but because you've built sustainable habits that nourish both your body and mind.

Take Sarah, for example. For years, she struggled to maintain a consistent workout routine, bouncing between fitness fads and extreme regimens that left her burned out. Eventually, Sarah found her stride by incorporating activities she genuinely enjoyed—morning walks in her neighborhood, weekend hikes with friends, and a weekly yoga class. Instead of forcing herself into high-intensity workouts she dreaded, she found a rhythm that felt natural. Her days no longer revolved around the pressure to "get fit," but rather the simple joy of moving her body in ways that felt good and sustainable.

Then there's David, who used to think healthy eating meant giving up his favorite foods and living on salads. But over time, he learned that nourishment wasn't about restriction—it was about balance. He started experimenting in the kitchen, creating meals that were both nutritious and satisfying. Cooking became a way for him to connect with the food he was eating, turning it into a mindful and enjoyable experience. David found that by focusing on fueling his body with wholesome foods, he could still enjoy occasional indulgences without guilt. His energy levels soared, and he finally felt at ease with his relationship to food.

For others like Anna, mental clarity and emotional resilience became the cornerstones of well-being. Between running her business and managing her home, Anna often felt overwhelmed by stress. But instead of powering through, she started setting aside just a few minutes each day for mindfulness and deep breathing exercises. Some mornings, she journaled her thoughts; on other days, she simply sat in silence, taking in a moment of calm before the busy day began. These small, intentional practices helped Anna maintain clarity in the face of challenges and develop emotional resilience—tools that made all the difference when life threw her curveballs.

And then there's James, who used to brag about how little sleep he could get by on. But after years of feeling foggy and rundown, he realized that sleep was the missing piece to his well-being puzzle. He started setting a consistent bedtime, creating a calming pre-sleep routine, and making his bedroom a haven for rest. As he began prioritizing restorative sleep, James noticed an immediate shift—not only was his energy higher, but his focus and productivity also skyrocketed. It became clear that sleep wasn't a luxury; it was a necessity for his success.

Finally, think about Emma, whose vision of well-being involved more than just physical health. She found joy in her hobbies—painting, spending time with friends, and traveling whenever she could. For Emma, well-being was about living a life filled with meaning and joy, engaging in activities that made her feel alive and connected. These moments of fulfillment were just as important to her health as any workout or meal plan.

Why Health and Well-being Matter in Your Vision of Freedom

Your health and well-being are at the core of experiencing personal growth and true freedom. Without physical strength, energy, and mental clarity, the ability to fully pursue your passions, enjoy your accomplishments, and live on your terms becomes severely limited. Neglecting your health can lead to burnout, stress, and a diminished capacity to reclaim your time and focus on what truly matters.

By integrating health and well-being into your vision, you're not just ensuring short-term success, you're creating a life that's sustainable, fulfilling, and rich with energy. It's about building a lifestyle where your body supports your ambitions, your mind fosters creativity and calm, and your emotional resilience helps you navigate challenges with strength and grace.

Consider Sarah, a driven entrepreneur who spent years building her business while ignoring her health, thinking that success required constant hard work. The toll became unavoidable—chronic fatigue, stress, and illness soon caught up with her. It wasn't until she refocused on her well-being—prioritizing sleep, regular exercise, and mindfulness—that Sarah began to thrive. Her energy returned, her productivity soared, and she rediscovered joy in work and life.

As you refine your vision of *Your Time, Your Way*, think about how these elements fit into your daily routine. What small steps can you take to nurture your long-term health and happiness today? How can you design your life to honor both your physical and mental well-being?

By prioritizing your health, you're laying the foundation for a life of freedom—one that's vibrant, meaningful, and fully under your control. It's not just about succeeding in your work; it's about thriving in all areas of your life.

Relationships and Social Life: The Heartbeat of Your Ultimate Lifestyle

When envisioning your ultimate lifestyle, it's essential to recognize the profound role that relationships and social connections play in your overall happiness and fulfillment. Success and personal achievements may be important, but the relationships you cultivate—both personal and professional—often bring the deepest meaning to your life. These connections form the emotional foundation that supports you during challenges, celebrates your victories, and enriches your daily experiences.

Whether it's your partner, family, friends, or professional network, these relationships are what make life vibrant and purposeful. They offer a sense of belonging, provide emotional security, and remind you that you don't have to walk the path to success alone.

These social connections are at the heart of every fulfilling life—relationships that help you thrive, grow, and truly enjoy the freedom you've worked so hard to create.

The Role of Relationships in Your Ultimate Lifestyle

Relationships are at the heart of your perfect life. Consider the people who mean the most to you: your family, friends, colleagues, and community. These individuals lift you up, inspire you, and share in your journey. In your vision of freedom, these relationships are present and thriving, offering mutual support and fulfillment.

Healthy, meaningful relationships provide a sense of belonging, connection, and emotional support—essential for a balanced and satisfying life. Whether sharing a meal with loved ones, collaborating with colleagues on meaningful projects, or enjoying time with good friends, these moments of connection bring joy and purpose to your days.

As you craft your vision of freedom, reflect on these relationships' role in your life. Are you surrounded by people who encourage and uplift you? Do your relationships contribute to your well-being, or do they drain your energy? In your ideal lifestyle, the people you choose to spend time with add value, encouraging your growth and helping you become the best version of yourself.

Nurturing Meaningful Connections

Meaningful relationships don't happen by accident; they require intention, effort, and care. These connections form the foundation of a fulfilling life and nurturing them is essential for living in alignment with your vision of freedom. Consider how your relationships, both personal and professional, can help you thrive. Instead of focusing on how many people you know, reflect on the depth and quality of your connections. Imagine a smaller, close-knit circle of friends, family, and colleagues who share your values and support your growth. Investing your energy in these relationships, rather than spreading yourself thin, will pay off in ways that a wide network of superficial connections never could.

Take the story of Emily, for instance. As a business owner juggling multiple priorities, she often found herself surrounded by acquaintances but feeling a lack of true connection. It wasn't until she consciously shifted her focus toward her closest relationships that she began to feel more fulfilled. She started spending more quality time with her family and a handful of trusted friends. Emily realized that deepening these connections brought her more joy and satisfaction than any business success ever had. Her experience serves as a reminder that it's not about the number of people in your life but the quality of the relationships you nurture.

In our fast-paced world, being present with the people who matter to you is one of the greatest gifts you can offer. Picture sitting down with a loved one, putting away your phone, and giving them your undivided attention. This simple act of being fully engaged during a conversation shows how much you value the relationship. It's through these moments of presence that relationships grow stronger.

Shared experiences also play a crucial role in building and maintaining strong connections. Whether it's a family trip, a regular catch-up with friends, or collaborating on a meaningful project with colleagues, these moments create lasting memories. They form the glue that holds relationships together, fostering deeper trust and connection. Imagine the joy of looking back on these shared experiences, knowing they've strengthened the bonds that mean the most to you.

Open and honest communication is at the heart of every healthy relationship. Expressing your thoughts and feelings clearly and listening with empathy when others do the same builds trust and mutual understanding. Conflicts are inevitable, but working through them respectfully strengthens the relationship rather than weakening it. In your vision of freedom, these relationships provide comfort and support grounded in mutual respect.

Another critical aspect of meaningful relationships is the encouragement of personal growth. Surround yourself with people who celebrate your successes and challenge you to be better. Be that same source of encouragement for others. Imagine a network of friends and colleagues who push you to reach your potential while you do the same for them. You grow and thrive together, creating a supportive environment where everyone can succeed.

However, nurturing relationships doesn't mean you can't set boundaries. In fact, healthy boundaries are vital for maintaining balance. Picture yourself confidently establishing limits that prevent burnout and keep your relationships respectful and balanced. By respecting your own needs and those of others, you preserve the integrity of these connections.

Finally, consider the broader community you belong to. Meaningful relationships extend beyond your inner circle. Engage with your community by giving back, whether through volunteering or acts of service. These connections provide a sense of purpose and fulfillment, reminding you that life is richer when you contribute to the well-being of others.

If you take just one step today to improve your relationships, start with intentional presence. Be fully engaged with those around you. These small, consistent actions can transform your connections and bring you closer to living the life of freedom and fulfillment that you envision.

Why Relationships Matter in Your Vision of Freedom

The relationships you cultivate are the heartbeat of your ultimate lifestyle. They bring love, joy, support, and meaning to your life, enriching your journey and making it far more fulfilling. As you design your vision of freedom, it's essential to remember that your success and happiness are deeply intertwined with the people you choose to share your life with. These connections will be the foundation upon which your experiences are built.

Incorporating strong, meaningful relationships into your vision ensures that your life is rich not only in personal achievements but also in deep connection, love, and mutual support. These are the relationships that will cheer you on during victories, catch you when you stumble, and walk beside you through every step of your journey. Prioritizing these connections will enhance every aspect of your path toward freedom, making your successes all the more meaningful.

Setting Clear and Achievable Goals: The SMART Goals Framework

As you create your vision of freedom, setting clear and achievable goals is essential. Think of your goals as stepping stones that guide you from where you are now to where you want to be. Without a solid plan, even the best intentions can drift aimlessly. However, not all goals are created equal—some are vague, others unrealistic. To truly move forward with purpose, your goals need to be well-defined and actionable. This is where the SMART Goals Framework becomes invaluable, offering a practical approach to ensure your goals are not only ambitious but also achievable.

The SMART Goals Framework

The SMART framework is a widely recognized tool that helps you craft goals that are clear, realistic, and most importantly, attainable. Let's break down what SMART stands for:

- Specific: Your goal needs to be precise. A vague goal like "I want to be healthier" doesn't offer much guidance. Instead, think in specific terms—what exactly do you want to accomplish, and why? For example, "I will go for a 30-minute walk every morning to improve my fitness" is clear and focused.

- Measurable: Progress is a great motivator, and measuring your success keeps you on track. A goal like "I will save $500 each month" is measurable because you can easily track your progress month by month. It's about having a clear target that allows you to evaluate your advancement.

- Achievable: While it's important to stretch yourself, your goals should still be within your capacity to achieve. Ask yourself if the goal is realistic given your current resources, time, and energy. Setting yourself up for success means finding a balance between ambition and realism.

- Relevant: Every goal should align with your broader vision of freedom. If your ultimate goal is more time with your family, a relevant goal might be, "I will work no more than 40 hours a week to ensure I have quality time with loved ones." It's about focusing on goals that truly matter to you and contribute to your overall purpose.

- Time-bound: Without a deadline, a goal can easily become a "someday" aspiration. Deadlines create urgency and help you prioritize. For example, "I will launch my new website by the end of the next quarter" is time-bound and gives you a specific timeline for action.

Applying the SMART Framework to Your Vision of Freedom

Now that you're familiar with the SMART framework (and hopefully, you've already started using this tool after reading my first book), it's time to apply it directly to your vision of freedom. Begin by identifying the key elements that define your ultimate lifestyle—whether it's achieving financial independence, improving your health, or building stronger relationships. Break each aspect of your vision into specific goals aligning with the SMART criteria.

For instance, if your vision includes the flexibility to travel, you might set a SMART goal such as: "I will build a remote business over the next 12 months that generates $10,000 per month, allowing me to travel for at least three months each year." This goal is specific, measurable, achievable, relevant, and time-bound, turning a vague desire into a concrete, actionable plan.

Applying the SMART framework transforms your vision of freedom from an abstract idea into a series of intentional steps. Each goal you set becomes a focused milestone, bringing you closer to the life you've envisioned. This structured approach keeps you motivated and ensures that all your efforts align with your long-term dreams of freedom and fulfillment.

Crafting a Roadmap to Achieve Your Goals

Once you've identified both your short-term and long-term goals, the next crucial step is to create a roadmap that connects them. This roadmap acts as your strategic guide, laying out the steps necessary to move toward your ultimate vision of freedom. Here's how you can craft an effective, actionable roadmap:

1. Start with Your Long-Term Goals: Begin by clearly defining your long-term goals—those major milestones you want to achieve over the next five, ten, or twenty years. Write them down and keep them visible somewhere you can review them regularly. These long-term goals are your guiding stars, offering direction and helping you stay focused on the bigger picture as you navigate the journey ahead.

2. Break Down Long-Term Goals into Short-Term Actions: After outlining your long-term goals, break them down into manageable, actionable short-term steps.

These smaller goals should be specific actions you can take in the next few weeks or months that contribute directly to your long-term vision. For instance, if your long-term goal is to start your own business, short-term actions could include conducting market research, drafting a business plan, or setting aside savings for startup costs.

3. Prioritize Your Goals: Not all goals are created equal, so prioritize them based on their importance and the impact they will have on your overall vision. Focus first on the goals that will bring you the closest to your ultimate objectives. Ensure that each short-term goal you pursue is a stepping stone that directly contributes to a long-term outcome.

4. Create a Timeline: Develop a timeline that lays out when you intend to achieve each short-term and long-term goal. Setting specific deadlines helps you stay on track and maintain momentum. For example, if your long-term goal is to become debt-free within five years, your timeline might include paying off smaller debts in the first year and tackling larger ones progressively in subsequent years.

5. Monitor Your Progress: Regularly track your progress toward both your short-term and long-term goals. Celebrate small wins along the way, and don't hesitate to adjust your roadmap as needed. Life can throw unexpected changes your way, and flexibility is key. By monitoring your progress, you remain accountable and ensure that every step you take is moving you closer to your vision of freedom.

6. Stay Motivated: Keeping your vision front and center is vital, especially when challenges arise. Regularly revisit your long-term goals to remind yourself why you started this journey in the first place. Use each short-term success as fuel to maintain your momentum, knowing that every small step brings you closer to the life you've envisioned.

Bringing It All Together

By distinguishing between short-term and long-term goals and crafting a clear roadmap, you're creating a structured path toward your vision of freedom. Short-term goals provide those immediate actions and quick wins that keep you motivated, while long-term goals represent the bigger milestones that shape your ultimate lifestyle. Together, they create a cohesive strategy that guides you from where you are now to where you want to be.

Remember, the journey to freedom is a marathon, not a sprint. A well-crafted roadmap will keep you focused, help you navigate challenges, and allow you to steadily move closer to the life you've always dreamed of. Every goal—whether short-term or long-term—serves as a vital step in your journey, bringing you closer to the freedom and fulfillment you seek.

Overcoming Limiting Beliefs: Breaking Free from What Holds You Back

As you work toward your vision of freedom, some of the biggest obstacles you'll face aren't external—they're internal. Limiting beliefs are those deeply ingrained thoughts and assumptions that can prevent you from achieving your goals or living the life you truly desire. These beliefs often operate beneath the surface, subtly influencing your decisions, actions, and overall mindset. To break free from these mental barriers, the first step is to identify them and understand how they might hold you back.

Identifying Limiting Beliefs

Limiting beliefs often stems from past experiences, societal expectations, or deeply rooted fears. They manifest as self-doubt or negative thoughts that convince you certain goals are out of reach. The tricky part is that these beliefs often feel like undeniable truths when, in fact, they're just perceptions that can be challenged and overcome.

Here are some signs that you may be dealing with limiting beliefs:

- **Thinking in absolutes**: You often tell yourself, "I can't," "I'm not good enough," or "This is just the way things are."

- **Avoiding risks**: You shy away from trying new things due to a fear of failure or judgment.

- **Procrastination**: You put off important tasks or find excuses for why you can't pursue certain goals.

- **Comparing yourself to others**: You frequently compare yourself to others and feel like you're falling short.

- **Doubting your ability**: You set goals, but deep down, you doubt your ability to achieve them.

By recognizing these patterns in your thoughts, you can begin to challenge and break free from the beliefs that are holding you back.

Common Limiting Beliefs That Can Hinder the Pursuit of Freedom

Limiting beliefs are unique to each person, but certain ones are common roadblocks for many people on their journey toward freedom. Let's explore a few of these that might be holding you back:

1. "I'm Not Good Enough" This belief is one of the most pervasive and destructive. It stems from the fear that you lack the skills, intelligence, or talent to achieve your goals. When you believe you're not good enough, you hesitate to take on new challenges, limiting your growth and potential. Whether in your career or personal life, this belief can block opportunities that could lead you to the freedom you're seeking.

2. "I Don't Deserve Success" Rooted in guilt, low self-worth, or imposter syndrome, this belief convinces you that success is meant for others, but not for you. You may feel unworthy of your dreams and unconsciously sabotage your progress, creating unnecessary obstacles. Recognizing that you deserve success is crucial to moving forward toward your goals.

3. "I Can't Afford to Take Risks" Fear of risk often keeps people stuck in safe but unsatisfying situations. While it's natural to weigh the pros and cons of a decision, the belief that any risk is too dangerous can prevent you from stepping out of your comfort zone and seizing new opportunities. Growth and freedom often require calculated risks, but believing that you can't afford any risks at all will limit your potential.

4. "It's Too Late for Me" This belief can emerge with age or after experiencing setbacks. You might think that you've missed your chance or that it's too late to

start something new. But the reality is, it's never too late to pursue your passions or make significant changes in your life. Believing otherwise can hold you back from the personal growth and freedom you deserve.

5. "Success Requires Sacrifice" While hard work is often part of achieving success, this belief can lead to the assumption that you must sacrifice your happiness, health, or relationships to get there. This all-or-nothing mindset can keep you from finding a balanced approach to your goals—one that allows you to thrive without losing sight of what's truly important in life.

6. "I'm Afraid of What Others Will Think" The fear of judgment or criticism from others can be a powerful limiting belief. You may worry that pursuing your true desires will lead to disapproval or make you stand out in ways that feel uncomfortable. But living authentically is the key to true freedom, and being held back by the opinions of others can prevent you from reaching your full potential.

Why Overcoming Limiting Beliefs is Crucial for Freedom

Limiting beliefs act as mental barriers, trapping you in a cycle of self-doubt, fear, and inaction. These beliefs prevent you from fully embracing your potential and hold you back from pursuing the life you envision. By identifying and challenging them, you begin to dismantle their hold and replace them with empowering beliefs that fuel your growth and success.

Breaking free from limiting beliefs is essential for achieving true freedom because these beliefs are often the invisible chains that keep you stuck. When you free your mind from these constraints, you open up a world of possibilities. With a mindset unburdened by self-imposed limits, you can take bold, decisive steps toward your goals, living a life that aligns with your deepest values and aspirations.

In the next section, we'll dive into practical methods for reframing and transforming these limiting beliefs. These strategies will help you cultivate a mindset that empowers you to pursue and achieve your vision of freedom.

Exercise: Uncovering Limiting Beliefs in Your Mindset

For the next exercises that will help you challenge and overcome your limiting beliefs, head over to the workbook available on the website (www.RogerGBbest.com/workbooks). These exercises are designed to guide you through practical steps in reframing your mindset, and they could be the key to unlocking your full potential. Don't hesitate—commit to this work and watch how it transforms your path to freedom!

Story: The Entrepreneur Who Reframed Failure

Meet David, a passionate entrepreneur with a vision of building his own tech startup. From an early age, David was captivated by technology and innovation, spending years refining his skills and saving enough money to finally take the leap. However, when the day arrived to launch his first product, things didn't unfold as he had hoped.

Despite months of hard work and preparation, the launch was a disappointment. Sales were far below expectations, and customer feedback wasn't positive. David found himself feeling like a failure. He had invested his time, energy, and finances into this project, and now it seemed like it had all been for nothing.

As doubt crept in, David began to internalize the belief: "I'm not cut out for this. I've failed, and I might never recover." This limiting mindset began to affect his every move. He hesitated to take risks, constantly second-guessed himself, and even contemplated giving up his dream.

But then David attended a workshop that changed everything. The speaker discussed the importance of reframing failure and shared stories of entrepreneurs who had faced multiple setbacks before achieving their breakthroughs. David realized that failure wasn't an endpoint but a stepping stone—an opportunity to learn and grow.

With a new perspective, David reflected on his initial product launch. Rather than seeing it as a definitive failure, he asked himself, "What lessons can I take from this? How can I improve for next time?" He studied customer feedback, fine-tuned his marketing strategy, and identified areas for improvement.

Instead of holding onto the belief "I'm not cut out for this," David redefined it to "This experience is helping me grow, and I will use what I've learned to succeed in the future."

Armed with a refreshed mindset and renewed energy, David went back to the drawing board, redesigned his product, adjusted his marketing, and prepared for a relaunch.

This time, things were different. Customers noticed the improvements, and sales picked up. But the real victory was in David's transformation. By reframing his setbacks, he had cultivated resilience and developed a growth-oriented approach to entrepreneurship.

In the following years, David's startup thrived. He launched new products, faced new challenges, and continued to grow—both personally and professionally. His belief that setbacks are valuable learning experiences became the cornerstone of his success, driving him forward with every obstacle he encountered.

David's story is a reminder that failure is not the end of the road. By reframing limiting beliefs, he was able to transform a perceived failure into the foundation for his long-term success. His journey shows that growth, resilience, and progress come from how we choose to interpret and learn from our experiences.

Conclusion

As we wrap up this chapter, take a moment to reflect on the transformative journey we've embarked on together. We began by digging deep into what freedom truly means to **you**—not just as a general concept, but as a vision that is personally tailored to your passions, purpose, and long-term aspirations. Defining this vision clearly is essential because it becomes your guiding star, leading you toward a life that feels both fulfilling and authentically yours.

You've explored powerful tools like vision boards and visualization exercises to bring your ideal lifestyle into focus. This isn't about daydreaming; it's about creating a tangible roadmap, an inspiring framework that will guide your decisions and actions as you progress toward your goals.

We also dove into the key pillars of an ultimate lifestyle, emphasizing work-life balance, health, and meaningful relationships. These are not just extras—they form the solid foundation upon which true freedom and fulfillment rest. Without them, achieving lasting personal growth can feel out of reach.

In addition, we discussed the importance of setting clear and achievable goals using the SMART framework, ensuring that your ambitions are backed by actionable steps.

By distinguishing between short-term and long-term goals, you learned how to craft a roadmap that connects your daily actions to your broader vision of freedom.

Finally, we explored the internal work needed to unlock your full potential, focusing on the importance of identifying and overcoming limiting beliefs. Equipped with practical tools to reframe these beliefs, you are now ready to replace them with empowering perspectives that will propel you forward on your personal and professional journey.

Now, it's time to step into action. This chapter has laid the foundation, but the true transformation begins when you put these concepts into practice. Start by clearly defining **your** vision of freedom—one that aligns with your passions, values, and purpose. Engage in powerful visualization exercises or create a vision board to bring your dreams to life. Then, take the crucial step of setting both short-term and long-term goals that support this vision, and begin taking those first, tangible steps toward achieving them.

Remember, your journey toward freedom is a process, not a race. Each small action moves you closer to the life you've envisioned, even if progress feels slow at times. Don't wait for the perfect plan or timing—start where you are, with what you have. Embrace the journey, learn from setbacks, and keep your focus fixed on your ultimate goal.

This is **your** life, **your** vision, and **your** path to freedom. Take control, define your future, and start building the life you've always dreamed of. The possibilities are endless when you believe in your vision and take consistent, intentional action toward making it a reality.

Call to Action: Start Creating Your Vision of Freedom

Now that you've explored what freedom means to you and how it can shape your ideal lifestyle, it's time to take the first concrete steps toward bringing that vision to life. The concepts we've discussed aren't just abstract ideas—they form the foundation upon which the life you've always dreamed of can be built. But, like any foundation, it only serves its purpose when you begin laying the bricks of action.

True transformation doesn't happen by waiting for the perfect moment. It happens when you start, here and now, with what you have. So take action today—start defining your vision with clarity, set meaningful goals, and begin shaping the life you truly desire.

Take Action Today

Don't wait for the perfect moment to start—begin today. Gather your materials for your vision board, set aside dedicated time for visualization, and start answering the key questions that will bring your vision of freedom into sharper focus. The sooner you begin, the sooner you'll start seeing meaningful changes in your life.

Remember, your vision of freedom isn't just a far-off dream—it's a destination within your reach. With intentional and consistent action, you can turn that vision into reality. By taking these first steps, you're laying a solid foundation for a life that fully reflects your values, passions, and deepest desires.

Your journey toward freedom starts now. Embrace it with open arms, knowing that you hold the power to create the life you've always envisioned. Each step forward—one vision, one goal, one action at a time—brings you closer to the life you've always dreamed of living.

Chapter Three
Uncovering the Myths of Hard Work and Burnout

In a world that glorifies the hustle, many of us have been conditioned to believe that relentless hard work is the ultimate key to success. We've been taught that the more hours we grind, the more sacrifices we make, the closer we'll get to achieving our dreams. But what if this constant push for more is actually holding us back? What if the notion that success requires endless hustle is a myth—a harmful one that leads to burnout, diminished productivity, and a life that feels anything but free?

In this chapter, we're going to challenge some of the most deeply ingrained beliefs about hard work and success. We'll examine why the idea that hard work alone guarantees success is not only flawed but also potentially damaging. We'll uncover the reality of burnout—how it can sneak up on even the most passionate entrepreneurs and leave you feeling drained, disillusioned, and disconnected from your goals. We'll also take a closer look at the misconceptions surrounding productivity, revealing that working more doesn't always mean achieving more.

> *Success is not the result of endless hours of work; it's the result of the right work, done efficiently and purposefully. – Roger Best*

But this isn't just about debunking myths—it's about redefining hard work in a way that supports personal growth, balance, and freedom. We'll explore how to shift from a mindset of constant hustle to one that embraces smart, sustainable effort. You'll learn to develop work habits that not only drive success but also safeguard your well-being, allowing you to protect your energy and enthusiasm for the work you do.

By the end of this chapter, you'll have a deeper understanding of what it truly means to work hard—and more importantly, how to work in a way that aligns with your vision of freedom. It's time to let go of the myths that have been holding you back and embrace a healthier, more sustainable approach to achieving your goals, on your terms.

The Story of John and the Brick Wall

In a world that glorifies the hustle, many of us have been conditioned to believe that relentless hard work is the ultimate key to success. We've been taught that the more hours we grind, the more sacrifices we make, the closer we'll get to achieving our dreams. But what if this constant push for more is actually holding us back? What if the belief that success requires endless hustle is a myth—a dangerous one that leads to burnout, diminished productivity, and a life that feels anything but free?

In this chapter, we're going to challenge some of the most deeply ingrained beliefs about hard work and success. We'll examine why the idea that hard work alone guarantees success is not only flawed but potentially damaging. We'll uncover the harsh reality of burnout—how it can creep up on even the most passionate entrepreneurs, leaving you drained, disillusioned, and disconnected from your goals. We'll also take a closer look at the common misconceptions around productivity, revealing that working more doesn't always translate to achieving more.

We are going to reshape the way you approach hard work so it nurtures your personal growth, well-being, and sense of freedom. We'll explore how to shift from a mindset of constant hustle to one that embraces smart, sustainable efforts. You'll learn to develop work habits that not only drive success but also protect your energy, passion, and overall well-being.

We'll point you to a new understanding of what it truly means to work hard—and, more importantly, how to work in a way that aligns with your vision of freedom and fulfillment. It's time to let go of the myths that have held you back and embrace a healthier, more sustainable approach to achieving your goals, on your terms.

The Myth of Hard Work Equals Success

The idea that hard work is the ultimate key to success is woven deeply into our cultural and societal fabric. It's a belief passed down through generations and frequently upheld as an unshakable truth. From a young age, we're taught that with enough effort, we can achieve anything. This narrative is reinforced by stories of self-made individuals who, through sheer determination, supposedly rose to greatness. You'll find several of these examples in my first book, *From Hamster Wheel to Hammock: A Guide to Taking Back Your Day*. But where did this belief originate, and how did it become so deeply ingrained in our collective mindset?

Historical Context: The Glorification of Hard Work

To understand the origins of this myth, we need to look back at the Industrial Revolution of the 18th and 19th centuries. During this transformative era, factories and mass production reshaped economies, and the concept of hard work became deeply tied to one's identity as a responsible citizen. Workers were expected to endure long hours under grueling conditions, and success was measured by one's capacity to persevere in the face of hardship, all in pursuit of economic advancement.

This mindset was further solidified by the Protestant work ethic, which emerged during the early modern period, especially in Northern Europe and the United States. This belief system emphasized hard work, discipline, and frugality as markers of moral virtue and paths to both spiritual salvation and earthly success. As this ethic became embedded in Western society, it reinforced the idea that persistence and effort were the ultimate keys to prosperity.

By the late 19th and early 20th centuries, the cultural narrative of self-made men like Andrew Carnegie and John D. Rockefeller, who built vast fortunes through relentless effort, added another layer to the glorification of hard work. Their stories were often oversimplified, focusing on personal grit while minimizing the roles of opportunity, timing, and labor exploitation. These narratives helped cement the enduring belief that hard work alone guarantees success—a myth that continues to shape modern perceptions of entrepreneurship and achievement.

Cultural and Societal Pressures

Fast forward to today, and this myth still thrives—amplified by societal expectations and the pressure to constantly hustle. In our culture, being busy is often mistaken for being successful or important. Social media only fuels this narrative, flooding us with images and posts celebrating the grind—late nights, early mornings, and the constant drive to do more, achieve more, and be more. If you're not working yourself to exhaustion, it's easy to feel like you're somehow falling behind or failing.

Societal expectations reinforce this belief from an early age, conditioning us to think that success demands sacrifice, long hours, and personal trade-offs. This pressure is especially strong in certain industries and cultures where overwork is not just expected but celebrated. Take, for example, Japan's 'karoshi,' or 'death by overwork,' which tragically underscores the extreme consequences of glorifying hard work without regard for well-being.

Workplace pressures further fuel this myth. Employers often demand more from their employees, and the competitive nature of modern economies leads individuals to push themselves past their limits. We're told that success is directly tied to how much effort we put in—regardless of whether that effort is sustainable or aligned with our overall well-being.

> *Working hard without direction is like running on a hamster wheel—you expend energy but go nowhere. - Roger Best*

The Fallacy of the Myth

But here's the often-overlooked truth: while hard work matters, it is far from the only ingredient for success. The belief that more hours automatically lead to better outcomes is a flawed concept. In reality, success depends on a variety of factors—effective strategy, seizing opportunities, the right timing, and yes, even luck. Without aligning hard work with smart decisions and innovation, even the most tireless effort can go to waste.

Moreover, believing that success requires endless hustle can be damaging. It often leads to burnout, chronic stress, and a life that feels imbalanced and unfulfilling. When we buy into this myth, we risk sacrificing our health, relationships, and happiness—chasing an ideal that may not even deliver the satisfaction we're seeking.

one In the rest of this chapter, we'll continue examining how this hard work myth plays out in our daily lives and how we can redefine our approach to work. We'll explore ways to cultivate success that support both our goals and our well-being. It's time to challenge the societal pressures that keep us trapped in the cycle of relentless hustle and adopt a more holistic, sustainable mindset toward success.

Reality Check: Hard Work vs. Success – What the Research Says

The belief that hard work alone leads to success is deeply ingrained in our culture, but the reality is more nuanced. Research and personal experience have revealed that while effort is essential, it's just one part of the equation. When I was younger, I would have argued against this idea, convinced that relentless effort was the key to success. Long workdays, late nights, and pushing myself to the limit seemed like the only way to prove my dedication. But over time, I learned the hard way that hard work without balance can lead to burnout and diminish both your productivity and well-being.

The idea that working smarter, not just harder, is more effective may seem counterintuitive, but it's supported by research. Studies have shown that after a certain point, the productivity gained from additional hours diminishes significantly. This means that working longer doesn't always equate to producing better results. For example, a study conducted by Stanford University revealed that productivity per hour declines sharply when the workweek exceeds 50 hours. In fact, those who work 70 hours a week produce little more with those extra 20 hours than someone working 50 hours does.

Additionally, other findings highlight the importance of cognitive flexibility, emotional intelligence, and effective decision-making in achieving success. Hard work that isn't paired with thoughtful strategy can result in wasted effort and missed opportunities. Research from Harvard Business Review also suggests that leaders who focus on high-impact activities, delegate effectively, and take time for reflection tend to achieve greater long-term success than those who rely solely on relentless effort.

In my own life, I realized that success isn't solely determined by how much I work but how effectively I prioritize my time, my energy, and my well-being. Here are some key findings that challenge the myth of hard work as the sole path to success:

- **The Law of Diminishing Returns**: Working beyond a certain number of hours results in reduced productivity. Studies show that 50 hours a week is often the point where more work yields less value.

- **Strategic Effort Beats Constant Effort**: Smart, focused effort on the right tasks produces far greater results than working long hours on everything. Prioritization is key.

- **The Role of Rest and Recovery**: Adequate rest, breaks, and downtime not only prevent burnout but also boost creativity and problem-solving abilities, essential elements of long-term success.

These findings show that hard work is necessary, but it must be combined with balance, strategy, and rest to truly achieve sustainable success. Here's a little more about this myth:

The 10,000-Hour Rule — More Than Just Hard Work

The 10,000-hour rule, popularized by Malcolm Gladwell in *Outliers*, has become synonymous with the idea that sheer time and effort are enough to master any skill. However, recent research provides a more nuanced understanding, suggesting that it's not just the number of hours spent but how those hours are used that makes the difference.

The core of mastery lies in *deliberate practice*, a concept emphasized by psychologist Anders Ericsson, whose work influenced Gladwell's rule. Deliberate practice involves structured, purposeful effort aimed at improving specific aspects of a skill. Unlike regular practice, which can be repetitive and passive, deliberate practice targets weaknesses, requires continuous feedback, and often involves discomfort as it stretches your abilities. The goal is to push your limits and refine techniques through focused intentional effort.

Another important consideration is the *quality of those practice hours*. While 10,000 hours can give a rough estimate of the time investment required, factors such as mentorship, access to resources, innate talent, and the opportunity for reflective learning play significant roles in the journey to mastery. The absence of these critical elements can turn those hours into wasted time, where no meaningful progress is made despite the effort.

Research also shows that individuals often plateau without feedback or goal-oriented improvement, regardless of how much time they put in. In fact, simply "working hard" without a strategic approach can lead to inefficiency, resulting in burnout rather than mastery. This highlights the danger of interpreting the 10,000-hour rule too literally—it's not about long hours of work alone but the *effective use* of those hours.

To truly progress, a combination of deliberate practice, consistent self-assessment, and quality resources is necessary. In the absence of these factors, you may find yourself caught in a cycle of busy work, with high effort but minimal results—a reality that can drain motivation and hinder long-term success.

The Role of Work-Life Balance in Productivity

The role of work-life balance in productivity is a topic that challenges long-held beliefs about the relationship between work hours and output. Numerous studies, including those conducted by the Organization for Economic Cooperation and Development (OECD), show that shorter, more focused work hours can lead to higher productivity.

Take Germany, for example. With an average workweek of 34 to 35 hours, German workers consistently rank among the most productive globally. This is due in large part to a cultural emphasis on efficiency during work hours and the prioritization of work-life balance. German workers focus intently on their tasks, reduce distractions, and are encouraged to rest adequately outside of work. This approach not only enhances concentration but also improves the quality of work.

In stark contrast, countries like South Korea and Japan, where long work hours are the norm, often experience diminishing returns in terms of productivity. In South Korea, the average workweek extends to nearly 40 hours, but the country's productivity rates are significantly lower than those of nations with shorter workweeks. Similarly, Japan's "karoshi" (death by overwork) phenomenon illustrates the extreme consequences of a culture that equates long hours with success. Despite the grueling hours, productivity remains subpar, highlighting the inefficiency of overwork and the physical and mental toll it takes on employees.

The underlying problem is that longer work hours lead to exhaustion, increased mistakes, reduced creativity, and lower overall work quality. Over time, chronic stress from overwork results in burnout, which further erodes productivity. These findings underscore a critical truth: working smarter, not harder, is the key to sustainable productivity. Balancing work with adequate rest and personal time allows individuals to recharge, stay focused, and consistently produce high-quality work.

In conclusion, fostering a work culture that values balance, focused work hours, and rest can significantly enhance productivity, benefiting both individuals and organizations alike.

The Impact of Burnout on Performance

Burnout is a well-documented consequence of chronic overwork, and its impact on job performance can be profound. When employees consistently push themselves beyond their limits without adequate rest or recovery, they risk entering a state of physical, emotional, and mental exhaustion—commonly referred to as burnout. This condition doesn't just affect the individual; it ripples through the entire organization, leading to a cascade of negative outcomes.

Research published in the journal *PLOS ONE* provides a stark illustration of how burnout affects employees' productivity and job satisfaction. The study found that employees experiencing burnout are significantly less productive than their well-rested counterparts. This decline in productivity is often due to the depletion of mental and physical resources, making it harder for employees to maintain focus, creativity, and efficiency in their work. Tasks that once felt manageable become overwhelming, leading to a slowdown in output and a decline in the quality of work.

Burnout also increases the likelihood of errors and mistakes. As employees become more fatigued, their cognitive functions, such as attention, memory, and decision-making, begin to suffer. This cognitive impairment means that even routine tasks can be mishandled, and critical decisions may be made poorly. The accumulation of small errors can lead to significant setbacks for a business, affecting everything from customer satisfaction to project timelines and overall company reputation.

Furthermore, the emotional toll of burnout often leads to a sense of disengagement and detachment from work. Employees who were once highly motivated and committed may begin to feel indifferent or even resentful about their jobs. This emotional withdrawal can lead to a lack of collaboration and communication within teams, further exacerbating the decline in productivity and overall workplace morale.

The study also highlighted a critical issue for organizations: increased turnover. Employees suffering from burnout are more likely to leave their jobs, either by choice or because their performance deteriorates to the point where they are let go. High turnover rates can be devastating for companies, leading to increased costs associated with recruiting, hiring, and training new employees. Additionally, the loss of experienced staff can result in a loss of institutional knowledge and disrupt ongoing projects, further undermining long-term success.

Companies with high levels of employee burnout not only suffer from lower overall productivity but also face significant challenges in maintaining a stable and engaged workforce. The cumulative effect of burnout—reduced productivity, increased errors, emotional disengagement, and higher turnover—can create a vicious cycle where the remaining employees are forced to pick up the slack, leading to even greater levels of stress and burnout across the organization.

Addressing burnout is essential in protecting the long-term viability and success of the company. Organizations that prioritize employee health, provide adequate support, and foster a culture of balance and well-being are more likely to see sustained productivity, lower turnover rates, and higher levels of employee satisfaction. In contrast, companies that ignore the warning signs of burnout may find themselves facing a steep decline in both employee performance and overall business success.

The Myth of Multitasking

The myth of multitasking, long believed to be a path to greater efficiency, is increasingly debunked by scientific research. Many people operate under the assumption that juggling multiple tasks at once saves time and boosts productivity. However, studies like those conducted by Stanford University have shown the opposite to be true—multitasking actually hampers productivity and cognitive performance.

In the Stanford study, researchers found that individuals who frequently multitask struggle more with filtering out irrelevant information. This inability to focus on what matters leads to a cluttered attention span and constant distractions. The act of switching between tasks itself—whether answering emails while in a meeting or texting during a conversation—requires significant cognitive energy. This process, known as "task switching," depletes mental resources, reducing one's capacity to focus deeply on a single task.

Another consequence of multitasking is that it impairs one's ability to sustain attention on more complex or creative tasks. Critical thinking, problem-solving, and other tasks requiring high-level mental effort suffer when our brain is pulled in multiple directions. As a result, instead of completing one task efficiently, people often end up with multiple half-finished tasks and scattered thoughts, ultimately slowing down overall progress.

This myth extends beyond the workplace into daily life. For example, checking social media during family time or constantly switching between apps can prevent you from fully enjoying or engaging in the present moment, leading to feelings of stress and dissatisfaction.

Research suggests focusing on one task at a time to truly boost productivity and improve the quality of work. Deep, focused work not only leads to better outcomes but also helps reduce the stress that multitasking tends to exacerbate.

By shifting from multitasking to a single-tasking approach, you can enhance your cognitive performance, make fewer errors, and feel more accomplished both professionally and personally.

The Importance of Strategic Effort and Innovation

The importance of strategic effort and innovation cannot be overstated in today's competitive and fast-paced business environment. A study conducted by the National Bureau of Economic Research (NBER) highlights a critical insight: while hard work is undeniably valuable, it is not the sole determinant of long-term success. In fact, innovation and strategic decision-making play a far more significant role in shaping a company's future.

The research revealed that companies focusing exclusively on working harder—pushing employees to the limit and emphasizing the quantity of work over quality—often find themselves outpaced by competitors who prioritize innovation and strategic thinking. Innovation helps companies stay ahead by adapting to changing market conditions and meeting evolving customer needs. Without it, even the hardest-working companies risk falling behind, especially in industries driven by constant advancements.

Strategic decision-making is equally important. Companies skilled at long-term planning, market analysis, and resource allocation are better equipped to anticipate challenges and seize opportunities. This proactive approach, rather than reactive, enables businesses to thrive. Companies focusing only on relentless hard work might find themselves merely reacting to changes instead of shaping their future through informed decisions. This can lead to missed opportunities and inefficient resource use.

The study also emphasizes the role of adaptability. In a rapidly changing market, companies that embrace flexibility and cultivate a culture that encourages creativity and experimentation are more likely to succeed. This mindset often sparks innovation, leading to new products, services, and business models. On the other hand, organizations that prioritize hard work over adaptability risk becoming rigid, stifling innovation, and missing strategic growth opportunities.

Ultimately, the NBER findings underscore the need for working smarter, not just harder. Companies that foster innovation, adaptability, and strategic thinking are more likely to achieve sustainable success. For both individuals and leaders, the takeaway is clear: hard work alone is not enough. True success requires critical thinking, strategic planning, and an openness to new ideas. By focusing on smart effort, businesses and individuals alike can achieve more with less while staying competitive in a constantly evolving market.

The Role of Rest and Recovery

The research by NBER shows that businesses that prioritize relentless hard work—pushing employees to their limits and focusing on quantity over quality—are often outpaced by competitors who emphasize innovation and strategic thinking. For entrepreneurs, this means that true growth comes not from endless hustle but from adapting to changing markets and consistently finding smarter ways to work. This strategic approach allows you to meet evolving customer needs while maintaining the personal freedom you desire.

Strategic decision-making is also crucial for entrepreneurs seeking long-term success while safeguarding their time and energy. By focusing on long-term planning, resource allocation, and market analysis, you can anticipate challenges and seize new opportunities, allowing for sustainable growth without the burnout that comes from constant grind.

Adaptability plays a key role in achieving freedom. Companies, and individuals, who embrace flexibility and foster creativity are more likely to innovate successfully, leading to new products, services, and opportunities. On the flip side, entrepreneurs who prioritize effort over adaptability may become rigid, stifling innovation and missing out on potential breakthroughs.

Ultimately, the NBER findings underscore the idea of working smarter, not just harder. As an entrepreneur, true personal and professional growth comes from combining effort with innovation, adaptability, and strategic thinking. This approach ensures you not only achieve success but also have the freedom to shape your journey *your way*, on your terms.

A More Holistic View of Success

These statistics and research findings reveal a critical truth: while hard work is undeniably a factor in achieving success, it's far from the only one. Success is multifaceted, shaped by a careful balance of deliberate practice, strategic effort, innovation, access to opportunities, and maintaining a healthy work-life balance.

As an entrepreneur or leader, these factors are even more crucial. Your ability to innovate, make strategic decisions, and maintain sustainable energy and focus is not just important, it's vital to both your success and the success of your business. Managing your time, energy, and resources directly impacts your company's culture and growth. If you neglect balance and strategic thinking in your own life, you risk personal burnout and leading your organization down an unsustainable path.

As you continue on this journey, it's essential to apply these lessons to your leadership approach. Strive for a method that prioritizes working smarter, leveraging opportunities, and creating an environment that supports long-term growth for both yourself and your team. Remember, the way you manage your personal freedom and well-being sets the tone for your organization's success. By leading with intentionality, balance, and purpose, you create a thriving business where you and your employees can reach your full potential.

Work Smarter, not Harder: The Hall of Fame for Hustle-Free Heroes

Success stories often highlight relentless effort and long hours, but many individuals have achieved remarkable success by working strategically and managing their time wisely. These examples show that innovation, balance, and leveraging resources can be just as critical as hard work.

1. Warren Buffett: The Oracle of Omaha

Warren Buffett is known for his strategic approach, spending much of his day reading, thinking, and reflecting. He attributes his success not to endless hours of work, but to making a few well-thought-out decisions. Buffett exemplifies how working smart and making time for reflection can lead to enormous success.

2. Richard Branson: The Adventurous Entrepreneur

Richard Branson is another example of someone who achieved success by focusing on what matters most and delegating responsibilities. He enjoys life while building his business, trusting his team to handle operations. Branson's story shows that you can thrive by maintaining a balanced lifestyle and focusing on innovation rather than getting bogged down in daily tasks.

3. Tim Ferriss: The 4-Hour Workweek

Tim Ferriss built his career by questioning traditional notions of hard work. Through his *4-Hour Workweek* philosophy, he advocates for efficiency, automation, and focusing on high-impact activities. Ferriss demonstrates how working smarter and prioritizing essential tasks can lead to success and personal freedom.

4. Sara Blakely: The Founder of Spanx

Sara Blakely became the youngest self-made female billionaire by solving a specific problem and leveraging creativity and risk-taking. She didn't rely on working extreme hours but instead focused on strategic effort. Blakely's journey shows the power of balancing work and life while staying focused on what truly matters.

5. Tony Hsieh: Zappos and the Power of Culture

Tony Hsieh built Zappos into a billion-dollar company not by driving his team to work long hours, but by creating a positive company culture. His focus on customer service and employee happiness demonstrates how success can be achieved by nurturing a supportive environment.

These examples illustrate that success doesn't always come from working extreme hours or pushing oneself to the brink of exhaustion. Instead, success often stems from strategic thinking, innovation, leveraging resources, and maintaining a healthy work-life balance. These individuals demonstrate that by focusing on what truly matters, delegating, and making intelligent decisions, it's possible to achieve remarkable success without subscribing to the myth that hard work alone is the key to success.

The Burnout Syndrome: When Hard Work Takes a Toll

In today's fast-paced world, where the hustle is often celebrated as a badge of honor, burnout has quietly become a widespread issue. Many ambitious individuals push themselves beyond their limits, convinced that the only path to success is through relentless effort. But this constant drive can backfire, leading to a state of deep physical, emotional, and mental fatigue known as burnout. Recognizing and understanding burnout isn't just essential for your health—it's also key to maintaining long-term success without sacrificing your well-being.

Understanding Burnout

Burnout is much more than just feeling fatigued after a demanding day or needing a break following a particularly challenging week. It's a chronic condition that develops gradually, often taking root without any immediate warning. Burnout occurs when you've been subjected to prolonged periods of stress, continuously pushing yourself without sufficient rest or recovery. It stems from being overextended emotionally, physically, and mentally, ultimately leaving you feeling exhausted, detached, and overwhelmed by your responsibilities.

The impact of burnout stretches beyond feelings of tiredness. It can severely diminish your productivity and creativity, lead to strained relationships, and deteriorate your overall quality of life. What might begin as a drive to achieve and succeed can quickly morph into a cycle where your efforts result in diminishing returns, and the passion you once had for your work—or for life in general—begins to fade.

Physically, burnout can manifest as constant fatigue, frequent illnesses due to a weakened immune system, and even headaches or gastrointestinal issues. Mentally, it can erode your ability to concentrate, sap your motivation, and contribute to feelings of helplessness or cynicism. Emotionally, burnout can create a sense of detachment, a lack of empathy, or even lead to anxiety or depression.

Recognizing burnout early is key to mitigating its long-term effects. Identifying the warning signs—such as emotional exhaustion, reduced performance, or detachment from work—can empower you to take action before burnout takes a firm hold. Strategies for preventing burnout include setting clear boundaries between work and personal life, prioritizing self-care, engaging in regular physical activity, and seeking social support when needed.

By understanding the true nature of burnout, you can start making intentional changes to protect both your well-being and your long-term success, ensuring that you're able to sustain your drive without sacrificing your health or happiness.

Definition and Stages of Burnout

Burnout doesn't strike suddenly—it develops progressively over time, often creeping in without being immediately recognized. Understanding the stages of burnout can help you catch it early and take action before it becomes overwhelming.

1. The Honeymoon Phase – This is where everything feels fresh and exciting. You're highly motivated, fueled by passion and optimism. You may be working long hours or taking on extra responsibilities, but it doesn't feel burdensome yet. However, while you're running on adrenaline, you might also be sowing the seeds of burnout by overcommitting or neglecting self-care in favor of work.

2. Onset of Stress- As the honeymoon phase fades, stress begins to emerge. You might notice that your energy levels are dropping and tasks that once excited you now feel more demanding. Productivity may start to dip, and feelings of irritability or frustration can surface. Although you're still pushing through, the wear and tear of constant pressure are becoming evident, both mentally and physically.

3. Chronic Stress -At this stage, stress becomes an almost constant companion. You may experience physical symptoms like headaches, digestive issues, or trouble sleeping. Emotionally, you may feel increasingly anxious, frustrated, or disconnected. Work starts to feel overwhelming, and you may find yourself withdrawing from colleagues, friends, or social activities. This phase is marked by a growing sense of helplessness as efforts to cope seem less effective.

4. Burnout -When burnout fully sets in, you hit a state of emotional, physical, and mental exhaustion. Cynicism and detachment from work, colleagues, and even personal interests take over. You may struggle with decision-making, and your productivity can plummet. You might also experience a steep decline in self-esteem, feeling inadequate or incapable. By this stage, burnout has a severe impact on your health, relationships, and overall well-being.

5. Habitual Burnout – If left unaddressed, burnout can evolve into a chronic condition. At this point, the exhaustion, disengagement, and sense of inadequacy become ingrained in daily life. This phase can lead to long-term health problems such as depression, anxiety, and chronic fatigue, and it can have significant consequences for your career, potentially resulting in prolonged absences or an inability to perform effectively.

Personal Story

I've gone through every stage of burnout—not just once, but multiple times. For years, I didn't even realize what was happening. All I knew was that something felt off and just wrote that off to being tired. Looking back, the signs were glaringly obvious to everyone around me, but I was blind to them at the time. I'd become short-tempered, irritable, and frankly, not very pleasant to be around. There were days when the idea of staying in bed sounded more appealing than just about anything, and that was completely out of character for me.

At the time, I shrugged it off as just being tired or maybe a bit overworked. I didn't realize how deep it went until later, when my body started giving me unmistakable signals. I remember one especially low moment when I began passing out every time I stood up too quickly. That's when I finally saw a doctor, who told me I had a bleeding ulcer. He prescribed Tagamet—back when you still needed a prescription for it—and a second medication that I didn't pay much attention to at first.

Within a few days, I felt dramatically better, which caught me off guard. I mentioned the shift to a friend who happened to be an RN, and she asked to see what I'd been prescribed. When she saw the second medication, she smiled and explained that it was an antidepressant. That explained the sudden mood lift, but at the time, I didn't care what it was. I just knew it made me feel better, and that was enough.

I wish I could say that burnout was a one-time thing, but it's not something you conquer and leave behind forever. You have to recognize it, face it head-on, identify the underlying causes, and make necessary changes to prevent it from recurring. I've faced it again, but the following time(s) I had learned to recognize the early warning signs and take proactive steps before things spiral out of control. I've also become more mindful of the situations and stressors in my life that could lead to burnout so I can adjust before I hit that breaking point again. That experience taught me an invaluable lesson: pushing yourself to the brink is never worth it, no matter how urgent or important the goal seems in the moment. Prioritizing well-being over relentless hustle is the key to sustaining long-term success.

My story might sound familiar to you. Maybe you've felt that same creeping sense of exhaustion and overwhelm, but you keep telling yourself you're just tired. The truth is burnout doesn't announce itself with flashing lights. It sneaks up, and by the time you realize what's happening, it can already have a firm grip on your health, relationships, and peace of mind. The real growth comes in recognizing those early signs and choosing to prioritize your well-being before burnout makes that choice for you.

The Impact of Burnout: A Toll on Every Aspect of Life

Burnout has far-reaching effects that can infiltrate every corner of your life, from your physical health to your emotional well-being and even your professional success. When left unchecked, burnout can work its way into every aspect of your life, both personal and professional.

Physical Consequences

Burnout can take a serious toll on your body. Prolonged stress and exhaustion can weaken your immune system, making you more susceptible to illnesses. Chronic fatigue is a common symptom, where no amount of sleep seems to restore your energy levels. You may also experience frequent headaches, muscle tension, gastrointestinal problems, or irritable bowel syndrome as your body reacts to constant stress. Over time, the physical wear and tear can lead to more severe health issues, such as heart disease, hypertension, and diabetes. The relentless pressure and lack of rest leave your body in a constant state of fight-or-flight, which is unsustainable and damaging in the long run. And, yes, it can even lead to bleeding ulcers.

Mental Consequences

The mental impact of burnout is equally concerning. Burnout often leads to decreased cognitive function, making it difficult to concentrate, remember important details, or make decisions. You might find yourself more forgetful, struggling to focus on tasks, or feeling overwhelmed by even the simplest responsibilities. This mental fog can also lead to a lack of creativity and problem-solving ability, which are crucial for both personal growth and professional success. Over time, chronic burnout can contribute to the development of mental health disorders such as anxiety and depression, creating a cycle that's hard to break. And, as I just said in my personal story, it can lead to sleep habit that are way outside the norm.

Emotional Consequences

Emotionally, burnout can leave you feeling detached and disengaged. You might start to lose interest in activities you once enjoyed or feel emotionally numb when faced with challenges. Cynicism and a pervasive sense of pessimism often accompany burnout, as stress erodes your resilience and optimism. This emotional toll can lead to strained relationships with friends, family, and colleagues as you become more irritable, withdrawn, or even hostile. The sense of fulfillment you once derived from your work or personal achievements may begin to fade, leaving you feeling empty and unmotivated.

Impact on Personal Life

In your personal life, burnout can create a disconnect between you and the people you care about. As burnout saps your energy and emotional reserves, you may find it harder to be present with your loved ones, leading to feelings of isolation or guilt. Your patience may wear thin, leading to conflicts at home or with friends. Burnout can also reduce your ability to enjoy leisure activities, hobbies, or downtime, as the constant stress makes relaxation seem impossible. Over time, this can strain your relationships and erode the support network you need to recover from burnout.

Impact on Professional Life

Professionally, the consequences of burnout can be devastating. As your productivity decreases, so does the quality of your work. Tasks that used to be routine may now feel insurmountable, leading to missed deadlines, mistakes, or a general decline in performance. This decline can affect your reputation, job satisfaction, and career progression. You may start to feel disengaged from your work, losing the passion and drive that once motivated you. In the long run, burnout can derail your business, making it difficult to achieve your professional goals.

The Far-Reaching Effects of Burnout

So, as you see, burnout is not just a fleeting feeling of exhaustion; it's a serious condition that affects your physical, mental, and emotional health. It can strain your relationships, diminish your professional performance, and undermine your overall quality of life. Understanding the impact of burnout is an early step in taking action to circumvent it. By recognizing the signs early and changing how you approach your work and life, you can protect yourself from the damaging effects of burnout and build a healthier, more sustainable path to success.

Misconceptions About Productivity: The Busy Trap

In our fast-paced world, it's easy to equate being busy with being productive. However, these two concepts are vastly different. Productivity is about achieving meaningful results and moving closer to your goals, while busyness is often just about filling time with activity—sometimes to the detriment of real progress. Understanding the difference between the two is crucial for anyone looking to maximize their effectiveness and avoid the pitfalls of merely "keeping busy."

The Difference Between Being Busy and Being Productive

Being Busy: When you're busy, your day is packed with tasks, meetings, and to-do lists, and it might seem like you're accomplishing a lot. However, busyness often involves doing things that are urgent but not necessarily important. It's easy to fall into the trap of filling your schedule with activities that give the illusion of productivity but don't actually move the needle on your most important goals. Busy people often find themselves exhausted at the end of the day yet frustrated because they haven't made significant progress on the things that really matter.

Being Productive: On the other hand, productivity is about focusing your time and energy on tasks that contribute to your long-term goals and create real value. Productive people prioritize their work based on importance rather than urgency. They are selective about what they take on, ensuring that their efforts align with their objectives. At the end of the day, productive individuals may have fewer tasks checked off their list, but the tasks they completed were high impact, moving them closer to their goals.

Common Traps That Create the Illusion of Productivity

1. The To-Do List Trap

- **The Illusion:** Creating a long to-do list and checking off items feels productive. There's a sense of accomplishment in seeing a list dwindle, but the reality is that not all tasks on the list are equally valuable.

- **The Reality:** Many people fill their to-do lists with low-priority tasks that are easy to complete but don't contribute significantly to their goals. This gives a false sense of achievement while the important work remains undone.

2. The Meeting Overload Trap

- **The Illusion:** Attending or scheduling numerous meetings can make you feel like you're in the thick of things, actively contributing and staying informed. It seems like a necessary part of getting things done.

- **The Reality:** Meetings can often be time sinks, especially if they lack a clear purpose or agenda. Too many meetings can interrupt your flow, leaving you with little time for focused, productive work. Often, these meetings could be replaced by a simple email or brief conversation, freeing up valuable time for tasks that matter.

3. The Multitasking Trap

- **The Illusion:** Juggling multiple tasks at once seems like a way to get more done in less time. It's easy to think that handling several things simultaneously is the epitome of efficiency.

- **The Reality:** Multitasking actually reduces your productivity. When you switch between tasks, your brain takes time to adjust, leading to lower efficiency and more mistakes. It's far more effective to focus on one task at a time, complete it, and then move on to the next.

4. **The Email Inbox Trap**

    - **The Illusion:** Constantly checking and responding to emails feels like you're staying on top of things and managing your responsibilities in real-time.

    - **The Reality:** Email can become a never-ending task that disrupts your focus and eats into your day. The constant influx of messages creates a reactive mode, where you spend your time responding to others' needs instead of working on your priorities. Productivity requires setting boundaries around email and allocating specific times to manage it.

5. **The Firefighting Trap**

    - **The Illusion:** Dealing with crises as they arise and putting out fires makes you feel indispensable and productive, as you're actively solving problems and keeping things running.

    - **The Reality:** Constant firefighting indicates a lack of planning and foresight. It's a reactive approach that prevents you from focusing on proactive, strategic work that could prevent these crises from occurring in the first place.

Focus on What Matters

Understanding the difference between being busy and being productive is essential for anyone looking to achieve meaningful success. It's not about how much you do but what you do and how it contributes to your goals. By avoiding common productivity traps and focusing on high-impact tasks, you can ensure that your efforts lead to real results rather than just the illusion of progress.

Quality Over Quantity: The Power of High-Impact Activities

I can assure you, as we strive for success, it's easy to get caught up in the mindset that doing more—checking off more tasks, attending more meetings, or putting in more hours—naturally leads to better outcomes. I say "I can assure you" because I've lived this scenario firsthand. I was constantly on the go, always meeting clients, ensuring every detail was covered, and always in motion. As my southern dad would say (and did frequently tell me), "You're running around with your shirttail standing straight out behind you." In case you're not familiar with Southern sayings, that means I was always moving at a fast run.

But through experience, I learned that real productivity and success don't come from the sheer volume of work or how fast you're moving. True progress comes from focusing on the quality of your efforts. Even more, prioritizing high-impact activities over a long list of low-value tasks is the key to meaningful progress and achieving your goals.

I can't recall exactly where I first heard this story—probably on one of those great cassette tapes from Brian Tracy, Jim Rohn, or Wayne Dyer—but the lesson stuck with me. It's about a successful self-made businessman from the early 1900s, and I've come to know it as "The $50,000 Idea."

The story goes that a young consultant approached this businessman, eager to work with his company. Despite having little to offer in terms of credentials, he gave the businessman one piece of advice and promised to return in 30 days to ask for whatever the businessman thought the advice was worth. His suggestion was simple but powerful: have each senior manager start their day by listing everything they needed to accomplish, then rewrite that list in order of importance. The goal was for each manager to focus on the first item until it was either completed or delegated—whether they finished one, two, or three tasks didn't matter, as long as they tackled the most important one first.

Each day, the list would begin with the unfinished tasks from the day before, re-prioritized. The consultant stressed that people often want to feel accomplished, so they tend to check off the easier tasks first. But in doing so, the high-impact tasks—the ones that truly move the needle—often get pushed aside.

Ultimately, this advice was worth $50,000—a huge sum in the early 1900s, and even more by today's standards. It highlights the crucial truth that knocking off small tasks might feel satisfying, but if the most important tasks aren't being tackled, true productivity is elusive. Prioritizing what matters most is the real key to success.

Why High-Impact Activities Matter

Efficiency and Effectiveness: High-impact activities are those tasks that significantly contribute to your long-term goals. These are the actions that move the needle, creating substantial value in your personal or professional life. By concentrating on these activities, you ensure that your time and energy are spent on what truly matters. I addressed this in great detail in my first book (From Hamster Wheel to Hammock – A Guild to Taking Back Your Day), but one technique that is really effective is The Eisenhower Matrix. With a little thought and planning, you'll be far more efficient and effective than you will by spreading yourself thin across numerous low-priority tasks with little overall impact.

Maximizing Results: When you focus on high-impact activities, you're making a conscious decision to work smarter, not harder. This means you'll need to identify the few tasks that yield the greatest results and give those higher-impact tasks the attention they deserve. It's the difference between making progress on a major project that can advance your business versus getting bogged down in administrative work that, while necessary, doesn't propel you forward. The Pareto Principle, or the 80/20 rule, encapsulates this idea well: 80% of your results often come from 20% of your efforts. By zeroing in on that crucial 20%, you maximize your effectiveness.

I've been there and have lived through the objections myself: "Those low-impact tasks still need to be done, so this approach just doesn't work. I'm the only one who can do it. I don't have anyone else for that job." The list of excuses can go on and on. But here's the challenge: try doing the important things first, and you'll find that the time-sucking tasks will find their place. Don't get me wrong, they still need to be handled, but when you tackle the critical tasks first, some of those time-consuming activities, like redoing something that wasn't done right the first time or working on a task with all the information in place, become easier and quicker. This approach not only gives you more time to get other things done, but it can also lead to increased revenue—allowing you to eventually delegate those lower-priority tasks and take them off your plate.

Better Decision-Making: Focusing on high-impact activities also enhances your decision-making process. When you know which tasks have the greatest potential to drive success, you're better equipped to make strategic choices about where to invest your time and resources. This clarity allows you to avoid the distractions of busy work and prioritize actions that align with your goals. It also helps you say "no" to tasks or projects that may consume your time but offer little in return, preserving your energy for what truly matters. Again, I cover these items in more detail in my first book.

Sustainable Success: Concentrating on quality over quantity is not just about achieving short-term gains; it's about building a foundation for long-term success. High-impact activities are often those that contribute to sustainable growth—whether it's developing new skills, cultivating important relationships, or innovating within your field. By investing in these areas, you set yourself up for continued success, avoiding burnout and frustration from constantly chasing after low-value tasks.

Implementing a Quality-First Approach

To shift your focus from quantity to quality, start by identifying the tasks that have the most significant impact on your goals. Ask yourself:

- What are the key activities that drive my success?
- Which tasks contribute directly to achieving my long-term objectives?
- What can I eliminate or delegate to free up more time for high-impact work?

Once you've identified these tasks, make them a priority in your daily schedule. Allocate your best hours—when you're most focused and energized—to working on these activities. Protect this time from distractions and interruptions, ensuring that you can and do give these tasks the full attention they deserve.

It's also important to regularly review and reassess your priorities. As your goals evolve, so too will the activities that have the greatest impact. Stay flexible and be willing to adjust your focus as needed, always with an eye on maximizing the quality of your efforts.

The Power of Focusing on What Matters Most

The path to success isn't paved with endless tasks and long hours; it's built on a foundation of high-impact activities that align with your vision and values. By prioritizing quality over quantity, you not only boost your productivity but also ensure that your efforts lead to meaningful, lasting results. In a world that often glorifies busyness, choosing to focus on what truly matters is a powerful way to reclaim your time, achieve your ambitions, and maintain a balanced, fulfilling life on your terms.

Steve Jobs and Apple's Focus on Simplicity

When Steve Jobs returned to Apple in 1997, the company was on the verge of collapse, burdened by an overwhelming number of products and a lack of clear focus. Recognizing that the path to success lay not in doing more, but in doing better, Jobs streamlined Apple's product line from over 350 items to just 10 core offerings. He concentrated Apple's resources on a few high-impact products—the iMac, iPod, iPhone, and later the iPad—transforming the company into an innovation powerhouse.

This 'less is more' approach allowed Apple to focus its creativity and engineering expertise on perfecting a few game-changing products, ultimately revolutionizing the tech industry. Jobs' strategy demonstrated that by focusing on what truly matters, Apple could achieve more—proving that success doesn't come from doing everything, but from doing the right things with excellence. His vision set a new standard for innovation and showed that prioritization is key to sustainable growth, a lesson entrepreneurs can apply to their own journeys of personal growth and business success.

Redefining Hard Work: Embracing the Smart Work Revolution

For generations, we've been conditioned to believe that hard work is the ultimate key to success. The narrative of grinding day in and day out—sacrificing sleep and pushing through exhaustion—has been so ingrained in our culture that it feels like the only path forward. But as we've seen, this relentless approach often leads to a negative outcome: burnout, diminished productivity, and a life that feels more like a hamster wheel than a journey toward fulfillment. It's time to redefine what hard work really means and shift our focus toward working smarter, not harder.

Smart Work Over Hard Work: A New Perspective

O.K., the concept of working smarter isn't new, but the *New Perspective* we're talking about is all about *you*—not just a strategy. Once this perspective becomes part of who you are, it will transform how you view your life and habits, leading to lasting, life-changing effects. Smart work is about maximizing your efforts to achieve the best possible results with minimal wasted time and energy. It's not about cutting corners or avoiding hard work altogether—it's about being strategic, thoughtful, and intentional in how you approach your tasks and goals.

The key to working smarter revolves around prioritizing high-impact activities, leveraging your strengths, and optimizing your workflow. It's about focusing on what truly matters and finding ways to streamline or delegate everything else. When you work smarter, you're not just making progress toward your goals—you're doing so in a way that's sustainable, balanced, and aligned with your long-term vision of freedom and fulfillment.

The Principles of Working Smarter

At the heart of smart work is the ability to prioritize effectively, which is both an art and a science. It's about recognizing that not all tasks are created equal—some will propel you forward in significant ways, while others may seem urgent or time-consuming and offer little real value in the grand scheme of your goals. The key is to distinguish between the tasks that truly matter and those that can be delegated, delayed, or dismissed altogether.

Prioritization and Focus

Prioritization begins with a clear understanding of your long-term objectives and the steps needed to achieve them. When you truly grasp your goals, it becomes easier to identify the tasks that have the greatest impact and deserve your immediate focus. These high-priority tasks—whether securing a major client, completing a key project, or developing a new skill—are the ones that move the needle and push you closer to achieving your vision.

By concentrating your efforts on high-impact activities, you can achieve more in less time because you're working on tasks that align directly with your goals. This focus is what separates productive work from busy work—tasks that may feel urgent but don't contribute meaningfully to your progress.

As an entrepreneur, mastering prioritization is crucial, given the multiple responsibilities you juggle daily. Whether it's negotiating, managing a team, or building your brand, focusing on the tasks that matter most ensures your business thrives without burning you out.

This approach also requires discipline—the ability to say 'no' to distractions and tasks that don't directly serve your goals. While these smaller tasks might clamor for attention, smart work means recognizing that clearing your to-do list isn't as valuable as making meaningful strides toward your most significant objectives.

Smart prioritization also involves flexibility. The priorities you set today may shift tomorrow, as new opportunities arise or circumstances change. By staying proactive, rather than reactive, you ensure that your efforts are always focused on what drives the most value. This focus enables you to not only succeed but to do so sustainably, paving the way for long-term success and fulfillment.

Leveraging Strengths and Delegation

As an entrepreneur, leveraging your strengths and those of your team isn't just a business strategy; it's a way to reclaim your time and energy, ensuring that you focus on the high-impact tasks that truly drive your business forward. In my experience, trying to do everything yourself only leads to burnout and a diminished quality of life. If you want to break free from 60–80-hour workweeks, leveraging is something you need to embrace.

Working smart means recognizing where your strengths lie and maximizing them. Whether it's strategic thinking, leadership, or technical expertise, honing in on your unique abilities allows you to produce your best work in less time. Smart work involves not only focusing on what you do best but also recognizing areas where you're less effective and delegating those tasks to individuals who are more capable.

This isn't shirking responsibility; it's optimizing efficiency. When you delegate tasks that fall outside your strengths, you're improving your business outcomes and creating space for personal growth and balance. This is especially crucial for entrepreneurs, as it helps avoid burnout and creates a lifestyle where both your business and personal life can thrive.

Effective delegation requires trust and clear communication. It's about empowering your team to take ownership of their roles while freeing you to focus on what truly matters, growing your business and living your life on your terms. By recognizing and leveraging your strengths, you set yourself up for long-term success while maintaining a work-life balance that supports your personal freedom."**

These changes keep the original message intact but tie it more closely to the themes of time management, entrepreneurial freedom, and working smarter, which are central to *Personal Growth for Entrepreneurs: Your Time, Your Way*.

Time Management and Efficiency

Time is your most precious and finite asset; once spent, it cannot be replenished. Unlike money or material resources, time is limited, making it crucial to manage it with intention and purpose. Effective time management lies at the heart of smart work, separating those who stay busy from those who achieve meaningful results. Structuring your time thoughtfully can significantly enhance productivity, reduce stress, and help maintain a healthy work-life balance.

One of the most powerful strategies for managing time wisely is incorporating periods of deep work into your routine. As defined by Cal Newport, deep work is focused, distraction-free attention dedicated to complex, demanding tasks. These periods of concentrated effort lead to your highest-quality output, where creativity thrives, problems are solved, and significant progress is made.

To successfully integrate deep work into your schedule, protecting these periods from interruptions is essential. This means setting clear boundaries, turning off notifications, and making it known to colleagues that you're in "do not disturb" mode. The goal is to create an environment where you can concentrate fully, free from the distractions that fragment attention and derail progress.

I once came across a simple plastic door sign with a rotating disk to display different messages like "Please Knock" or "Do Not Disturb." For years, I kept an open-door policy, thinking it was best for my team to always have access to me. But over time, I realized the constant interruptions weren't serving anyone well. So, I got one of these signs, and it made a noticeable difference. Now, when I need deep focus, I flip it to "Do Not Disturb." It's a simple but effective way to manage interruptions and protect focus. These signs are easily found online for just a few bucks—and trust me, they're worth it.

While deep work is important, it's equally vital to recognize the need for breaks to recharge your energy. The brain isn't designed to sustain intense focus without rest. Short breaks can refresh your mind and prevent burnout, keeping you productive throughout the day. Techniques like the Pomodoro Technique, where you work for 25 minutes followed by a 5-minute break, help maintain momentum while keeping energy levels up.

Another essential tool in time management is time blocking. This technique allocates specific chunks of time to particular tasks or activities. Instead of a vague to-do list, time blocking gives structure and clarity to your day. Each block is dedicated to a task—whether it's deep work, meetings, or exercise—creating a roadmap that keeps you on track and ensures every hour is spent with intention.

Time blocking also allows you to align tasks with your natural energy levels. If you're most focused in the morning, schedule deep work sessions then. For me, that's typically very early, before the sun rises and before my team starts working. Conversely, you can reserve less demanding tasks for times when your energy dips, like after lunch. Matching tasks to your energy levels helps maximize efficiency and ensures you're performing at your best when it matters most.

Incorporating these strategies—deep work, regular breaks, and time blocking—can transform how you approach your day. Instead of feeling overwhelmed by a never-ending list, you'll have a clear plan that prioritizes what matters, respects your need for rest, and uses your time wisely. Managing time well is about making deliberate choices, focusing on high-impact activities, and creating a balanced rhythm that allows you to work smarter, not harder.

Strategies to Maximize Efficiency and Effectiveness

1. The 80/20 Rule (Pareto Principle)

- Apply the 80/20 rule to identify the 20% of tasks that produce 80% of your results. Focus your efforts on these high-impact activities and minimize time spent on less important tasks. This principle helps you concentrate your energy where it matters most, leading to greater productivity with less effort.

2. Batching Similar Tasks

- Group similar tasks together and tackle them in one session. This reduces the mental load of switching between different types of tasks and allows you to get into a flow state where you can work more efficiently. For example, set aside specific times for responding to emails, making phone calls, or completing administrative tasks rather than spreading them throughout the day.

3. Eliminating Time Wasters

- Identify and eliminate activities that don't add value to your goals. This might include excessive meetings (one of my pet peeves), unnecessary social media use, or tasks that could be automated. By cutting out these time-wasters, you free up more time for meaningful work.

4. The Two-Minute Rule

- If a task will take less than two minutes to complete, do it immediately. This prevents small tasks from piling up and cluttering your to-do list. While it might seem minor, this strategy can help keep your workload manageable and prevent small tasks from becoming distractions.

5. **Mindful Breaks and Rest**

- Incorporate regular breaks into your schedule to maintain energy and focus throughout the day. Short, mindful breaks can help you recharge, reducing the risk of burnout and increasing your overall productivity. Techniques like the Pomodoro Technique, where you work for 25 minutes and then take a 5-minute break, can help maintain momentum while keeping you refreshed. My technique for this is to use a water glass or coffee cup. When I reach out for a drink/sip from either one and it's empty, it's time to stretch my legs and refill.

Embrace the Shift to Smart Work

Redefining hard work as smart work is about working with intention, efficiency, and balance. It's recognizing that success isn't measured by the number of hours you put in, but by the value you create during those hours. By focusing on high-impact activities, leveraging your strengths, managing your time effectively, and continually improving your approach, you can achieve more while maintaining your well-being. Embrace the shift to smart work and discover a more sustainable, fulfilling path to success. Be sure to regularly take a good look at yourself and make sure you are still on track. It's easy to fall back into the trap of being focused on how much you get done and how long you work as your measure of accomplishment.

Leveraging Strengths and Delegating Weaknesses: The Power of Focus

As we reach the final section of this chapter, it's time to delve into one of the most crucial aspects of working smarter: leveraging your strengths and delegating your weaknesses. Recognizing what you excel at and focusing your efforts is a key strategy for maximizing your effectiveness. Equally important is delegating tasks outside your core strengths to others better suited for them. This approach enhances your productivity and helps build a stronger, more capable team around you.

Recognizing and Utilizing Your Strengths

The foundation of working smart lies in understanding and capitalizing on your unique strengths. These strengths include anything from strategic thinking, problem-solving, and creativity to leadership, communication, or technical expertise. When you focus on tasks that align with your natural abilities, you're not just working—you're thriving. You're more likely to enter a state of flow where you're deeply engaged and performing at your best, leading to higher-quality work and greater satisfaction.

Recognizing your strengths requires self-awareness and reflection. Take the time to identify the areas where you consistently excel and where your efforts yield the best results. These are the activities that energize you, where you feel most confident and capable. By concentrating on these tasks, you're able to make a significant impact with less effort, as you're working in harmony with your natural talents.

But leveraging your strengths doesn't just mean focusing on what you're good at—it also means strategically positioning yourself in roles and projects where those strengths can shine. This might involve looking for opportunities that align with your skills or reshaping your current responsibilities to better fit your strengths. The more you can align your work with what you do best, the more effective and fulfilled you'll be.

Effective Delegation and Outsourcing: The Art of Letting Go

Okay, I'll admit that this one is tough, but it's vital to if you ever want to get to that proverbial hammock. This will start with leveraging your strengths and recognizing where your weaknesses lie. No one is equally skilled at everything, and attempting to do it all can lead to burnout, frustration, and inefficiency. Delegation and outsourcing can save the day.

Effective Delegation: Delegation is goes far beyond offloading work because you don't want to do it, it helps you make sure that each task is handled by the person most capable of doing it well. Effective delegation involves identifying tasks that fall outside your strengths or that can be more efficiently handled by someone else. For instance, if you excel at big-picture strategy but struggle with the finer details, delegating administrative tasks to someone who thrives in that area allows you to focus on what you do best.

Effective delegation also requires clear communication and trust. When you delegate a task, you need to provide clear instructions, detail your expectations, and provide the necessary resources for the person to succeed. It's important to trust that they will handle the task competently and give them the autonomy to do so. Micromanaging defeats the purpose of delegation and can undermine your team's confidence and effectiveness. Instead, make sure that the individual to which yu have delegated a task/project to is prepared for that task. If not, train them to do it or give them the procedures to get it don. When you have laid the foundation, delegate with confidence, offer support as needed, and focus on the results rather than the process.

Outsourcing: In addition to delegating within your team, outsourcing can be a powerful tool for managing tasks that require specialized skills or that are outside the core functions of your business. Outsourcing allows you to tap into expertise you may not have in-house, such as graphic design, IT support, accounting services, or specialized marketing services. By outsourcing these tasks, you ensure that they are handled by professionals who are experts in their field, freeing up your time to focus on your core strengths.

When outsourcing, it's important to select partners or service providers who understand your goals and can align their work with your vision. Just as with delegation, clear communication is key. Provide detailed briefs and maintain regular communication to ensure the work progresses as expected. Outsourcing can save you time, reduce costs, and allow you to scale your efforts without stretching yourself too thin.

How to Implement Delegation and Outsourcing

Implementing delegation and outsourcing effectively requires a strategic approach:

1. **Identify Tasks for Delegation:** Start by reviewing your workload and identifying tasks that don't align with your strengths or could be better handled by someone else. Consider tasks that are time-consuming but not high impact, as well as tasks that require specialized skills you don't possess.

2. **Choose the Right Person:** Select someone with the skills and capacity to take on the task. Consider their strengths, workload, and areas of expertise. Ensure that the person is not only capable but also motivated to succeed.

3. **Communicate Clearly:** When delegating, be clear about what needs to be done, the expected outcomes, and any deadlines. Provide the necessary resources and support, and make sure the person understands the importance of the task.

4. **Trust and Empower:** Once you've delegated a task, trust the person to get it done. Avoid micromanaging; instead, check in periodically to offer support and ensure things are on track. Empower your team to take ownership and make decisions.

5. **Evaluate and Adjust:** After the task is completed, take the time to review the results and provide feedback. Use this experience to refine your delegation process, making adjustments where necessary to improve efficiency and effectiveness.

6. **Consider Outsourcing:** For tasks that are outside your team's expertise, explore outsourcing options. Research potential partners or service providers, and choose those who align with your goals and values. Establish clear communication channels and set expectations to ensure a successful partnership.

The Path to Greater Success

Leveraging your strengths and delegating your weaknesses is not just a tactic for getting more done—it's a strategic approach to maximizing your impact and ensuring sustainable success. You create a more efficient, productive, and fulfilling work environment by focusing on what you do best and entrusting other tasks to those who are better equipped. This approach allows you to work smarter, not harder, and positions you—and your team—for greater achievements.

Work-Life Integration: Blending Professional Success with Personal Fulfillment

As we've explored various strategies for working smarter, it's important to recognize that true success only comes to fruition when it aligns well with your overall life. This is where the concept of work-life integration comes into play. Unlike the traditional idea of work-life balance, which suggests keeping work and personal life in separate, neatly divided compartments, work-life integration embraces the idea that these areas of your life can and should coexist harmoniously.

What is Work-Life Integration?

Work-life integration is the practice of blending your professional responsibilities with your personal life in a way that allows you to meet the demands of both without feeling overwhelmed or having to sacrifice one for the other. It's about finding a rhythm that suits your unique situation, where work and personal activities are interwoven throughout the day in a way that feels natural and sustainable.

Rather than trying to keep work and life separate, work-life integration encourages you to align your work with your personal values and lifestyle. This might mean adjusting your work hours to fit your family's schedule better, incorporating personal activities into your workday, or finding ways to pursue personal passions alongside your career goals.

The Importance of Work-Life Integration

The traditional nine-to-five workday and the rigid separation between work and personal life are becoming increasingly outdated, especially in today's world, where remote work and flexible schedules are more common. Work-life integration recognizes that life doesn't always fit into neat compartments and that blending work with life can lead to greater satisfaction and productivity.

For entrepreneurs and leaders, work-life integration can be particularly important. Your work is often closely tied to your identity and personal goals, making it difficult to switch off completely at the end of the day. Instead of struggling to achieve a perfect balance, work-life integration allows you to create a more fluid approach where work and life complement each other.

When you integrate your work with your personal life, you're more likely to experience:

- **Greater Flexibility:** You can adjust your schedule to accommodate both work and personal commitments, reducing the stress of trying to fit everything into a strict time frame.

- **Increased Fulfillment:** By aligning your work with your personal values and interests, you create a sense of purpose that permeates both areas of your life.

- **Enhanced Productivity:** When work and life are integrated, you can structure your day to match your natural energy levels and personal priorities, leading to better focus and output.

- **Reduced Burnout:** Integrating work and life helps you avoid the "all or nothing" mentality, where you're either fully immersed in work or trying to escape it. This balanced approach can help prevent burnout by allowing you to address both work and personal needs throughout the day.

How to Achieve Work-Life Integration

Achieving work-life integration requires a conscious effort to design your day and structure your responsibilities in a way that supports both your professional and personal goals. Here are some strategies to help you get started:

1. **Identify Your Priorities**

    - Start by identifying what's most important to you in both your work and personal life. What are your core values, and how can they be reflected in how you spend your time? Understanding your priorities will help you make decisions that support a harmonious integration of work and life.

2. **Create a Flexible Schedule**

    - Embrace the flexibility that work-life integration offers. Instead of adhering to a rigid schedule, create a flexible plan that allows you to move between work and personal activities throughout the day. This might involve setting specific times for focused work, as well as for family, exercise, or hobbies.

3. **Set Boundaries**

    - While integration encourages a blend of work and life, it's still important to set boundaries to prevent one from overtaking the other. For example, designate certain times of the day or week when you're completely off the clock, or create physical boundaries by having a dedicated workspace.

4. **Leverage Technology**

- Use technology to your advantage to help manage both work and personal commitments. Tools like shared calendars, task management apps, and communication platforms can help you stay organized and ensure that nothing falls through the cracks.

5. **Take Time to Recharge**

    - Prioritizing your time to simply recharge should be a part of your work-life integration strategy. Ensure that you're making time for activities that recharge you, whether it's exercise, meditation, or simply taking a walk. When you take care of yourself, you're better equipped to handle the demands of both work and life.

6. **Incorporate Personal Passions into Your Work**

    - Find ways to bring your personal passions into your work. Whether it's through side projects, collaborations, or incorporating hobbies into your professional life, this integration can make work feel more fulfilling and aligned with your interests.

7. **Communicate with Your Team**

    - If you're leading a team, communicate your approach to work-life integration and encourage others to find their own balance. Foster a culture where flexibility is valued, and where team members feel empowered to manage their work in a way that supports their personal lives.

Embracing a Holistic Approach to Success

Work-life integration isn't about trying to do it all or blending work and life into one indistinguishable blur. Instead, the goal is to find a rhythm that works for you and allows you to achieve your professional goals while living a fulfilling personal life. By embracing this holistic approach, you create a sustainable model for success where work and life enhance each other rather than compete. As you continue on your journey, remember that true success is about living a life that's balanced, fulfilling, and true to your values.

Mindful Work Practices: Cultivating Focus and Reducing Stress

Incorporating mindfulness into your workday is a powerful way to reduce stress, increase focus, and enhance overall productivity. Mindfulness is the practice of being fully present in the moment and aware of your thoughts, feelings, and surroundings without judgment. Integrating mindfulness into your work practices allows you to create a more intentional, centered approach to your daily tasks, leading to greater clarity and effectiveness.

Mindfulness helps you break the cycle of constant multitasking and distractions that often lead to stress and burnout. It encourages you to slow down, focus on one task at a time, and approach your work with a calm, clear mind. This improves the quality of your work and allows you to enjoy the process rather than constantly feeling rushed or overwhelmed.

Practical Tips for Being Present and Intentional at Work

1. **Start Your Day with Intention**

   - Begin each workday with a few minutes of mindful reflection. Set clear intentions for the day, focusing on what you want to achieve and how you approach your tasks. This simple practice can help you start your day with purpose and clarity, setting a positive tone for the hours ahead.

2. **Practice Deep Breathing**

   - Throughout your day, take regular breaks to practice deep breathing. Deep breathing helps calm your nervous system, reduces stress, and brings your attention back to the present moment. Even just a few minutes of focused breathing can reset your mind and improve your ability to concentrate.

3. **Single-Tasking**

   - Instead of multitasking, focus on one task at a time. When you're working on a project or responding to emails, give that task your full attention. If your mind starts to wander, gently bring it back to the task at hand. This practice of single-tasking enhances your focus and ensures that you're fully engaged with your work.

4. **Mindful Transitions**

   ○ Pay attention to the transitions between tasks or meetings. Before moving on to the next item on your agenda, take a moment to pause, breathe, and clear your mind. This mindful transition helps you let go of the previous task and approach the next one with a fresh perspective.

5. **Mindful Communication**

   ○ Practice mindfulness in your interactions with colleagues and clients. Listen actively, without interrupting, and respond thoughtfully. Being fully present in conversations fosters better understanding, reduces miscommunication, and strengthens relationships.

6. **Create a Mindful Workspace**

   ○ Design your workspace to promote mindfulness. Keep your desk organized and free from distractions. Consider adding elements that help you stay grounded, such as plants, calming colors, or a small reminder to take deep breaths. A mindful workspace can create a sense of calm and focus.

7. **End Your Day with Reflection**

   ○ Conclude your workday with a few minutes of mindful reflection. Review what you've accomplished, acknowledge any challenges, and let go of any lingering stress. This practice can help you transition smoothly from work to personal time, reducing the likelihood of bringing work-related stress home with you.

Embracing Mindfulness for a Balanced Work Life

Incorporating mindful work practices into your daily routine can significantly reduce stress, improve focus, and enhance your overall well-being. By being present and intentional in your work, you not only increase your productivity but also create a more fulfilling and balanced work life. Mindfulness is a simple yet powerful tool that can help you navigate the demands of your professional life with greater ease and satisfaction.

Conclusion

As we conclude this chapter, it's evident that the traditional belief in hard work as the only route to success is not just outdated but can be harmful. The endless grind, glorified by hustle culture, often leads to burnout, diminished productivity, and a sense of imbalance in life. Instead, we've explored a more sustainable and smarter approach that prioritizes high-impact activities, leverages your unique strengths, and integrates work with a fulfilling personal life.

Working smarter means being intentional with your time, focusing on tasks that move the needle, and recognizing that success is more about how effective you than how much you do. It involves embracing continuous improvement, delegating tasks that don't align with your strengths, and incorporating mindfulness to create a harmonious balance between your professional and personal goals.

Encouragement to Reflect and Challenge Preconceived Notions

Now that you've explored the principles of working smarter take a moment to reflect on your current work habits. Challenge the traditional notions you may hold about hard work—are you equating long hours with success? Are there areas in your life where smarter, more strategic work could replace exhausting efforts?

Consider how you can align your approach with the strategies we've discussed. Focus on identifying your strengths, prioritizing high-impact tasks, and delegating or letting go of less meaningful responsibilities. Embrace the understanding that true success isn't about the number of hours you put in—it's about the quality and focus you bring to your efforts.

Remember, real success is measured not by how much you do, but by the effectiveness and intentionality of your work. By adopting these shifts, you'll achieve more without sacrificing your well-being, paving the way for long-term fulfillment. Take that first step today—evaluate your work habits and make intentional changes that lead to a more balanced, productive, and successful life.

Call to Action: Reflect, Reevaluate and Realign

As you reach the end of this chapter, it's time to take a step back and reflect on your current beliefs and practices about hard work. Ask yourself: Are your efforts truly leading you towards success, or are they just keeping you busy? Are you working in a way that's sustainable, or are you inching closer to burnout with every passing day? It's crucial to pause and reassess how you approach your work and life—because the path you're on today will shape your future.

I challenge you to take a moment to think critically about the way you work. Are you prioritizing the tasks that genuinely matter, or are you getting bogged down in the details? Are you leveraging your strengths, or are you spending too much time on tasks that could be better handled by someone else? These are important questions to consider as you move forward.

Go to and grab the workbook.

Chapter Four
Purpose-Driven Goals
Setting Yourself Up for Success

IN A WORLD THAT often emphasizes achieving more, it's easy to get caught in the cycle of setting and chasing goals that may not truly resonate with who we are. But what if the key to lasting success and fulfillment isn't just about setting goals, but about setting the *right* goals—those that align deeply with your purpose and values? This chapter is all about helping you identify, set, and pursue purpose-driven goals that not only propel you toward success but also bring meaning and satisfaction to your life.

Purpose-driven goals go beyond the surface level—they're not just about hitting a target or checking off a list. Instead, they align your ambitions with your core values and the bigger picture of what you want your life to represent. When your goals are rooted in a strong sense of purpose, each step toward achieving them feels more intentional, impactful, and, ultimately, fulfilling.

I must admit, in my earlier days, I wrote down plenty of goals that lacked real purpose. I'd hear someone mention a goal and think, "That sounds like a good one," and then adopt it as my own. However, I found that those goals seldom made much of a difference in my life. They seemed like something I wanted, but they never moved the needle. At times, I even started to think that maybe goal-setting didn't really work.

But then, I'd achieve one of *my own* goals—those that truly resonated with me—and be reminded of the power of goal-setting. What I didn't realize at the time was that the goals I struggled with weren't really mine. I had adopted them from others, and they were little more than printed words on a page. The more I thought about it, the more I realized these goals didn't connect with my true desires or values.

As I reflected on why these goals never took hold, I noticed patterns. My mind would wander whenever I focused on them, or doubt would creep in, making me feel they were unachievable. Or worse, they'd slip to the back of my mind, and I wouldn't invest the necessary time or energy into pursuing them. These goals weren't truly mine, and I wasn't driven to achieve them.

Interestingly, some of these adopted goals eventually reappeared later—when they genuinely resonated with me. And this time, I achieved them. This taught me an invaluable lesson: just because a goal sounds worthy doesn't mean it's the *right* goal for you.

My encouragement here is to take a close look at your goals and make sure they genuinely matter to you. Goals require time and energy, even if it's just the time spent visualizing them and creating a plan to achieve them. Personally, I believe that a higher power—whether you call it God, the Universe, or something else—guides us toward the right goals. But regardless of your beliefs, the important thing is to let that power or your intuition work within you.

If you find yourself writing down goals that never seem to lead anywhere, take a moment to ask yourself if they're truly goals that ignite a fire within you. If they don't, it's time to let them go and focus on what truly matters to *you*.

Let's move forward and explore what it really means to have purpose-driven goals and why they are essential for long-term success. We'll delve into how to uncover the driving forces behind your ambitions and help you clarify your sense of purpose. Once you have that clarity, we'll guide you in setting meaningful, achievable goals that align with your true desires. From there, we'll discuss how to create a roadmap for success, ensuring your goals are not just dreams but actionable steps toward a fulfilling life. Finally, we'll explore how to overcome obstacles along the way and maintain momentum toward your vision.

By the end of this chapter, you'll have the tools and insights to set yourself up for success—success defined not only by external achievements but by a deep sense of purpose and fulfillment.

> *"Efforts and courage are not enough without purpose and direction."*—John F. Kennedy

Understanding Purpose-Driven Goals

Purpose-driven goals are deeply aligned with your core values, passions, and the bigger vision you hold for your life. These goals are not simply about achieving a specific outcome or checking off a to-do list; they are about making a meaningful impact that reflects who you are at your core. With purpose-driven goals, you're fueled by an inner sense of direction, giving you clarity and motivation that goes beyond external rewards. They link your daily actions to a larger narrative guided by your beliefs, values, and aspirations.

On the other hand, **generic goals** tend to be more surface-level and often lack the depth or personal significance that makes a goal truly meaningful. These are the types of goals that may look good on paper—perhaps borrowed from someone else's vision or shaped by societal pressures—but they don't connect with your inner drive. Generic goals are typically motivated by external factors, such as achieving a certain status, meeting others' expectations, or hitting arbitrary milestones. While they can lead to accomplishments, they often fall short in reaching the place that you really want to be. You know, your version of the Hammock Lifestyle.

The primary distinction between purpose-driven and generic goals lies in their foundation. Purpose-driven goals are deeply rooted in your personal "why," driven by a desire to live authentically and make choices that reflect your true self. This connection to your purpose fuels both motivation and clarity, giving you the resilience needed to stay committed, even when challenges arise.

In contrast, generic goals might offer a fleeting sense of accomplishment but often leave you feeling unfulfilled, wondering why you pursued them in the first place. Without a solid link to your deeper purpose, it's easy to lose motivation or feel detached from the outcome of your efforts.

The significance of purpose-driven goals cannot be overstated. When your goals align with your values and purpose, every step toward achieving them feels intentional and meaningful. You're not simply working toward a destination—you're crafting a life that harmonizes with your core desires. This alignment results in greater satisfaction, increased motivation, and a clear sense of direction, both personally and professionally.

Ultimately, purpose-driven goals empower you to live a life true to who you are, guiding you toward a form of success that isn't measured by external standards but by the fulfillment and sense of accomplishment you feel within.

The Impact of Purpose-Driven Goals

Purpose-driven goals have the power to transform both your personal and professional life. Unlike generic goals, which often feel like obligations or tasks to be checked off, purpose-driven goals are deeply connected to your core values and passions. This alignment energizes your motivation, enhances your sense of fulfillment, and ultimately leads to more meaningful and impactful results. Let's explore how these benefits come to life when your goals reflect your true purpose.

Increased Motivation

One of the most significant advantages of purpose-driven goals is the natural increase in motivation. When your goals align with your deeper values, you're not just working toward arbitrary targets—you're pursuing something that truly matters to you. This intrinsic motivation is far more powerful than external rewards, such as money or recognition. It's the kind of drive that keeps you going, even when the road gets tough, because your actions are fueled by a clear sense of purpose.

For entrepreneurs, this can be a game-changer. When your goals are tied to a vision you're passionate about—whether it's building a business that makes a real impact, developing a product that solves genuine problems, or fostering a company culture that empowers your team—you'll find yourself more willing to put in the effort, take risks, and push through challenges. This connection to purpose gives you the relentless drive to see your goals through to completion.

Sense of Satisfaction

If your goals don't make you happy, staying committed when challenges arise is hard. Purpose-driven goals, however, bring a deeper sense of satisfaction that keeps you motivated, even in tough times. Achieving a goal connected to your values that goes beyond simply reaching a milestone will lead you toward realizing a vision that resonates with who you are. Chasing dreams and goals that make you happy comes from knowing your work is part of something bigger and aligned with your core beliefs.

For instance, an entrepreneur building a sustainable business model feels rewarded not just by profits but by the positive environmental impact. Similarly, mentoring the next generation brings fulfillment through the success of others, not just personal gains. This sense of satisfaction enhances your achievements and reinforces a purpose-driven journey, making it more rewarding and sustainable.

Better Results

Finally, purpose-driven goals often lead to better results. When you're truly passionate about your goals, you're more likely to invest the time, energy, and creativity needed to achieve them. You're also more resilient, more open to finding innovative solutions, and more committed to the long-term, all of which drive higher-quality outcomes.

Purpose-driven goals help you stay focused even in the face of setbacks because you're driven by a deeper connection to your values. The desire to see your vision come to life pushes you to find ways to overcome obstacles, leading to better, more sustainable outcomes than those produced by generic goals that lack personal significance. Moreover, the authenticity and passion behind your goals often attract others who share your vision—whether they're team members, partners, or customers—leading to stronger collaborations and increased support.

The Power of Purpose

Purpose-driven goals aren't just about achieving success—they're about achieving meaningful, fulfilling success that aligns with your core self. When your goals are rooted in your purpose, you experience increased motivation, a deeper sense of fulfillment, and better outcomes. You're not just more productive—you're more passionate, more connected to your work, and more likely to see your vision through to the end.

As you set your own goals, take the time to reflect on what truly drives you. What are the values and passions that fuel your ambitions? How can you align your goals with these deeper motivations? By focusing on purpose-driven goals, you'll not only achieve more but also do so in a way that enriches your life and positively impacts those around you.

By The WAY

As you dive into setting your purpose-driven goals, don't forget one crucial step: writing down your big "why." We've discussed this before, both in this book and in *From Hamster Wheel to Hammock*, but it's worth repeating. Your "why" is the foundation of your purpose—it's the driving force behind everything you do. Without a clear understanding of your "why," it's challenging to create goals that resonate with your deeper values and passions.

Take the time to reflect on what motivates you, what you're passionate about, and what kind of impact you want to make in the world. Write these thoughts down and keep them where you can see them regularly. This clarity will guide you as you set your purpose-driven goals, ensuring they align with your true self. Remember, it's not just about what you want to achieve—it's about why you want to achieve it. When your goals are connected to your "why," they become more meaningful, motivating, and ultimately, more attainable.

Simply put: **Don't create a goal that sounds good, or that you found somewhere else. Set your goals on those things that make your heart beat faster and keep you up at night!**

Discovering Your Purpose

While I'd love for everyone reading this book to dive into my earlier work, and the future ones I have in the pipeline, my goal is for this book to stand strong on its own. So, let's start by laying the foundation for discovering your purpose. Before you can set purpose-driven goals, you must take a crucial first step: uncovering what truly drives you. This is the bedrock upon which all meaningful goals are built. Your purpose is the underlying force behind everything you do—it's what gets you out of bed in the morning, fuels your ambitions, and serves as the compass that guides your decisions.

Discovering your purpose means understanding the values, passions, and motivations that resonate most deeply with you. It involves uncovering what truly matters and aligning your actions with those core principles.

For entrepreneurs, understanding your purpose is especially powerful. It can transform a business from being just a way to make money into a vehicle for making a difference. When your work aligns with your purpose, it becomes more fulfilling and more impactful. You're no longer just chasing profits—you're pursuing a mission that has the potential to change both your life and the lives of others.

In this section, we'll explore how to embark on the journey of discovering your purpose. We'll reflect on your values, passions, and past experiences, and explore how these elements can come together to reveal your unique purpose. By the end of this section, you'll have a clearer understanding of what drives you, allowing you to set goals that are truly aligned with who you are and what you want to achieve.

Finding your purpose may not always be quick or straightforward, but it's one of the most important steps toward living a life of meaning and success. Let's begin the journey of uncovering what really drives you, so you can start setting purpose-driven goals that lead to true fulfillment.

It's Time for an Exercise

As you continue your journey toward discovering your true purpose, it's important to dive deeper into self-reflection and exploration. To help you with this, I've created a comprehensive workbook that offers additional exercises and guidance. In the workbook, you'll find several self-reflection questions designed to help you uncover your passions and values, journaling prompts to fine-tune your purpose, and a mind-mapping exercise titled *Discovering Your Purpose*.

If you don't already have the workbook, you can easily download it at . This resource will guide you through these powerful exercises, helping you gain the clarity you need to set purpose-driven goals that truly resonate with your vision for life. Take advantage of this extra content to ensure you're fully aligned with what drives and motivates you.

Now, let's take the next step together toward your purpose-filled future!

Aligning Goals with Purpose

Aligning your goals with your purpose is essential for creating a fulfilling and successful life. Once you've identified your true passions and core values, the next step is ensuring that every goal you set is a reflection of what truly matters to you. Goals aligned with your purpose give meaning to your work and keep you motivated, even when faced with challenges. Success becomes far more meaningful when it aligns with your values and feels deeply connected to who you are. Instead of simply chasing achievements, you are pursuing goals that truly resonate with your inner drive and vision for your life.

When your goals are aligned with your purpose, each task becomes more than just an item to check off—it's a meaningful step toward realizing your vision. To make this alignment work, it's crucial to continually reflect on your goals and ask yourself if they are guiding you toward the life you want. This requires an ongoing commitment to authenticity and self-awareness, as well as the courage to adjust your goals when they no longer serve your deeper purpose.

In this section, we'll explore how to evaluate and refine your goals to ensure they are in sync with your values and passions. You'll learn strategies to create purpose-driven goals that challenge you while keeping you inspired. This approach will give you a clear and intentional path forward, ensuring that your pursuit of success is deeply connected to what truly matters to you. By aligning your goals with your purpose, you'll have a roadmap that leads to a more meaningful, impactful, and fulfilling life.

Setting Purpose-Driven Goals

Setting purpose-driven goals is about more than simply jotting down what you want to achieve; it's about ensuring your ambitions are closely aligned with your core values and passions. When your goals reflect your purpose, they become more than just tasks to accomplish—they become milestones that resonate deeply, fueling both your commitment and drive.

Start by grounding your goals in the purpose you've defined for yourself. Think of this as creating goals that mirror what truly matters to you, rather than goals that are just part of a checklist. These purpose-driven objectives are often big-picture and inspiring, encouraging you to step outside your comfort zone and tackle challenges that stretch your abilities. These aren't just random goals—they're designed to move you closer to the life and impact you envision.

Breaking down these ambitious goals into actionable steps is essential to avoid overwhelm. Each step toward your larger objective should feel manageable, creating a steady sense of accomplishment as you work through each piece. This process is not about achieving everything at once but about consistently building momentum, one achievable task at a time.

Staying connected to your "why" is critical as you move forward, especially when challenges arise. Revisiting your purpose regularly can help keep your motivation strong and focused, transforming obstacles into manageable setbacks rather than insurmountable roadblocks. Celebrating each milestone, however small, reinforces this connection to your larger vision and keeps your progress satisfying and tangible.

Along the way, it's essential to remain flexible. Purpose-driven goals may evolve as you grow, and staying adaptable ensures you can refine your path without losing sight of what matters most. Remember, this journey isn't about reaching a final destination as quickly as possible; it's about aligning your path with your purpose, creating a life filled with meaningful progress, and building success that feels right every step of the way. For more on building purpose-driven goals and detailed steps to support your journey, visit .

Case Studies: Successful Alignment of Goals with Purpose

To truly grasp the power of aligning goals with purpose, let's explore two more real-life examples complementing those shared earlier. These case studies highlight how purpose-driven goals not only drive business success but also foster deep fulfillment and positive impact.

1. Sara Blakely and Spanx: Empowering Women Through Innovation

Sara Blakely, founder of Spanx, aligned her entrepreneurial goals with a clear purpose: empowering women by helping them feel confident in their skin. This mission pushed her to innovate in the women's undergarment industry, leading to the creation of Spanx, which has revolutionized how women dress and feel.

Blakely's purpose wasn't just about filling a market gap but about making a genuine difference in women's lives. This connection between her purpose and goals didn't just lead to financial success—it built a brand that deeply resonates with its audience. By staying true to her purpose, Blakely has become a role model for aspiring female entrepreneurs while building a company that improves the confidence of women worldwide.

2. Howard Schultz and Starbucks: Building a Community-Focused Experience

Howard Schultz, former CEO of Starbucks, pursued a purpose-driven vision that went beyond simply selling coffee. Schultz wanted Starbucks to be a "third place" between home and work, where people could gather, relax, and connect. His goal was to create a sense of community through the Starbucks experience.

By aligning this goal with his purpose, Schultz led innovations like free Wi-Fi, an inviting atmosphere, and ethical sourcing practices. Starbucks transformed from a small coffee shop to a global brand known for fostering community and connection. The success of Starbucks is a testament to the power of aligning business goals with a larger purpose that resonates emotionally with customers.

Creating a Vision Statement

Head over to the workbook to begin crafting your vision statement—a powerful tool for clarifying your long-term goals, values, and the future you want to create, whether for yourself or your business. A well-thought-out vision statement serves as your guiding star, influencing and inspiring every decision and action you take. This step-by-step guide in the workbook will walk you through how to write a compelling vision statement that aligns with your purpose, sets a clear direction, and keeps you motivated along the way.

Get started at www.RogerGBbest.com/workbooks .

Example Vision Statements

Please head over to the workbook to walk through the full process, but here are a few examples to get you started with crafting your own vision statement—both personal and business-focused:

Personal Vision Statement:

- "My vision is to live a life of purpose, continuously growing and learning, while using my creativity and compassion to inspire and empower others to achieve their dreams."

- "My vision is to live a balanced life where personal growth, meaningful relationships, and contribution to the community are prioritized. I aim to nurture my passions, challenge myself continually, and cultivate a lifestyle that reflects my core values of integrity, kindness, and lifelong learning."

Business Vision Statement:

- "Our vision is to revolutionize sustainable fashion by creating stylish, eco-friendly products that inspire consumers to embrace sustainability, while leading the industry toward a greener future."

- "Our vision is to create a sustainable future by innovating in clean energy solutions that empower individuals and businesses to reduce their carbon footprint.

We aim to be a global leader in renewable energy technologies, fostering environmental responsibility while delivering value to our stakeholders."

Vision Statements can, and should, go beyond the basic and should be directed at what is expected within one. I have the standard examples above because are more focused one requires more input. But here's our vision statement for one of the companies I own.

BizTek Vision Statement

- At BizTek, we believe that technology is a catalyst for transformation. Our vision is to empower businesses to reach their full potential through innovative solutions that drive efficiency, growth, and long-term success. We believe that true innovation doesn't just solve problems—it opens doors to new possibilities. That's why we are committed to combining deep industry expertise with cutting-edge technology, because we know that businesses deserve more than just tools—they need solutions that evolve with them.

- At the heart of our vision is the belief in trust and integrity. We know that businesses thrive when they can rely on their partners, and we are dedicated to being that steadfast partner. We operate with transparency and collaboration, understanding that the best outcomes are achieved together.

- We also believe in safeguarding the future. In an ever-changing digital world, we are relentlessly protecting our clients' data and critical infrastructure against security threats because we understand the value of their assets and the importance of peace of mind. Our commitment is to help our clients confidently navigate the complexities of the modern business landscape, ensuring their success today and securing their future for tomorrow."

Writing a personal or business vision statement is a critical step toward achieving long-term success and fulfillment. By following the guide, you create a vision that not only inspires but also acts as your north star, guiding you toward a future that reflects your values, purpose, and aspirations. Importantly, your vision statement is not static—it should evolve as you grow and as your goals shift. Regularly revisiting and refining it ensures your vision remains aligned with your current journey and ambitions.

A well-crafted vision statement is essential because it lays the foundation for all your goal-setting efforts. It serves as a compass, providing clarity and direction in a world full of distractions. With a clear vision, every goal you set becomes a meaningful step toward a future that resonates with your core values. Without that clarity, it's easy to veer off course, chasing goals that may not lead to lasting satisfaction or fulfillment. In contrast, a clear, motivating vision keeps you on track, inspires continuous growth, and helps you make decisions that align with your deeper purpose.

When your vision is clear, it provides the necessary focus and drive to pursue long-term objectives with passion and commitment. It becomes the touchstone against which you measure your progress and adjust your strategies, ensuring that each step you take is in service of your overarching goals.

Bridging Purpose-Driven Goals and SMART Framework: A Holistic Approach to Success

Purpose-driven success involves building a life and career that feels deeply rewarding and reflect your core values. It aligns your goals with what truly matters, leading to a sense of accomplishment that goes beyond simply checking off tasks. This alignment creates a foundation for lasting satisfaction and personal fulfillment. The SMART Goals Framework acts as the practical roadmap to get you there. When combined, these two approaches ensure that your goals aren't just boxes to check off; they are meaningful milestones that guide you toward the future you envision.

1. Purpose as the "Why," SMART Goals as the "How" – Your purpose is the guiding star, the deep reason behind everything you do. But purpose alone won't get you where you need to go—this is where SMART goals come in. Purpose provides the "why," but SMART goals define the "how." They translate your larger mission into specific, actionable steps that give clarity and structure to your journey.

2. The Power of Specificity in Purpose-Driven Work -Setting purpose-driven goals using the SMART framework ensures that each step is tied to your bigger vision. For instance, if your purpose is to make a positive social impact through entrepreneurship, a SMART goal could be as specific as *"Launch a program that provides 100 mentorship* *opportunities to local startups within the next year."* The purpose remains your guiding principle, while the SMART framework gives you the precision to achieve it.

3. Measurability Brings Purpose to Life – Tracking progress is crucial in making sure you're advancing toward your larger mission. When your purpose is tied to a measurable goal, you can celebrate small wins and course-correct when necessary. For example, a purpose-driven company aiming to *"reduce its environmental impact"* might set a measurable goal like *"Reduce waste by 15% in six months."* This makes your broader vision tangible and achievable.

4. Achievability and Sustainability – Purpose-driven work can sometimes lead to overly ambitious goals, where you might feel the pressure to achieve big things all at once. The "Achievable" aspect of SMART goals keeps you grounded, ensuring that your goals are ambitious yet attainable. This is essential for long-term success, preventing burnout and frustration as you make progress in meaningful ways.

5. Relevance Ensures Purpose Alignment – The relevance of a goal is where purpose-driven work truly shines. Every SMART goal must align with your values and long-term mission. This keeps you from getting sidetracked by short-term gains or distractions that don't serve your purpose. If your vision is to create a business that supports underserved communities, setting a relevant goal like *"Develop partnerships with three community organizations over the next year"* ensures that you remain focused on what really matters.

6. Time-Bound Goals Create Urgency for Your Purpose – Purpose can sometimes feel like a lifelong mission, but without deadlines, you may never take action. Time-bound goals ensure that you're consistently moving forward. They transform your purpose from an abstract idea into a series of concrete steps. By giving yourself a deadline, such as *"Increase client satisfaction ratings by 10% within six months,"* you create momentum and maintain accountability to your long-term vision.

Bringing it All Together: Purpose-Driven SMART Goals

When combined, the SMART framework and your purpose create a powerful system for achieving meaningful success. The SMART approach turns your vision into actionable steps, while your purpose ensures those steps are aligned with your deepest values. Together, they form a holistic strategy for creating a life and career that not only achieves results but also brings fulfillment, impact, and alignment with who you are.

For more detailed exercises, templates, and examples on how to craft your SMART goals in alignment with your purpose, head over to the workbook at www.RogerG Bbest.com/workbooks . There, you'll find guided steps to start applying the SMART framework to your own purpose-driven goals, making each goal a stepping stone toward lasting success and fulfillment.

I know that examples frequently make things clearer to my clients, as they have for me, over the years. So here ae are examples of how broad purpose-driven aspirations can be transformed into SMART goals:

Example 1: Aspiration - Improve Access to Education

Broad Aspiration: "I want to improve access to education in underserved communities."

SMART Goal: "Partner with three local nonprofits to launch a free online tutoring program for 200 high school students in underserved communities within the next year, with the goal of improving their standardized test scores by 15%."

- **Specific:** Launch a free online tutoring program.

- **Measurable:** Reach 200 students and aim for a 15% improvement in test scores.

- **Achievable:** Partnering with three nonprofits makes it feasible.

- **Relevant:** Directly aligns with the goal of improving access to education.

- **Time-bound:** To be accomplished within one year.

Example 2: Aspiration - Promote Environmental Sustainability

Broad Aspiration: "I want to promote environmental sustainability in my business."

SMART Goal: "Reduce the company's energy consumption by 25% over the next 18 months by upgrading to energy-efficient lighting, installing solar panels, and implementing a company-wide recycling program."

- **Specific:** Reduce energy consumption by upgrading lighting, installing solar panels, and recycling.

- **Measurable:** Achieve a 25% reduction in energy consumption.

- **Achievable:** Specific actions (lighting upgrades, solar panels, recycling) make the goal attainable.

- **Relevant:** Directly supports the broader goal of promoting environmental sustainability.

- **Time-bound:** To be completed within 18 months.

Example 3: Aspiration - Support Local Economic Growth

Broad Aspiration: "I want to support local economic growth."

SMART Goal: "Develop and launch a small business mentorship program within the next 12 months, pairing 20 local entrepreneurs with experienced business leaders to help them grow their businesses by at least 10% over the following year."

- **Specific:** Create a mentorship program for local entrepreneurs.

- **Measurable:** Involve 20 entrepreneurs and aim for a 10% growth in their businesses.

- **Achievable:** Leveraging the experience of business leaders makes this feasible.

- **Relevant:** Directly contributes to the goal of supporting local economic growth.

- **Time-bound:** Program development within 12 months, with measurable growth over the following year.

Example 4: Aspiration - Foster Workplace Well-being

Broad Aspiration: "I want to foster well-being in the workplace."

SMART Goal: "Implement a company-wide wellness program within the next six months that includes weekly fitness classes, mental health resources, and a flexible work schedule, aiming to improve employee satisfaction scores by 20% by the end of the year."

- **Specific:** Introduce a wellness program with fitness classes, mental health resources, and flexible scheduling.

- **Measurable:** Increase employee satisfaction scores by 20%.

- **Achievable:** Specific, actionable steps make this goal feasible.

- **Relevant:** Aligns with the goal of fostering workplace well-being.

- **Time-bound:** Launch within six months, with satisfaction improvement by year-end.

Example 5: Aspiration - Advocate for Social Justice

Broad Aspiration: "I want to advocate for social justice."

SMART Goal: "Organize a series of five community workshops on social justice issues within the next year, aiming to engage at least 500 participants and increase local awareness of key social justice topics by 30%."

- **Specific:** Organize community workshops on social justice.

- **Measurable:** Engage 500 participants and increase awareness by 30%.

- **Achievable:** A series of five workshops is a feasible goal.

- **Relevant:** Directly supports the goal of advocating for social justice.

- **Time-bound:** To be completed within the next year.

By transforming broad purpose-driven aspirations into SMART goals, you create a clear and actionable path to achieving your vision. These examples demonstrate how to take an overarching purpose and break it down into specific, measurable, achievable, relevant, and time-bound steps that will guide you toward meaningful success.

Building a Roadmap to Success

With your purpose-driven goals clearly defined and structured using the SMART framework, the next step is building a strategic roadmap to guide you from where you are to where you aspire to be. This roadmap acts as a detailed blueprint, showing the specific steps, milestones, and resources you'll need to reach your goals.

Even the best-defined goals can feel overwhelming without a clear path forward. A strategic roadmap helps break down these goals into manageable steps, providing both clarity and direction. It allows you to keep your focus on the big picture while tackling the immediate actions required to move forward.

This section will explore how to create a roadmap that aligns with your purpose-driven goals. You'll learn how to prioritize tasks, set realistic timelines, and anticipate obstacles. By the end, you'll have a concrete plan that brings clarity and confidence to your journey toward success. Whether personal or business-related, this roadmap will keep you on track and ensure consistent progress.

Breaking Down Goals into Manageable Steps

To bring your purpose-driven goals to life, break them down into smaller, actionable steps. Think of this process as constructing a bridge—each step is a plank that moves you closer to your destination, one piece at a time.

Start by dividing your larger goal into smaller tasks. For example, if you're launching a new business, you wouldn't tackle it all at once. Instead, you would break it into steps such as market research, developing a business plan, securing funding, and building a marketing strategy. Each task is critical but far more manageable on its own.

Once you've identified these smaller tasks, prioritize them. Determine which tasks need immediate attention and which can follow. This helps focus your efforts and prevents you from being overwhelmed. It's about taking logical, sequential steps that lead you steadily toward your goal.

Next, assign realistic timelines for each task. Set deadlines that challenge but don't overwhelm you. Timelines help create urgency and keep you accountable, ensuring you stay on track. Don't forget to establish milestones along the way; celebrating even small wins will show progress and boost motivation.

Also, anticipate potential obstacles. Consider challenges that could arise and plan how you'll tackle them. This proactive approach helps you remain resilient and adaptable, ensuring that setbacks won't derail your plan.

By breaking down your goals into manageable steps, your roadmap becomes clear and actionable. This structured approach makes the journey to success less daunting and helps build momentum. Focusing on one step at a time ensures steady progress, turning your goals from possibilities into inevitabilities.

Tips for Creating Sub-Goals and Milestones

1. **Start with the End in Mind**
   - Begin by clearly defining your main goal. Understanding the end result you want to achieve makes it easier to identify the key steps needed to get there. Visualize the entire journey and then work backward to identify the sub-goals and milestones that will guide you.

2. Break Down Large Goals into Smaller, Actionable Steps

- Divide your main goal into smaller, manageable tasks that can be completed one at a time. Each sub-goal should represent a specific, actionable step toward your larger objective. This approach helps to make even the most ambitious goals feel achievable.

3. Prioritize Your Sub-Goals

- Once you've identified your sub-goals, prioritize them based on their importance and the order in which they need to be accomplished. Some tasks will naturally need to come first before others can be completed. Focus on what needs to happen first and build from there.

4. Make Your Sub-Goals SMART

- Apply the SMART criteria—Specific, Measurable, Achievable, Relevant, and Time-bound—to each sub-goal. This ensures that every step you take is clear, realistic, and aligned with your overall vision while also giving you a way to measure progress.

5. Set Clear Milestones

- Milestones are critical markers of progress. Set clear milestones at regular intervals to track your advancement. These should be specific achievements that signify you've reached a significant point in your journey, such as completing a key phase of a project or reaching a particular financial target.

6. Establish Realistic Timelines

- Assign deadlines to each sub-goal and milestone. Make sure these timelines are realistic, allowing for focused work while also considering any potential challenges or delays. Setting timeframes keeps you accountable and maintains momentum.

7. Celebrate Small Wins

- Recognize and celebrate the completion of each milestone. Celebrating small wins keeps you motivated and provides a sense of accomplishment as you move toward your larger goal. These celebrations can be simple but should mark your progress and keep your spirits high.

8. **Adjust as Needed**

   - Be flexible and open to adjusting your sub-goals and milestones as circumstances change. If you encounter obstacles or if new opportunities arise, don't hesitate to tweak your plan. Staying adaptable ensures that your roadmap remains relevant, practical, and effective as you progress.

9. **Document Your Progress**

   - Keep a record of your completed sub-goals and milestones. This documentation helps you track your progress and provides valuable insights into what's working well and what might need adjustment.

10. **Stay Focused on the Big Picture**

    - While working through sub-goals and milestones, regularly revisit your primary goal to ensure that every step you take is aligned with your overall vision. This helps you maintain perspective and stay connected to your ultimate purpose.

By following these tips, you'll be able to create sub-goals and milestones that effectively guide you toward achieving your larger goals. This structured approach makes your journey more manageable and keeps you motivated and on track as you work toward success.

Understanding Short-Term, Medium-Term, and Long-Term Goals

To effectively set purpose-driven goals, it's crucial to distinguish between short-term, medium-term, and long-term goals. Each plays a distinct role in guiding your progress, allowing you to create a balanced, actionable roadmap toward your ultimate vision. These goals don't operate in isolation—they work in concert to help you stay focused, motivated, and on track.

Short-Term Goals

Definition: Short-term goals are tasks or objectives that you aim to achieve within a relatively short period, typically within the next few days, weeks, or up to a year. These goals are often the immediate steps that keep you moving forward and provide quick wins that build momentum.

Purpose: Short-term goals are crucial for maintaining motivation and focus. They break down larger, more daunting goals into manageable actions, making it easier to see progress. These goals also help you build the habits and discipline needed to tackle more significant challenges.

Examples:

- Completing a specific project within a month.

- Learning a new skill relevant to your work within three months.

- Increasing your daily productivity by following a new time management technique for the next 30 days.

Tip: Ensure that your short-term goals are aligned with your medium- and long-term objectives. Each short-term goal should be a stepping stone toward achieving something greater.

Medium-Term Goals

Definition: Medium-term goals are objectives that you plan to achieve within the next one to three years. These are more substantial than short-term goals and often involve significant progress toward your long-term vision.

Purpose: Medium-term goals serve as the bridge between your immediate actions and your long-term aspirations. They provide a sense of direction and help you stay focused on the bigger picture while ensuring that your day-to-day efforts are aligned with your ultimate objectives.

Examples:

- Expanding your business into a new market within two years.

- Saving a specific amount of money for a major investment or purchase over the next 18 months.

- Completing a professional certification or degree within the next two years.

Tip: Medium-term goals should be specific and realistic, with clear milestones along the way. Regularly review these goals to ensure they remain aligned with your long-term vision as circumstances change.

Long-Term Goals

Definition: Long-term goals are the big-picture objectives you aim to achieve over an extended period, ranging from three to ten years or more. These goals represent the culmination of your efforts and are typically tied to your overall purpose and vision.

Purpose: Long-term goals are the ultimate targets that guide your overall strategy and decision-making. They are often ambitious and challenging, requiring sustained effort, perseverance, and a clear sense of direction. These goals give meaning to your short- and medium-term efforts, ensuring that everything you do is aligned with your broader aspirations.

Examples:
- Building a successful business that becomes a leader in your industry within ten years.
- Achieving financial independence by a certain age.
- Write and publish a book that shares your knowledge and experiences with a broad audience within five years.

Tip: While long-term goals are essential for providing direction, they should be flexible enough to adapt to changes in your circumstances or priorities. Regularly revisit and refine your long-term goals to ensure they continue to inspire and challenge you.

Integrating Short-Term, Medium-Term, and Long-Term Goals

Creating a cohesive roadmap to success involves thoughtfully integrating short-term, medium-term, and long-term goals. Each type of goal plays a distinct role, and when they work together effectively, they provide clear direction and sustained momentum. Here's how to bring them into alignment:

1. **Start with Your Long-Term Vision** – Begin by defining your long-term goals, which should be directly tied to your purpose and overall vision. These goals are the ultimate destination you're striving toward and should inspire and challenge you. Whether your long-term goal is to scale your business, achieve financial independence, or create a meaningful legacy, this step sets the foundation for your entire journey.

2. **Set Medium-Term Goals as Milestones** – Next, break your long-term vision into medium-term goals that represent significant progress toward that vision. Think of these goals as checkpoints or milestones that ensure you're staying on track. For example, if your long-term goal is to launch a nationwide business, a medium-term goal might be expanding to three new regions over the next two years. These milestones keep you motivated and focused on steady progress.

3. **Use Short-Term Goals for Immediate Action** – Short-term goals are where the rubber meets the road. These are your day-to-day or week-to-week actions that drive immediate progress. Whether it's completing a market analysis, attending a networking event, or developing a new skill, short-term goals provide the momentum needed to move toward your medium-term milestones. They also offer quick wins, which help you maintain enthusiasm and commitment to the larger vision.

4. **Regularly Review and Adjust** – As you work through your goals, regularly reviewing and adjusting them is essential. Check in on your short-, medium-, and long-term goals to ensure they remain aligned with your evolving purpose and vision. Be flexible enough to make adjustments when necessary—this helps you stay adaptable and resilient in the face of new opportunities or challenges.

By effectively integrating these types of goals, you create a balanced and strategic approach that ensures consistent progress toward your ultimate vision. Each type of goal plays a vital role in keeping you focused, motivated, and on track, guiding you toward sustainable, purpose-driven success. For more details on Short, Medium, and Long-Term goals, go to .

Creating Action Plans

Once you've defined your purpose-driven goals, the next critical step is developing detailed action plans that guide you toward achieving those goals. To create concrete steps toward your goals, it's essential to break each one down into manageable actions, prioritize key tasks, and set clear deadlines. Next, identify the resources or support you need, track your progress, and remain adaptable if circumstances shift. This structured approach allows you to maintain focus and achieve consistent progress.

For a detailed, step-by-step guide on building action plans tailored to your short-term, medium-term, and long-term goals, download the workbook at . Here, you'll find practical exercises designed to help you clarify your goals, set milestones, and create a roadmap that moves you closer to your vision with each step.

Whether you need help organizing your thoughts, setting up accountability systems, or simply tracking progress, the workbook offers a comprehensive toolkit to support your journey. Make sure to grab it and keep it handy as you continue developing your roadmap to success.

Resilience and Persistence: Your Power to Keep Moving Forward

Every journey toward meaningful goals will be filled with challenges, both expected and unexpected. It's during these times that **resilience** and **persistence** become your most valuable assets. Resilience goes far beyond bouncing back. Resilience takes you to a place where you've developed, and continue to develop, the strength to move forward, no matter the obstacles that might jump in front of you. Every setback is a learning experience, a moment to refine your approach and fortify your determination.

Think of resilience as a muscle. The more you use it, the stronger it becomes. You aren't born with it fully developed; it's something you build over time. With each challenge you face, you have the chance to strengthen that muscle. Every time you get back up after a fall, you reinforce your commitment to your goals, proving to yourself that you have what it takes to succeed.

Hand in hand with resilience is **persistence**—the determination to keep going even when the road gets rough. It's easy to stay committed when things are going well, but true persistence shows up when the going gets tough. It's the drive to push forward when motivation is low, progress feels slow, or obstacles seem impossible. Together, resilience and persistence create an unstoppable force, carrying you toward your goals no matter what stands in your way.

Staying Motivated and Overcoming Setbacks

Motivation is a powerful fuel for achieving your goals, but let's be honest—it can be fickle. It's natural to experience dips in motivation, especially when progress seems slow or when setbacks arise. To keep moving forward, keep your **purpose front and center**. Revisit the "why" behind your goals regularly. That core purpose is the fuel that keeps your persistence burning even when motivation flickers.

Setbacks aren't failures; they're opportunities to learn and grow. Each time you encounter an obstacle, you're being given the chance to fine-tune your approach and strengthen your resolve. Successful people aren't those who never face challenges; they're the ones who keep going despite them. The key is to see setbacks as **valuable feedback**—lessons that help you adjust your strategy and move closer to your goals.

A great way to maintain motivation is to **break down your larger goals into smaller, manageable tasks**. Each small win builds momentum and reinforces your progress. Celebrate these wins—big or small—they're the building blocks of success.

Flexibility and Adaptability in Your Approach

As much as you can plan, life is full of surprises. This is where **flexibility** and **adaptability** come in. Flexibility doesn't mean giving up on your goals; it means being open to changing your approach when necessary. It's about staying focused on the destination while being willing to explore different paths to get there.

Adaptability goes hand in hand with this. It's the ability to shift course when circumstances change, without losing sight of your overall vision. Changing direction doesn't mean you've failed—it means you're smart enough to recognize when adjustments are needed. When something isn't working, adaptability allows you to pivot and find a new solution. Remember, the river doesn't flow in a straight line—it bends, curves, and sometimes changes course, but it keeps moving forward. Your journey is the same.

Embracing the Journey

The pursuit of purpose-driven goals isn't just about the destination; it's about the transformation that happens along the way. **Resilience, persistence, motivation, and adaptability** aren't just tools to help you reach your goals; they're the qualities that shape you into a stronger, more capable individual. Every setback, every victory, every lesson learned contributes to your personal growth.

As you continue your journey, remember that the obstacles aren't meant to stop you—they're there to help you grow. The setbacks aren't failures—they're opportunities to rise again. Your plan doesn't have to be rigid—staying flexible and adaptable will keep you moving forward. And motivation doesn't have to be constant—it's your persistence and resilience that will get you through even when it's not easy.

Trust in yourself, trust in the process, and remember that each step you take brings you closer to the life you want to create. The road may not always be smooth, but every twist and turn is part of the adventure. Keep going, keep growing, and know that you already have everything you need to succeed.

Conclusion

We've covered a lot in this chapter—everything from resilience to persistence, flexibility, and motivation. If your head is spinning with ideas and strategies, don't worry—that's growth happening! It's easy to feel like you're standing at the base of a mountain, staring up and wondering how on earth you're going to climb it.

Here's the truth: you don't climb a mountain all at once. **One step at a time**, my friend. And all the strategies, tools, and mindsets we've talked about? They won't help you unless you start using them. So, here's my challenge to you—take what you've learned and put it into action.

Want some extra help with the first few steps? Head over to my website () and download the **workbook** that accompanies this book. It's full of exercises and journaling prompts designed to help you put these strategies into practice. Whether you're working through your goals, creating action plans, or building resilience, the workbook will be your guide.

Take things one step at a time. Break your goals into manageable pieces, and when things get tough, remember why you started this journey in the first place. Keep your eye on the bigger picture and don't forget to celebrate your progress along the way.

You have everything you need to succeed right now. The strategies, the mindset, and the purpose-driven goals—it's all within you, waiting for you to put it into action. So, get started, stay focused, and keep moving forward. You've got this!

Go out there and show that mountain who's boss!

Chapter Five

Simplification Strategies

Cutting Out the Noise

IN A WORLD CONSTANTLY vying for our time, attention, and energy, it's easy to feel overwhelmed by the sheer volume of tasks and distractions we face each day. Whether it's the relentless notifications on your phone, the ever-growing to-do list, or the competing demands of work and personal life, the noise can become deafening. And when you're surrounded by this constant barrage, it's hard to stay focused on what truly matters—your purpose, your goals, and your well-being.

Our goal here is to cut through that noise and reclaim clarity through the power of simplicity. But here's the key: simplicity is going to help you cut back on a lot of unnecessary "stuff" and move your focus onto what really matters. In the process, It will help you strip away the unnecessary and redirect your energy toward the things that genuinely contribute to your success and happiness.

We'll begin by exploring why simplicity isn't just a nice-to-have—it's necessary in today's fast-paced world. Then, we'll look at the common sources of noise that clutter your life and distract you from your goals. Whether it's the physical clutter in your workspace, the digital distractions on your devices, or the emotional clutter weighing on your mind, recognizing these sources is the first step toward eliminating them.

But identifying the noise is only half the battle. You'll also learn practical simplification strategies to apply to both your personal life and your business. These techniques will help you create the space—mentally and physically—to focus on what really matters. And once you've started simplifying, we'll talk about how to maintain that clarity and focus, so you don't slip back into old habits.

By the end of this chapter, you'll have the necessary tools to cut out the noise, streamline your life, and create a clear path toward your goals. It's time to let go of what's unnecessary and embrace a simpler, more focused way of living and working. Because simplicity isn't just about making life easier, it's about making it better.

The Power of Simplification: Warren Buffett's "20-Slot" Rule

Warren Buffett, one of the most successful investors of all time, is a strong advocate for simplification, especially when it comes to decision-making and setting goals. He's famously shared his approach to prioritizing with what he calls the "20-Slot" Rule.

Imagine having a punch card with only 20 slots for your entire life. Each time you make a major decision or pursue a big goal, you punch one slot. Once all 20 are punched, that's it—no more major decisions, no more big goals. It forces you to be incredibly selective about where you focus your time, energy, and resources.

Buffett's "20-Slot" Rule is a powerful metaphor for the necessity of simplification. By intentionally limiting your priorities, you're compelled to focus on only the most important things, the ones that really move the needle. This reduces overwhelm and distraction while dramatically increasing the chances of success in the areas you choose to prioritize. After all, when someone like Warren Buffett offers a piece of advice, it's probably worth taking to heart.

By borrowing this approach from Buffett's playbook, we're reminded that simplification isn't about doing less; it's about doing more of what truly counts. Buffett himself has achieved remarkable success by concentrating his focus on just a few high-impact decisions rather than spreading himself thin across countless projects. This kind of clarity has allowed him to channel his energy where it matters most, leading to extraordinary results.

In your own life, simplifying and zeroing in on your highest-impact goals and decisions will free up your time and energy for what really matters. It's not about cutting back—it's about letting go of what's unnecessary so you can give your full attention to what brings you the greatest results.

The Burden of Complexity

In today's fast-paced world, it's easy to get caught up in the web of complexity that seems to surround us at every turn. We juggle countless tasks, wade through endless information, and strive to meet increasing demands in both our personal and professional lives. While this complexity can sometimes feel inevitable, it comes with a heavy cost. The more complex our lives become, the more stress and inefficiency we invite, ultimately eroding our productivity and well-being.

Complexity brings stress in subtle yet powerful ways. When you're overwhelmed by too many responsibilities or bombarded with information, your mind struggles to keep pace. Each new task, decision, or distraction adds to the mental load, making it harder to focus, think clearly, or make effective decisions. This cognitive overload drains your energy, leaving you exhausted, frustrated, and far from your best.

It's not just stress—complexity also breeds inefficiency. When your to-do list is never-ending, and your attention is pulled in a dozen directions, prioritizing becomes a challenge. You may find yourself constantly switching between tasks, rarely completing anything, or worse, spending too much time on trivial matters instead of focusing on what's truly important. This scattered approach leads to wasted time and effort, with little to show for it at the end of the day.

In today's digital age, the constant flood of information—emails, notifications, social media, news updates—only adds to the complexity. While staying informed matters, the sheer volume of data we consume can quickly become paralyzing. This endless influx makes it difficult to separate what's meaningful from the noise, leading to decision fatigue and a dip in productivity.

But complexity doesn't just undermine productivity, it impacts your well-being, too. The chronic stress of a complex life can easily lead to burnout, anxiety, and even physical health issues. When you're constantly running on empty, it's easy to lose sight of the bigger picture, forget why you started in the first place, and feel disconnected from your purpose.

Recognizing the burden of complexity is the first step toward taking back control. When you understand how complexity creates stress and inefficiency, you can start making conscious choices to simplify. The goal is to clear away the clutter—both mentally and physically—that's been holding you back, so you can work and live in a way that's more focused, effective, and fulfilling.

In a world that often equates busyness with success, it takes courage to simplify. But the rewards are worth it: greater clarity, improved productivity, and a sense of peace that comes from knowing you're focusing on what truly matters. As we dive into simplification strategies in this chapter, keep in mind that the goal isn't just to cut out the noise, it's to create space for the things that bring you closer to your goals and enhance your well-being.

The Benefits of Simplification

At this point, everything around us seems designed to complicate! But if you've ever wished for a superpower, simplification is within reach—and it can make a profound difference in your daily life. Think of it like wiping the fog off a window: suddenly, everything becomes clear, and the path ahead is much easier to navigate. When you choose to cut through the clutter, both in life and work, the benefits aren't just noticeable—they're transformative. Simplification boosts your productivity, sharpens your decision-making, and touches every part of your life with a sense of clarity and calm that's hard to beat.

Let's dive into how embracing simplicity can lead to some pretty incredible results. I can almost hear Jimmy Cliff singing, *I Can See Clearly Now*. Too much? Maybe, but you get the idea!

Increased Clarity, Focus, and Productivity

Let's talk about what happens when you embrace simplification—it's like a breath of fresh air sweeping in. One of the first things you'll notice is this incredible sense of clarity. As you start stripping away the unnecessary—the distractions, the endless to-do lists, the constant noise—you begin to see what truly matters with razor-sharp focus. Instead of feeling pulled in a million directions, the path ahead becomes clear and defined. It's an empowering shift. With that clarity comes a newfound sense of direction and purpose, guiding your actions with intention and confidence.

And here's the magic part: clarity leads directly to focus. When your mind isn't bogged down by competing demands, you can channel your energy into the tasks and goals that actually matter. This is where true productivity comes to life. It's not about doing more; it's about doing the right things. You'll start seeing real results—not because you're working harder, but because you're working smarter. No more wasting time on trivial tasks that don't move the needle. You're directing your energy toward what truly counts, and that's where the magic happens.

Simplification doesn't just change how you work—it transforms how you live. By focusing on fewer, more meaningful activities, you'll find yourself achieving more with a sense of ease and efficiency that feels almost effortless. Your productivity won't just increase—it'll soar. Not because you're grinding through longer hours, but because you're making the best use of your time, energy, and resources.

So, if you're ready to feel more in control, more focused, and more satisfied with your achievements, it's time to embrace simplification. Start small, focus on what truly matters, and watch as your life and work transform in ways you never imagined. The results will speak for themselves.

Enhanced Decision-Making

Simplification also plays a key role in sharpening your decision-making skills. In a complex environment, making decisions can feel overwhelming. The more options, variables, and information you need to consider, the harder it becomes to choose the best path forward. This often leads to decision fatigue, where the sheer number of choices clouds your judgment and leaves you feeling stuck.

When you simplify, you reduce the number of decisions you need to make, and more importantly, you reduce the complexity of those decisions. With fewer distractions and greater clarity, you can evaluate your options more effectively and make decisions with confidence. Simplification allows you to prioritize—separating the essential from the non-essential—so you can focus on the decisions that matter most.

Improved decision-making isn't just about efficiency; it's about empowerment. When you're clear on your goals and priorities, you make choices that align with your values and purpose. This leads to better outcomes, greater control, and a boost in confidence as you move forward in your life with intention.

Reduced Stress

One of the most powerful benefits of simplification is the significant reduction in stress. In our modern lives, complexity is a major source of stress—whether it's managing multiple roles, navigating endless streams of information, or juggling countless responsibilities. This stress is mentally and physically draining, often leading to burnout and a decline in overall well-being.

Simplification provides a much-needed antidote to this overwhelm. By cutting down on the number of tasks, decisions, and distractions you face each day, you lighten your mental load. This creates room for rest, reflection, and creativity—all essential for maintaining your energy and sense of well-being. Simplification helps you stay focused on the present moment, rather than being constantly pulled in different directions by competing demands.

As the noise of complexity fades, you'll feel more at ease, more in control, and more connected to what truly matters. The stress that once felt overwhelming begins to melt away, replaced by a sense of calm and purpose. This reduction in stress doesn't just improve your mental health—it boosts your physical health as well, contributing to a stronger, more balanced sense of well-being.

The benefits of simplification are profound. By increasing clarity, focus, and productivity, enhancing decision-making, and reducing stress, simplification helps you live and work in alignment with your true priorities and purpose. It's not about doing less—it's about doing more of what truly matters. Every step you take toward a simpler life is a step toward greater fulfillment, success, and well-being.

Identifying Sources of Noise

In today's fast-paced world, it's easy to feel overwhelmed by the sheer volume of noise that surrounds us—both external and internal. This noise takes many forms, from the constant barrage of notifications and demands to the mental chatter that pulls our attention away from what truly matters. To reclaim clarity and purpose, it's essential to first identify these sources of noise. By understanding where this noise comes from, we can start cutting through the distractions and complexity that hold us back, opening the door to a simpler, more intentional life.

Internal Noise

When we think about the sources of noise in our lives, it's easy to focus on the external—the constant notifications, endless to-do lists, and the demands of work and family. But some of the most disruptive noise comes from within. Internal noise—those thoughts, feelings, and habits that cloud our minds—can be just as distracting, if not more so, than any external source. This internal noise creates mental clutter, contributes to complexity, and often prevents us from making real progress. Let's explore the different forms of internal noise and how they impact our ability to live and work with clarity and purpose.

Mental Clutter: Negative Thoughts, Anxieties, and Indecision

Mental clutter is like background noise that never seems to shut off. The constant chatter of negative thoughts, anxieties, and indecision can dominate your inner dialogue. This clutter doesn't just occupy mental space—it actively blocks your ability to focus, make decisions, and move forward.

Negative thoughts are a significant source of mental clutter. These voices in your head may tell you that you're not good enough, that you're bound to fail, or that you're wasting your time. Often rooted in self-doubt or past experiences, these thoughts can be incredibly difficult to silence. The more room they take up in your mind, the less space there is for positive, constructive thinking. They sap your confidence, cloud your judgment, and ultimately prevent you from taking action on your goals.

Anxieties are another form of internal noise. Whether it's fear of the unknown, worry about the future, or concern over what others think, anxiety can be paralyzing. It keeps you stuck in a cycle of "what ifs," unable to move forward because you're too focused on everything that could go wrong. This type of mental clutter is particularly harmful because it drains your energy and makes even small tasks feel overwhelming. Anxiety often leads to procrastination, as you delay taking action out of fear or uncertainty.

Indecision is yet another contributor to mental clutter. Faced with multiple options, the inability to choose can leave you feeling stuck. Indecision often stems from a fear of making the wrong choice, leading to paralysis by analysis. Instead of moving forward, you remain in a state of limbo, constantly second-guessing yourself. This mental clutter not only slows your progress but also creates unease and dissatisfaction.

Personal Habits that Contribute to Complexity

Beyond mental clutter, certain personal habits also create internal noise and add complexity to your life. Often ingrained over the years, these habits can be hard to recognize and even harder to change.

Perfectionism is one such habit. While striving for excellence is valuable, perfectionism often leads to unnecessary complexity. When you're fixated on making everything flawless, you overcomplicate tasks that could be simple. This not only consumes more time and energy than necessary but also creates stress and anxiety. Perfectionism can even lead to procrastination, as the fear of not getting something "just right" prevents you from starting or completing tasks.

Overcommitting is another habit that adds to internal noise. Saying "yes" to too many things—whether it's work projects, social engagements, or personal responsibilities—quickly leads to overwhelm. Overcommitting spreads your attention and energy thin, making it difficult to focus on what's truly important. This habit often stems from a desire to please others or a fear of missing out, but it ultimately creates a tangled web of obligations that are hard to manage.

Cluttered environments, both physical and digital, also contribute to internal noise. If your workspace is filled with unnecessary items or your computer is cluttered with files, it becomes harder to focus and be productive. Physical clutter often reflects mental clutter; when your surroundings are chaotic, your mind tends to be as well. Simplifying your environment can have a powerful impact on your mental clarity and well-being.

I have to admit, this has been a struggle for me over the years. I've often joked, "A clean desk is the sign of a sick mind." Personally, I liked the idea that "a messy desk is the sign of genius." But, as I mentioned in my first book, I once brought in high-dollar consultants to help me break through a wall in one of my businesses. What I didn't share was how they spent their first few hours with the door closed, going through everything on my desk and shelves. And let me tell you—they were ruthless.

They pulled the trash can out from under my desk and placed it front and center, as if to say, "This is where most of your stuff belongs." Each item was picked up with questions like, "What is this for?", "When was the last time you used it?", and "Is there a better place for this?" The process was relentless, but the results were eye-opening. Aside from a few items being filed away or passed on to someone else, most of it ended up in the trash. These consultants were serious about eliminating clutter, and they made it clear that a clean, organized workspace was non-negotiable if I wanted to break through the barriers I was facing.

Finally, I hate to admit it, but multitasking is one of the worst things you can do for efficiency. I've been guilty of it for years. I used to say, "If I didn't multitask, I'd never get anything done." I think I mentioned earlier—maybe in this book or the last—that I used to have an open-door policy, which meant I was constantly interrupted. I still have four monitors on my desk, and I'd have more if I had the space. For years, I used those screens to juggle multiple tasks: answering emails, working on projects, researching something for a client—the list goes on. I firmly believed in multitasking and defended it whenever the topic came up.

But, as they say, even old dogs can learn new tricks. Not only have I read countless studies on multitasking, but I also tested it for myself. I compared my productivity while multitasking versus focusing on one task at a time. The results were undeniable: multitasking leads to scattered thinking and reduced productivity. When you try to juggle multiple tasks, your attention is divided, and the quality of your work suffers. The constant switching between tasks creates mental fatigue and leaves you feeling more overwhelmed than accomplished. These days, my multiple monitors are still useful, but now I use them to give me more flexibility as I work on one thing at a time. (I currently have this document open on one screen, another workbook document for this book open on another, a browser open on the third for research, and a fourth with misc. foundational data.)

Internal noise—whether from mental clutter or personal habits—can be a significant barrier to clarity, focus, and progress. Negative thoughts, anxieties, and indecision create a whirlwind of mental activity that prevents you from moving forward with confidence. Meanwhile, habits like perfectionism, overcommitting, and multitasking add layers of complexity that make it harder to achieve your goals.

Recognizing these sources of internal noise is the first step toward simplifying your life. Addressing the mental clutter and personal habits that contribute to complexity will help create a clearer, more focused mindset. This, in turn, will allow you to approach your goals with greater clarity, purpose, and efficiency, setting the stage for a more fulfilling and productive life.

External Noise

While internal noise often stems from our thoughts, emotions, and habits, external noise comes from the environment and circumstances that surround us. This type of noise can be just as disruptive—if not more so—because it constantly bombards us from the outside, making it difficult to focus, stay organized, and move forward with purpose. Understanding the various forms of external noise is essential to simplifying your life and reclaiming the clarity needed to achieve your goals.

Environmental Distractions: Digital Noise, Physical Clutter, and Interruptions

In today's digital age, we're more connected than ever before. While this connectivity brings many benefits, it also creates a flood of digital noise that can be overwhelming. Digital noise includes the endless stream of emails, text messages, social media notifications, and news alerts that demand our attention. Every ping, buzz, or pop-up notification pulls you away from what you're doing, breaking your concentration and making it harder to return to a state of flow. These constant digital distractions not only reduce your productivity but also contribute to mental exhaustion as your brain is forced to switch between tasks constantly.

Physical clutter is another major source of external noise. The spaces we inhabit—whether at home, at work, or even in our cars—have a profound impact on our mental state. A cluttered environment creates a cluttered mind. When your workspace is filled with unnecessary items, piles of papers, or disorganized materials, it's harder to find what you need, stay focused, and work efficiently. Physical clutter also causes stress, constantly reminding you of unfinished tasks and disorganization. The more cluttered your surroundings, the more overwhelmed you're likely to feel, which can lead to procrastination and a lack of motivation.

Interruptions are yet another form of external noise that can significantly disrupt your progress. These interruptions can come from colleagues, family members, phone calls, or unexpected visitors. Even seemingly small interruptions can break your flow and make it difficult to regain focus, especially if you're working on something that requires deep concentration. Over time, these interruptions add up, leading to frustration and a decrease in productivity. They also contribute to a fragmented schedule, where you're constantly shifting between tasks rather than making meaningful progress on any one thing.

And let's not forget how environmental distractions chip away at our time, forcing us to work longer hours—something I've discussed a LOT in this book and my last one. I'm happy to report that I've finally turned off almost all my notifications and now schedule specific times for tasks that used to interrupt my day constantly. I've become one of the most disconnected people you'll ever meet, and it feels fantastic. Now, technology works for me—not the other way around.

Unnecessary Commitments and Tasks

Many of us fall into the trap of saying "yes" to too many things—whether it's additional work projects, volunteering for community events, or agreeing to social engagements that don't truly align with our priorities. While each individual commitment may seem manageable, they collectively create a burden that can quickly become overwhelming.

Unnecessary commitments eat away at your time and energy, leaving less room for the activities that matter most. They stretch you too thin, making it difficult to give your full attention to any one thing. When you're constantly running from one obligation to the next, there's little time left for reflection, creativity, or rest. This over-commitment often leads to burnout and a constant feeling of being behind, as you struggle to keep up with an endless list of tasks and responsibilities.

Similarly, unnecessary tasks—those that don't contribute meaningfully to your goals or well-being—also add to the noise in your life. These might include busy work, tasks that could be delegated, or activities you've taken on out of habit. While these tasks might seem small, they accumulate over time, consuming valuable resources that could be better spent on more important endeavors. Filling your schedule with low-impact activities reduces the time and energy available for high-impact, purpose-driven actions.

Wrapping It Up

The simple truth of this section is that it's easy to think we're doing a good thing when we are actually working against our own goals and progress. External noise, whether from environmental distractions like digital noise and physical clutter or from unnecessary commitments and tasks, can create significant barriers to clarity, focus, and progress. These forms of noise constantly pull you away from what truly matters, making it difficult to stay organized, motivated, and productive.

Recognizing and addressing these sources of external noise is crucial to simplifying your life. By reducing digital distractions, decluttering your environment, and learning to say "no" to unnecessary commitments, you can create a more focused, intentional, and effective approach to your goals. Simplification isn't about doing less; it's about eliminating the noise that holds you back, so you can do more of what truly matters.

Simplification Techniques for Personal Life

Welcome to the part of the chapter where we roll up our sleeves, dig through the piles, and finally tackle that junk drawer you've been avoiding for years. Yes, we're talking about decluttering—both your physical space and your life. Don't worry, though; we'll make this as painless—and hopefully as fun—as possible. By the end of this section, you'll be well on your way to creating a more streamlined, intentional living space that actually brings you joy instead of stress. And trust me, even if the process isn't exactly thrilling, the outcome will be worth it.

Let's be honest: most of us have more stuff than we know what to do with. We've all got that one closet—or maybe an entire room—filled with items we've convinced ourselves we *might* need someday. Spoiler alert: "Someday" probably isn't coming, and in the meantime, all that stuff is just taking up space and causing unnecessary stress. That's where the magic of decluttering comes in.

Our Move to Puerto Rico: The Ultimate Decluttering Adventure

Let me tell you a little story about how we took decluttering to the extreme when we decided to move to Puerto Rico. When most people think about moving, they imagine packing up a truck, maybe renting a storage unit, and hauling all their belongings to a new place. But not us. We decided to take the minimalist approach to a whole new level.

When we made the decision to trade in our mainland life for the island breeze of Puerto Rico, we realized something important: we didn't want to be weighed down by all the "stuff" we'd accumulated over the years. So, we did what any reasonable people would do—we sold our house, held an estate sale, and started fresh. And by "started fresh," I mean we moved to Puerto Rico with a grand total of six suitcases. Yes, you read that right. Six suitcases.

Now, before you start picturing us living in a minimalist monk's cell, let me clarify: we moved into a fully furnished place. On the island, it's pretty common to find homes that are "move-in ready," and ours was no exception. It came with all the furniture, dishes, and even all the beach towels we could ever need. All we had to do was show up with our suitcases and a couple of pairs of well-worn flip-flops.

But let me tell you, getting down to six suitcases wasn't easy. It felt like a game of "Keep, Toss, or Donate" on steroids. The fondue set we hadn't used since 1998. Gone. The stacks of old magazines we were *definitely* going to read someday? Outta there. The 47 coffee mugs with witty sayings or great logos we'd somehow collected over the years. Let's just say we kept two of our favorites and wished the rest well on their journey to new homes.

There's something incredibly liberating about letting go of all that stuff. When we arrived in Puerto Rico with just those six suitcases, it felt like a fresh start in every sense of the word. We weren't weighed down by clutter or overwhelmed by possessions. Moving in and unpacking took minutes, not days. Instead of figuring out where everything should go, we were free to enjoy our new surroundings, explore the island, and focus on what really mattered—like finding the best spot for mojitos.

Of course, I'd be lying if I said there weren't a few moments of stress when we realized we had really left behind that perfectly good blender. But you know what? It was worth it. Living with less has allowed us to appreciate what we have more. It's also made cleaning a breeze—seriously, when you only have a handful of possessions, dusting takes about five minutes, tops. O.K., that job honestly falls to the cleaners that come in once a week and there's all the stuff that came with the house, but I'm sure you get my drift.

So, if you're feeling overwhelmed by clutter or just need a fresh start, take it from us: sometimes, less really is more. You don't have to sell your house and move to an island (though I highly recommend it if you get the chance), but you *can* start by letting go of the things that don't add value to your life. Whether it's that sweater you haven't worn in five years or the collection of mismatched Tupperware you've been meaning to tackle, start small and see how it feels.

Decluttering might not sound glamorous but trust me—it can be life-changing. And who knows? It might just be the excuse you need to plan your own adventure, whether that's moving to Puerto Rico or finally taking that trip you've been dreaming about. And if you end up with only six suitcases to your name, don't worry—you'll be in good company. After all, who needs a blender when you've got a beach and plenty of others willing to make the drinks with the umbrella in them?

Decluttering Physical Space

Now that we've explored the importance of simplifying your life, it's time to roll up our sleeves and tackle decluttering your physical space. Our homes and workspaces can quickly become overwhelmed with random items that accumulate faster than we can manage. The result? Spaces that feel chaotic and stressful, making it difficult to stay organized, think clearly, or focus on what truly matters.

Decluttering your physical space is like giving your environment—and your mind—a fresh start. It's about transforming your surroundings into places that feel open, calm, and functional, rather than overwhelming and cluttered. But don't worry; I'm not going to just leave you with the concept of decluttering. We're going to dive into a step-by-step guide that will help you turn cluttered chaos into serene simplicity, one drawer, closet, or desktop at a time.

Ready to dive in? Let's get started!

Step-by-Step Guide to Decluttering Your Home and Workspace

Decluttering might sound like a chore, but trust me, it's more like a liberation movement for your home. Imagine finding your keys without having to dig through a mountain of random items. Or better yet, imagine opening a drawer and actually knowing what's inside. Revolutionary, right?

Step 1: Start Small, Dream Big First things first—don't try to tackle your entire house or office in one go unless you want to end up curled in a fetal position under your dining room table. Start with a small area, like that junk drawer or your desk. These are contained spaces where you can see progress quickly, and trust me, nothing feels better than seeing a clutter-free surface.

Step 2: The "Keep, Toss, Donate" Game This is where the fun begins. Grab three boxes or bags and label them "Keep," "Toss," and "Donate." Then, go through your items one by one. If you haven't used something in the past year and it doesn't make you smile, it's time to let it go. If it's broken, toss it. If it's still in good shape but not something you need, donate it. If it's something you use regularly or it brings you genuine joy, keep it. Simple, right?

Step 3: Rinse and Repeat Once you've tackled your first small space, keep the momentum going. Move on to the next drawer, shelf, or closet, and repeat the process. Remember, this isn't a sprint; it's a marathon. Decluttering takes time, but each step brings you closer to a simpler, more peaceful environment.

Step 4: Find a Home for Everything One of the secrets to staying decluttered is making sure that everything you decide to keep has a designated spot. When things have a home, it's easier to put them away, and you're less likely to accumulate new clutter.

The Minimalist Approach: Keeping Only What is Essential and Meaningful

Now, let's talk minimalism—not the stark, white-walled, one-chair kind, but the kind that helps you keep your sanity. I don't want to sound like Marie Kondo here, but I've found that the clutter constantly surrounding me makes it hard to look past that "stuff" and get focused. Minimalism will help you cut through all the busyness surrounding you and focus on what's essential and meaningful while letting go of the rest. Trust me, when you surround yourself with things that add value to your life, you will thank me.

Think of minimalism as curating your own personal museum. Every item you keep should tell a story or serve a purpose. That coffee mug that makes your mornings brighter? Keep it. The three extra sets of measuring cups you never use. Maybe not. The idea isn't to live in a bare, empty space but rather to create an environment where everything you see, use, and touch brings you joy or serves a clear purpose.

Minimalism doesn't mean you can't have things—it means you choose what you have intentionally. It's about quality over quantity and making your space a reflection of what truly matters to you. And let's be real: a clutter-free space is much easier to keep clean, which is a win for everyone.

Decluttering and embracing a minimalist approach might sound like a lot of work, but the payoff is huge. By simplifying your physical space, you're creating a more organized home or office and clearing out the mental clutter that comes with it. You'll be amazed at how much lighter and more focused you feel when you're not surrounded by unnecessary stuff. Plus, with less to clean and maintain, you'll have more time to focus on what matters—like finally reading that book you bought three years ago.

Now, let me be clear... other than the move to Puerto Rico, we don't make a habit of going full Marie Kondo in our lives. But I do want to stress the importance of choosing to find your place of clarity—and your desk or office is a great place to start. If you've known me for years, you've probably seen my desk piled up with almost no clear space. That was then—this is now! My desk is well organized.

I've got to admit this realization hit me hard during the move to Puerto Rico, and it's a lesson I quickly adopted as a personal choice going forward. I used to argue that my clutter was just my version of organization, and I could find any piece of paper (as long as no one tried to "help" clean up my mess) in two seconds flat. And honestly, I could. But here's what I realized: when the clutter was gone, my focus increased *profoundly*—and almost instantly.

So, grab some boxes, put on your favorite motivating playlist, and start simplifying your life—one drawer at a time. Trust me, your future self will thank me.

Digital Detox

In this digital age, our lives are constantly buzzing with notifications, messages, and social media updates. It's as if our devices have a direct line to our attention, pulling us away from whatever we're doing with every ping and buzz. While these digital connections can be valuable, they often become a source of distraction that makes it difficult to focus, be present, or even breathe. The solution? A digital detox—where we take a step back, reclaim our time, and regain control over the digital noise that surrounds us.

Digital distractions have a sneaky way of infiltrating every moment of our day. Whether it's the constant influx of emails, the lure of social media, or the never-ending stream of notifications, it can feel like we're always on call, always available, and always "on." This constant connectivity might seem necessary, especially in today's fast-paced world, but it often comes at the cost of our peace of mind and productivity. The more we allow these digital interruptions to dictate our time, the harder it becomes to focus on tasks that truly matter—whether it's work, personal projects, or simply spending quality time with friends and family.

My son recognized this problem in his own life not too long ago. He found that he was constantly checking Facebook on his phone—scrolling through updates, reacting to posts, and getting lost in the endless feed of information. It wasn't that Facebook was inherently bad, but it consumed more of his time and attention than he was comfortable with. So, in a move that I found both bold and inspiring, he decided to completely remove Facebook from his phone. Just like that—no more mindless scrolling, no more constant notifications. For a time, he disconnected from that digital distraction entirely.

The result? He found himself with more time and mental space to focus on things that truly mattered to him. Eventually, he reinstalled Facebook, but only because it was a valuable tool for connecting with prospects and clients. However, he didn't fall back into old habits. Instead, he set strict boundaries, only accessing the app at specific times during the day. By doing this, he maintained the benefits of his digital detox while still leveraging the platform for his work.

He's even taken this digital detox to another level. He's chosen to stop watching much of what he used to and is now extremely selective about what he does watch. He focuses on the important things—like family, handling business that needs his attention, and surrounding himself with content that helps him stay focused on what's good in his life. This shift has allowed him to be more intentional about how he spends his time and energy, creating a greater sense of balance and fulfillment.

Inspired by his experience, I took a hard look at my own digital habits. I realized that the constant barrage of notifications was pulling me away from my work, interrupting my focus, and stressing me out. So, I made a decision: I turned off notifications for almost all forms of digital media. No more email dings, social media pings, or news alerts pulling me out of the moment. Instead, I scheduled specific times to check these things, ensuring I stay informed and connected—but on *my* terms.

This small change made a huge difference. Without constant interruptions, I found it easier to stay focused on the task at hand—whether that was writing, working with clients, or just relaxing with a good book. I felt more in control of my time, and my stress levels dropped significantly. It wasn't about cutting off all digital connections, but about being intentional with how and when I engage with them. I still check my email messages and I still check in with social media once or twice a day. But I don't get those constant pings, or pop-ups on my computer or my phone. I can tell you it's worth being delayed on the occasional mail, or even someone thinks they really need to connect on Facebook or LinkedIn.

Creating a digital minimalist lifestyle doesn't mean you have to abandon technology altogether. All it really entails is making deliberate choices to reduce distractions and use technology in a way that supports your life rather than detracts from it. Whether turning off notifications, setting specific times to check emails and social media, or removing apps that don't serve you, small adjustments can lead to big improvements in focus, productivity, and overall well-being.

The digital world isn't going anywhere, and as I've already said, it's not inherently evil. But by controlling how we interact with it, we can reclaim our time, reduce stress, and create space for the things that truly matter and make a difference. Just like my son's decision to step back from Facebook or my choice to silence notifications, a digital detox can help you find balance in a world that's always connected. So go ahead, take a step back, turn off the noise, and see how much more you can accomplish when you're in control of your digital life rather than the other way around.

Streamlining Daily Routines

There's something almost magical about a well-oiled daily routine. When your habits and routines are working in harmony, the day seems to glide along effortlessly—like a perfectly choreographed dance where every step is in sync. You wake up, get through your morning routine, and hit the ground running, ticking off items on your to-do list with the precision of a Swiss watch. But, as we all know, life isn't always so predictable. Sometimes, despite our best-laid plans, life throws us a curveball, and suddenly, that beautifully crafted routine feels more like a tangled mess of missed steps and forgotten beats.

Streamlining your daily routines is about finding that sweet spot between efficiency and flexibility. It's about creating habits that help you move through your day with purpose and ease while recognizing that you sometimes need to pivot. After all, routines are there to serve you, not the other way around.

Let's start with the basics: when your daily habits are in sync, everything seems to fall into place. You know what needs to get done, and you've established a rhythm that allows you to move through the day smoothly. Maybe you begin with a cup of coffee and a few minutes of meditation, or perhaps you're the type who dives straight into work (though I highly recommend carving out some time to focus and plan). Whatever your approach, having a routine can save you from the mental drain of decision fatigue. When you already know what comes next, there's no need to waste brainpower figuring it out—you just move through your day almost on autopilot.

But here's where things get interesting: life has a way of throwing off our rhythm. Maybe you wake up to find the internet is down, and your plan to tackle emails immediately goes out the window. Or perhaps your kid decides that today is the perfect day to rebel against getting dressed for school, turning your calm morning routine into a circus act. It's in these moments that flexibility becomes just as important as having a routine in the first place.

Flexibility in your routines doesn't give you a license to abandon them at the first sign of trouble, but it does acknowledge that there are times when it is necessary and appropriate to adapt. It's about understanding that while routines are helpful, they're not set in stone. They should bend when life's currents shift, allowing you to adjust without losing footing.

Some days, your routine might go exactly as planned, with everything falling neatly into place. On other days, you might have to toss the schedule out the window and go with the flow. And that's okay. The key is to have routines strong enough to keep you on track but flexible enough to accommodate life's unexpected twists and turns.

Streamlining your daily routines helps you strike a balance. It's about creating a framework that supports your goals and helps you move through the day with ease, all while giving yourself the freedom to adapt when things don't go as planned. Efficiency is great, but so is resilience. When you can combine the two, your routines won't just make your life easier, they'll make it more enjoyable too.

So, embrace your routines, but remember to keep them flexible. After all, life is full of surprises, and the best routines are the ones that can dance to any tune, even when the music changes.

Simplification Techniques for Business

In the business world, where every minute counts and to-do lists seem to stretch into infinity, finding ways to simplify can feel like a lifesaver. But here's the catch—simplification doesn't mean cutting corners or doing less; it means doing what matters most and doing it well. It's about trimming the fat from your workday so you can focus on what truly moves the needle. And it all starts with mastering the fine art of prioritization and time management.

Prioritization and Time Management

Imagine your workday as a giant buffet—there's a lot on the table, and while it all might look appetizing, you can't possibly devour everything. This is where prioritization comes in. It's about picking the dishes that will truly satisfy your hunger and leaving the rest for another time (or another plate). And no, prioritization isn't just about staring at your list and hoping the most important tasks magically reveal themselves. It's about using tools and techniques that help you cut through the noise and focus on what truly matters.

One tried-and-true method for prioritization (and one that I particularly like) is the **Eisenhower Matrix**, a simple yet effective tool even a U.S. president swore by it. Here's how it works: you divide your tasks into four quadrants—Urgent and Important, Important but Not Urgent, Urgent but Not Important, and Not Urgent and Not Important. The magic happens when you realize that not everything on your list is urgent or important. In fact, some tasks can be delegated, delayed, or even ditched entirely. By sorting your tasks this way, you focus on what truly deserves your attention and avoid getting bogged down by the trivial stuff.

But prioritization is just the first step. Once you've figured out what's important, it's time to manage your time like a boss. This is where **time-blocking** and **batching** come into play—two techniques that can transform your productivity from chaotic to streamlined.

Time-blocking is like giving each task its own little slice of the day, ensuring that you're not trying to do everything all at once. Picture your day as a puzzle, and each time block is a piece that fits perfectly into the overall picture. Setting aside dedicated blocks of time for specific tasks eliminates the constant start-stop-start-again pattern that drains your energy. During these blocks, you focus solely on the task at hand, knowing that everything else has its own time slot waiting for it. The result? You get more done in less time, with far less stress.

Batching, on the other hand, is like time-blocking's efficiency-obsessed cousin. It's about grouping similar tasks and tackling them in one go rather than spreading them out across the day or week. Think of it like doing all your laundry in one load instead of washing each item separately (which, let's be honest, no one would ever do). When you batch tasks, whether it's answering emails, writing reports, or making phone calls—you can maintain focus, avoid context-switching, and breeze through your workload with far less friction.

I know what you're thinking: *"This all sounds great in theory, but my day never goes as planned!"* And you're right—life happens, especially in business. But here's the beauty of these techniques: they're designed to help you manage the chaos, not eliminate it. Prioritization, time-blocking, and batching are about giving you the structure you need to stay focused, even when things go off-script. And when you've got a solid framework in place, you can handle those curveballs with much more grace and less panic.

In the end, simplifying your business life is a tool that leads to a lifestyle. A lifestyle that helps you gain clarity and focus on doing those things that matter. By prioritizing your tasks, managing your time wisely, and using tools like the Eisenhower Matrix, time-blocking, and batching, you'll find that your workday runs smoother, your stress levels drop, and you have more energy to tackle the tasks that truly make a difference. So go ahead, give it a try—your future self will thank you, and who knows, you might even have time left to enjoy doing the things you love. You know, Hammock stuff vs. Hamster Wheel.

Streamlining Processes

Alright, you've mastered the art of prioritization and time management (you have, right?), and your daily routine is practically humming along. But there's still one big piece of the simplification puzzle we need to tackle: your processes. Now, I know what you're thinking—processes aren't exactly the stuff you'd write home about. But stick with me because streamlining your processes is like giving your business a tune-up. It's about ensuring every part runs as smoothly as possible so you can keep cruising toward your goals without unnecessary pit stops.

Streamlining processes is all about identifying and eliminating those pesky redundant tasks and non-value-added activities that quietly siphon away your time and resources. These things might have made sense at one point, but now they're just slowing you down. It's like the old habit of double-checking your work five times when once or twice would do—or keeping a paper trail for everything in an increasingly digital world. These little inefficiencies add up, and before you know it, they've created bottlenecks in your workflow.

The key to streamlining is getting brutally honest about what's really necessary. Ask yourself, "Is this activity actually helping me achieve my goals, or is it just something I've been doing out of habit?" If the answer is the latter, it's time to let it go. Imagine your business as a well-oiled machine, and every redundant activity is a rusty bolt—unnecessary and potentially problematic. The more you strip away, the more efficiently your machine will run.

But cutting out the fluff is only half the battle. The other half is implementing efficient systems and tools to keep everything running smoothly. We've already touched on systems and tools, so I won't belabor the point. But here's the thing: the best systems are the ones that make your life easier without adding extra layers of complexity. It's like finding that perfect kitchen gadget that actually speeds up your cooking instead of just taking up space in your drawer.

When it comes to implementing efficient systems, think of it like setting up a conveyor belt in your business. Everything should flow seamlessly from one task to the next without unnecessary stops or delays. The goal is to create a streamlined process that minimizes wasted time and maximizes output. And let's be honest—who doesn't want to get more done in less time?

Of course, the trick is not to fall into the trap of over-systematizing. It's easy to go overboard and end up with a system so complex that it becomes its own headache. The best systems are like a good jazz band—structured enough to keep everything on track but flexible enough to allow for some improvisation. You want a system that supports your work, not one that stifles it.

So, as you streamline your processes, remember: the goal isn't to strip everything down to the bare bones—it's to eliminate the unnecessary and implement the essential. By cutting out redundant activities and fine-tuning your systems, you're setting yourself up for a smoother, more efficient operation. And let's be real—when your processes are streamlined, not only does your work get easier, but you also free up time to focus on the big-picture stuff that drives your business forward.

Ultimately, streamlining processes is about creating a business that runs like a dream. So, take a deep breath, roll up your sleeves, and get ready to do some serious fine-tuning. Your future, less-stressed self will thank you for it, and your business will be all the better. After all, who doesn't love the sound of a well-oiled machine running at full throttle?

Effective Delegation: Empowering Your Team

By now, you've likely dipped your toes into the waters of delegation, and you know that it's not just about offloading tasks—it's about strategically empowering others to take ownership of their work. But as with anything in business, there's an art to effective delegation that goes beyond simply handing off a to-do list. You have to create an environment where your team members, or those you outsource to, feel both capable and motivated to deliver high-quality results.

When you delegate effectively, you free up your own time and allow your team to grow, develop new skills, and take greater ownership of their roles. But here's the catch: delegation without empowerment is like handing someone the keys to a car without teaching them how to drive. To ensure that the tasks you delegate are executed well, you need to equip your team with the tools, knowledge, and confidence they need to succeed.

Empowerment starts with clarity. When you delegate a task, it's essential to provide clear instructions, expectations, and context. Your team needs to understand not just *what* they're doing but *why* it matters. Delegating IS NOT micromanaging—quite the opposite. It is setting the stage so they know the destination and allowing them the freedom to choose the best route to get there. It's about trusting them to use their judgment and creativity while being available to provide guidance when needed.

However, empowerment goes beyond clear communication. It gives your team the autonomy to make decisions within the scope of their responsibilities. This might feel a bit uncomfortable at first—especially if you're used to being hands-on—but it's a crucial step in building a strong, capable team. When team members feel trusted to make decisions, they're more likely to take initiative, solve problems on their own, and bring new ideas to the table. And when they know they have your support, they're more likely to take calculated risks that could lead to innovative solutions.

Of course, effective delegation isn't just tossing tasks into the air and hoping they land in the right place. You've got to have the processes in place, and your team needs to understand the vision to ensure that the quality of work meets your standards. This is where regular check-ins and feedback come into play. You don't need to hover over your team's shoulders, but you do need to create opportunities for collaboration, and course correction. By providing constructive feedback, you help your team refine their work and develop their skills, all while maintaining the high standards that are essential to your business.

Here's the real secret sauce of effective delegation: You have to create a culture of ownership. When you empower your team to take full responsibility for their tasks, they become invested in the outcomes. They're not just completing tasks for the sake of it—they're contributing to the success of the business, and they know it. This sense of ownership leads to higher engagement, better performance, and ultimately, better results.

So, as you continue to delegate, keep in mind that while you're offloading work, you're also building a stronger, more capable team. You are giving your team the tools they need to succeed, trusting them to use their judgment, and providing the feedback and support that ensures you end up where you want to be. When you delegate effectively, you lighten your load AND empower your team to take your business to new heights. And that's a win-win for everyone involved.

Maintaining a Simplified Lifestyle

So, you've done the hard work. You've decluttered, streamlined, delegated, and turned your life and business into a lean, mean, simplicity machine. But as anyone who's ever tried to maintain a New Year's resolution can tell you, the real challenge isn't in making changes—it's in keeping them. Welcome to the final, and arguably most important, part of this journey: maintaining a simplified lifestyle.

Simplifying your life and business isn't a one-time event; it's a commitment, a way of living that requires consistency and discipline. Think of it like getting in shape—just because you hit your goal weight doesn't mean you can suddenly revert to old habits of midnight snacks and skipping workouts. We all know that's the root of people getting to their goal weight and then bouncing back up to where they were before. The same goes for simplicity. To keep the clutter at bay and the noise turned down, you need to cultivate habits that reinforce the changes you've made.

Consistency and Discipline: Developing Habits to Maintain Simplicity

The first step in maintaining a simplified lifestyle is developing the habits that will keep it that way. Habits are the unsung heroes of simplicity—they work quietly in the background, ensuring that clutter doesn't creep back in and that your streamlined processes stay, well, streamlined. But here's the thing about habits: they don't form overnight. They require consistency and a bit of discipline to take root.

Think back to the changes you've made—decluttering your space, managing your time more effectively, and delegating tasks. Now, imagine what would happen if you let those changes slide, even just a little. It's a slippery slope. One unchecked email turns into a thousand, one cluttered drawer becomes a whole room, and suddenly, you're back where you started. The key to avoiding this backslide is to make simplicity a habit, something you do without even thinking about it.

This might mean setting aside a few minutes each day to tidy up your workspace or regularly blocking out time to review your priorities and ensure you're still focused on what matters most. It's about building small, consistent actions into your routine that support the simplified life you've worked so hard to create. And while it might take some time to build these habits, once they're in place, they'll make maintaining simplicity almost effortless.

The Importance of Regular Reviews and Adjustments

Even with the best habits in place, life has a way of throwing curveballs, and what worked for you last month—or even last week—might not work today. That's why regular reviews and adjustments are crucial to staying on track. Think of it as a routine maintenance check for your simplified life, ensuring everything is still running smoothly and efficiently.

These reviews don't have to be complicated or time-consuming. It could be as simple as taking a few moments at the end of each week to reflect on what's working and what's not, making minor adjustments as needed. Maybe you've noticed that a new task has crept into your routine that doesn't add value, or perhaps a process that was once efficient has become cumbersome. Regular reviews allow you to course-correct before things get out of hand.

Adjustments are part of the deal when it comes to maintaining simplicity. As your life and business evolve, so too will your needs and priorities. The beauty of a simplified lifestyle is its flexibility—it can and should adapt to fit your current circumstances. So, don't be afraid to make changes, tweak your routines, and let go of what no longer serves you.

Maintaining a simplified lifestyle is a lot more about persistence than it is about perfection. It's about committing to the habits that keep your life and business running smoothly and being willing to adjust when things start to feel out of balance. With consistency, discipline, and a willingness to adapt, you can ensure that the simplicity you've worked so hard to achieve doesn't just stick around—it becomes the foundation for a more focused, intentional, and fulfilling life.

So, keep at it. Keep refining, keep adjusting, and keep enjoying the benefits of a life that's uncluttered, streamlined, and aligned with what truly matters. The effort is worth it because when you live simply, you live more fully—and that's a lifestyle worth maintaining.

Mindfulness and Intentionality

As we reach the final stretch of our journey toward a simplified life, it's time to focus on two key elements that will help you maintain your progress: mindfulness and intentionality. These concepts might seem a bit abstract, but they're the glue that holds everything together. Without them, it's too easy to slip back into old habits, letting the clutter and chaos slowly creep back in. But with mindfulness and intentionality at the helm, you can navigate life with a calm, focused mind and a clear sense of purpose.

Practicing Mindfulness to Remain Present and Focused

Mindfulness is like having a superpower in your back pocket—a way to bring your attention fully into the present moment, no matter what's going on around you. When you practice mindfulness, you're not just going through the motions or letting your mind race ahead to the next task. Instead, you're fully engaged in whatever you're doing, whether it's working on a project, having a conversation, or simply sipping your morning coffee.

Staying present isn't always easy, especially in a world constantly vying for your attention. But mindfulness is about training your mind to focus, noticing when it wanders, and gently bringing it back to the here and now. It's about noticing the details—the way the sunlight filters through your office window, the sound of your keyboard as you type, and the warmth of the coffee cup in your hand. It's that brief pause I take every time I look out of one of our windows or off our balcony. These small moments of awareness anchor you in the present and help you stay connected to what you're doing rather than getting lost in the noise of everything else.

Mindfulness also has a way of cutting through mental clutter. When you're fully present, you're less likely to be overwhelmed by endless to-do lists or the "what-ifs" that can cloud your mind. Instead, you can approach each task with clarity and calm, giving it your full attention and energy. This focused approach doesn't just make you more productive—it makes the experience of work and life more meaningful and, yes, more pleasurable.

Making Intentional Choices in All Areas of Life

Mindfulness naturally leads to intentionality, the practice of making deliberate, thoughtful choices in every area of your life. When you're intentional, you're not just reacting to whatever comes your way—you're actively shaping your life according to your values, goals, and priorities. This intentional approach is crucial for maintaining simplicity because it helps you avoid the traps of old habits and unnecessary complexity.

Intentionality means pausing before you say "yes" to a new commitment and asking yourself whether it aligns with your goals and truly adds value to your life. It's about consciously choosing how to spend your time, energy, and resources rather than letting them be dictated by external demands or pressures. When you make intentional choices, you're more likely to stay on the path of simplicity because you're regularly checking in with yourself to ensure your actions align with your priorities. It's easy to say "yes" to tasks, especially when they seem small or quick. But without filtering them through the lens of intentionality, these seemingly minor commitments can quickly add up and derail your goals and vision for the future.

This doesn't mean you need to overthink every decision, but rather that you bring a sense of purpose to your choices. Whether you're deciding how to spend your weekend, what projects to take on at work, or how to respond to a difficult situation, intentionality is about making choices that support the life you want to lead. It's about saying "no" when something doesn't serve you and fully committing when it does.

In the end, mindfulness and intentionality are like the twin pillars of a simplified life. Mindfulness keeps you grounded in the present, helping you focus and find meaning in your day-to-day experiences. Intentionality ensures that your actions align with your goals, preventing the drift back into old habits and unnecessary complexity. Together, they empower you to live with clarity, purpose, and a sense of calm, no matter what life throws your way.

So, as you move forward, remember to carry these practices with you. Stay present, make intentional choices, and build a life that reflects your values and priorities. Because when you live mindfully and intentionally, you don't just maintain simplicity—you thrive in it.

Conclusion

As we bring this chapter on simplification to a close, take a moment to reflect on how far you've come on your journey toward a more focused, intentional life. Simplification goes far beyond decluttering your space or streamlining processes—it allows you to create a life that aligns with your true priorities, where every action, every choice, and every moment is infused with purpose.

We've explored the importance of cutting out the noise—both internal and external—that so easily distracts and overwhelms us. We've dug into the practicalities of decluttering physical spaces, refining daily routines, and streamlining business processes. We've touched on the power of effective delegation and emphasized the need for consistency, discipline, and regular reviews to keep things on track.

But perhaps most importantly, we've delved into mindfulness and intentionality—the two practices that will help you maintain this simplified lifestyle in the long run. By staying present and making deliberate, thoughtful choices, you ensure that the simplicity you've worked so hard to achieve doesn't slip away when life gets busy.

Remember, simplification isn't a destination—it's an ongoing process. It's a commitment to living with clarity, focus, and intention, day after day. There will be times when things get messy, old habits creep back in, or life throws you a curveball. But with the tools and strategies you've learned in this chapter, you're well-equipped to handle whatever comes your way.

So, as you move forward, keep refining, simplifying, and returning to what truly matters. The more you do, the more you'll find that a simplified life isn't just easier—it's richer, more fulfilling, and ultimately, more aligned with who you are and what you want to achieve.

You've got this. Keep going, and enjoy the peace, clarity, and focus that come with living an intentionally simple life.

Encouragement to Implement

Now that you've made it through this chapter, you're armed with the knowledge and tools to bring real, lasting simplicity into your life and business. But here's the thing—knowing what to do is only half the battle. The real magic happens when you start taking action. So, I'm here to give you a nudge to get you moving because the best time to start simplifying your life is right now.

Imagine the relief of walking into a clutter-free home or sitting down at a streamlined, organized desk. Picture yourself tackling your workday with a clear sense of purpose, free from the constant pull of distractions and unnecessary tasks. Envision a life where you have more time, focus, and energy to spend on the things that truly matter to you. That's what's waiting for you on the other side of simplification.

This is your chance to create the life and business that serves your purpose and helps you get to where you want to be. The noise and clutter get in the way of progress and productivity. So, what are you waiting for? Start now, take that first step, and commit to making simplification a priority. Your future self will thank you, and you'll be amazed at how much lighter, clearer, and more fulfilled you'll feel. You've got this—let's make it happen!

Call to Action

Ready to take the next step in simplifying your life and business? Don't let this be just another chapter you read—turn it into action! Head over to www.RogerGBbest.com/workbooks and download the workbook explicitly designed for this book. It's packed with exercises that will help you put the strategies you've learned into practice. Start working through the exercises today and begin taking back your day, one step at a time. Your simplified, more intentional life is just a click away!

Chapter Six
The Art of Saying No
Protecting Your Time & Energy

LET'S FACE IT—SAYING "NO" can be tough. We're often conditioned to believe that the more we say yes, the more successful, helpful, or likable we'll be. But here's the truth: saying yes to everything often means saying no to the things that truly matter. Your time, energy, and peace of mind are all finite resources. If you're constantly giving them away, there's nothing left for the things that actually fuel your dreams and goals.

This chapter is all about reclaiming your time and energy by mastering *The Art of Saying No*. And believe me, it is an art. We're going to dive into why saying no is crucial for maintaining balance in both your personal life and business and how mastering this skill can unlock more time for what truly aligns with your priorities. You'll also learn how to say no in a way that doesn't leave you feeling guilty or unkind, and we'll tackle the fear and guilt that often come with setting boundaries.

You'll discover strategies to protect your energy and explore real-life scenarios where saying no can be a game-changer. We'll also discuss how saying no is vital to maintaining balance—not just superficially, but in a way that restores the mental space and clarity you need to keep moving forward.

By the end of this chapter, you'll have practical tools to prioritize your needs and goals without feeling overwhelmed or guilty. You'll realize that protecting your time and energy isn't selfish—it's essential. Get ready to embrace the power of no and start taking back control over how you spend your time and where you direct your energy. Because sometimes, saying no is the best way to say yes to the life you truly want.

Have you ever heard of Warren Buffett?

There's a well-known story about Warren Buffett and his personal pilot, Mike Flint, that perfectly illustrates the importance of saying no to protect your time and energy. One day, Flint asked Buffett for advice on how to prioritize his goals. Always the strategist, Buffett told him to write down his top 25 career goals. Once Flint completed the list, Buffett asked him to circle his top 5.

Then Buffett asked, "What about the other 20?"

Flint replied, "Well, they're still important, so I'll work on them intermittently while focusing on my top 5."

Buffett shook his head and said, "No. You've got it wrong. Everything you didn't circle just became your 'avoid at all costs' list. No matter what, these things get no attention until you've succeeded with your top 5."

The lesson is clear: when you say yes to too many things, even good things—you dilute your focus and energy. Buffett's point was that in order to protect your time and achieve what truly matters, you need to get comfortable saying no to anything that doesn't directly contribute to your highest priorities.

Let's not focus on doing more—let's focus on doing what counts.

Understanding the Importance of Saying No

Saying no can feel uncomfortable—maybe even selfish—but it's one of the most powerful tools you have for protecting your time, energy, and well-being. Every time you say yes to something, you're inevitably saying no to something else. And often, that "something else" is your own priorities—whether it's your personal well-being, your goals, or the relationships that matter most to you. This is where the real issue lies: constantly saying yes can leave you drained, overwhelmed, and stretched too thin to focus on what truly deserves your attention.

Why does saying no matter so much? The answer lies in the concept of boundaries. Boundaries are essential for maintaining both mental and physical health. Without them, you run the risk of burnout, losing control of your schedule, and getting caught in a cycle of endless commitments that leave little room for what's truly important. Think of your time and energy like a bank account—every yes is a withdrawal, and if you're not careful, you'll find yourself overdrawn and exhausted.

By setting boundaries and learning to say no, you protect these valuable resources. It's about recognizing that your energy is finite and needs to be spent wisely. When you take on too much, especially tasks or responsibilities that don't align with your priorities, you're robbing yourself of the opportunity to focus on what really matters. And this doesn't just apply to business—it's about personal well-being, too. It's about having time to rest, recharge, and connect with the people and activities that bring you joy.

Boundaries also give you space to breathe and reflect. When you're constantly saying yes to everyone else, you're never giving yourself the chance to step back, assess where you are, and adjust your course if needed. Protecting your time and energy allows you to stay connected to your goals and make progress where it counts.

In a world that often glorifies being busy, saying no can feel like a radical act—but it's also an important investment in your personal health and focus. It's about reclaiming control over your life and ensuring that you're not running yourself into the ground for things that don't serve your purpose. When you say no to what drains you, you make room for what fuels you. You give yourself permission to focus on high-priority tasks, personal well-being, and the goals that truly move the needle in your life.

So, saying no isn't selfish—it's necessary. It's the key to preserving your energy for what matters and building a life that aligns with your true values and aspirations.

Common Barriers to Saying No

Saying no sounds simple in theory, but in practice, it can feel like one of the hardest things to do. We all want to be kind, helpful, and cooperative, but sometimes, those good intentions become the very things that make it difficult to protect our time and energy. Let's face it: there's a lot that can get in the way of a good, solid no. Whether it's the fear of disappointing others, guilt, or the pressure to be seen as a team player, these barriers can make saying no feel impossible.

Fear of Disappointing Others

One of the most common barriers to saying no is the fear of letting people down. We worry that by saying no, we'll disappoint someone—whether it's a colleague, a friend, or a family member. Sometimes, we even equate their disappointment with personal failure. This fear can make it incredibly difficult to say no, even when we know we're overcommitting ourselves. But here's the truth: constantly saying yes to avoid disappointing others usually leads to disappointing yourself. You can't pour from an empty vessel, and when you're stretched too thin, you end up doing a disservice not only to yourself but also to the people who genuinely need your time and focus.

Guilt and Social Pressures

Then there's guilt—good old guilt. We've all been there. You feel guilty for turning down a request because you don't want to seem selfish or unhelpful. Society often reinforces this guilt, pushing the idea that saying yes is the polite, generous thing to do. You might even feel pressured by social norms or expectations, especially in professional settings, where saying yes is often seen as being a team player or going above and beyond. But here's what we need to remember: saying no isn't about being selfish—it's about knowing your limits and protecting your resources. If you're constantly giving without ever refueling, you won't be able to give your best to anything or anyone.

Misunderstanding the Concept of Kindness and Cooperation

Many of us mistake saying yes for kindness. We think that to be cooperative and helpful, we have to agree to everything that comes our way. But true kindness and cooperation don't mean running yourself into the ground for others. In fact, saying no can sometimes be the kindest thing you can do—for both yourself and the person asking. When you say no to something you can't fully commit to, you're respecting both your time and theirs. You ensure that when you do say yes, it's because you can give it your full attention and energy. It's also about being honest with yourself and those around you. Authentic cooperation happens when you're working from a place of balance and purpose, not obligation and exhaustion.

These barriers—fear, guilt, and misunderstanding kindness—are real, but they don't have to control your decisions. Learning to say no is about recognizing that your time and energy are limited resources that deserve protection. When you start to see boundaries as an act of self-respect rather than a rejection of others, saying no becomes easier and more empowering. In the end, you'll find that the people who genuinely value you will respect your boundaries, too.

The Need for Validation

Okay, let's be totally honest here—sometimes we say yes because it feeds our sense of self-worth. We like to feel needed, helpful, and valuable, and saying yes to every request can become a way to affirm that we're doing something right—that we're essential to the people around us. It feels good in the moment to be the go-to person who can handle anything. But here's the catch: while saying yes might boost your ego in the short term, it can deplete your energy and leave you with little time for what truly matters in the long run. We often confuse being busy with being important, when in reality, constantly saying yes can leave you overworked and underappreciated. True self-worth doesn't come from how much you can take on; it comes from knowing your limits and protecting what's most valuable—your time, energy, and well-being.

Identifying Priorities

Before you can confidently say no to the things that don't serve you, you have to get crystal clear on what does. That's where identifying your priorities comes in, and it all starts with knowing your values and goals. When you take the time to understand what truly matters—whether in your personal life or business, you create a filter for everything that demands your time and energy. If something doesn't align with your core values or help you move toward your goals, it's easier to recognize that it's not worth your yes.

Think about it this way: without a clear sense of your priorities, life can feel like a constant juggling act, with everything competing for your attention. You end up feeling scattered, overwhelmed, and unsure of where to focus your energy. But when you define what's most important—whether it's spending time with family, building your business, or caring for your mental health—you create a compass to guide your decisions.

Clarifying your values and goals is essential to identifying priorities. If you value balance and time with loved ones, that will guide the commitments you accept. If your goal is to grow your business or focus on personal development, you'll prioritize opportunities that align with those ambitions. Knowing your priorities isn't just about organizing your schedule; it's about protecting your time and energy for what truly counts. When you're clear on your values, the things that drain you or pull you off course become much easier to let go of.

And here's the key: once you've identified your priorities, saying no becomes a lot less painful. You're not just rejecting a request—you're choosing to protect the things that align with your bigger picture. You're saying yes to what matters most; that clarity leads to real progress and fulfillment.

Clarifying Your Values and Goals

Clarifying your values and goals is like setting the foundation for everything else. It's not just about knowing what you want; it's about understanding why you want it and how it fits into the bigger picture of who you are and where you're headed. Without this clarity, it's easy to get pulled in a thousand different directions, chasing after things that don't really matter or align with what's most important to you.

Your values are the things you hold most dear—the guiding principles that shape your decisions, behaviors, and relationships. They're deeply personal and unique to each of us. For some, it might be family, health, or creativity; for others, it might be growth, freedom, or making an impact. These values act like a compass, helping you navigate through life's opportunities and challenges. When you're clear on your values, making choices becomes easier because you have a clear sense of what feels right and what doesn't.

Goals, on the other hand, are the specific outcomes you want to achieve—the tangible milestones that move you closer to the life you envision for yourself. But here's the thing: goals without values are hollow. If you're chasing goals that don't align with your core values, you'll end up feeling disconnected and unfulfilled, even if you achieve them. That's why it's so important to ensure your goals are rooted in your values. When they are, every step you take toward achieving them feels meaningful and connected to who you are.

Clarifying your values and goals isn't a one-time thing; it's ongoing. As you grow and evolve, your priorities will shift, and that's okay. The key is to regularly check in with yourself and ask: "Does this align with who I am and what I really want?" When you do this, you gain the power to make decisions that serve you and lead you closer to the life you truly want to live. With clarity, you no longer feel like you're just going through the motions—you're moving with purpose.

Exercises to identify personal and professional priorities:

For these exercises, please go to www.RogerGBest.com/workbooks

Aligning Commitments with Long-Term Goals and Values

When it comes to living a life that feels meaningful and purposeful, alignment is everything. You can set the biggest goals and have the clearest values, but if your daily commitments don't line up with them, you'll always feel off track. We often get so caught up in the whirlwind of day-to-day responsibilities that we lose sight of the bigger picture. That's why it's so important to regularly check in with yourself and ask, "Do my commitments reflect my long-term goals and values?"

Let's face it—most of us are juggling more than we'd like. Between work, family, social obligations, and everything else life throws at us, it's easy to fall into the trap of saying yes to things that don't really matter. The problem is, every time you say yes to something that doesn't align with your long-term goals or values, you're taking time and energy away from the things that do align with them. It's like planting seeds in someone else's garden while neglecting your own.

The key to aligning your commitments is understanding your long-term goals and the values guiding you. Your goals represent the destination you're working toward, while your values serve as the compass that helps you stay on course. When you're clear on both, it becomes easier to see which commitments serve those goals and which are just distractions.

Not every opportunity or request is meant for you, even if it seems worthwhile on the surface. Saying yes to everything can leave you overwhelmed and scattered, constantly chasing after things that don't actually bring you closer to the life or career you want. Instead, when you align your commitments with your goals and values, each step you take feels more intentional and fulfilling.

The beauty of this alignment is that it creates a sense of flow. When your commitments reflect your long-term vision, you're no longer just ticking items off a to-do list—you're actively building the life you want. Your daily actions feel purposeful, and the energy you put in gives back because it's directed toward something meaningful.

The challenge lies in saying no to what doesn't fit. But remember, every no is a yes to something more important. We're really talking about protecting your time and energy for what truly matters. When you start aligning your commitments with your goals and values, you'll not only make progress faster, but you'll also feel more connected to the journey. Your life becomes a reflection of what's most important to you, and that's when real fulfillment starts to take shape.

The Impact of Overcommitting

When it comes to living a meaningful and purposeful life, alignment is everything. You can set the biggest goals and have the clearest values, but if your daily commitments don't line up with them, you'll always feel off track. We often get so caught up in the whirlwind of day-to-day responsibilities that we lose sight of the bigger picture. That's why it's so important to regularly check in with yourself and ask, "Do my commitments reflect my long-term goals and values?"

The truth is—most of us are juggling more than we'd like. Between work, family, social obligations, and everything else that ends up on our calendars, it's easy to fall into the trap of saying yes to things that don't really matter. The problem is, every time you say yes to something that doesn't align with your long-term goals or values, you're taking time and energy away from what does.

The key to aligning your commitments is first understanding your long-term goals and the values that guide you. Your goals represent the destination you're working toward, while your values serve as the compass that keeps you on course. When you're clear on both, it becomes easier to see which commitments serve those goals and which are distractions.

Not every opportunity or request is meant for you, even if it seems worthwhile on the surface. Saying yes to everything can leave you overwhelmed and scattered, constantly chasing after things that don't actually bring you closer to the life or career you want. Instead, when you align your commitments with your goals and values, each step you take feels more intentional and fulfilling.

The beauty of this alignment is that it creates a sense of flow. When your commitments reflect your long-term vision, you're no longer just ticking items off a to-do list—you're actively building the life you want. Your daily actions feel purposeful, and the energy you put in gives back because it's directed toward something meaningful.

The challenge lies in saying no to what doesn't fit. You're actually protecting your time, energy, and the dream of fulfilling your dreams (you know, those things that truly matter) when you keep your calendar clear enough to chase after those dreams every day. When you start aligning your commitments with your goals and values, you'll not only make progress faster, but you'll also feel more connected to the journey. Your life becomes a reflection of what's most important to you, and that's when real fulfillment starts to take shape.

Consequences of Spreading Oneself Too Thin

Spreading yourself too thin might initially feel like a badge of honor; you're busy, in demand, and juggling a hundred things at once. But over time, the reality hits: when you try to do it all, you end up doing very little well. The impact of taking on too much can be subtle at first, but it accumulates, slowly eroding your energy, focus, and overall well-being.

One of the first signs is the constant feeling of being overwhelmed—your mind races to keep track of deadlines, commitments, and tasks. Instead of feeling accomplished at the end of the day, you're left exhausted and anxious, knowing tomorrow's list is just as long. There's no sense of completion, just an ongoing cycle of trying to catch up, which leaves you mentally drained and physically tired.

Your quality of your work suffers too. When you're spread too thin, you can't give any single task the attention it deserves. You rush through things just to check them off the list, cutting corners, making mistakes, and delivering work that doesn't reflect your best effort. It's frustrating because, deep down, you know you could do better if you just had the time and space to focus. But that focus is impossible when your energy is scattered across too many commitments.

On a personal level, spreading yourself too thin impacts your relationships and overall happiness. You're so busy that you barely have time for the people who matter most—family, friends, or even yourself. Those important connections get pushed aside because there's always another task, another project, another obligation demanding your attention. And the time you need to recharge and take care of yourself disappears under the weight of your commitments, leaving you burned out and disconnected.

Perhaps the most damaging consequence is how it pulls you away from your long-term goals and values. You get so caught up in the day-to-day busyness that you lose sight of what truly matters. Instead of working toward the life or career you envision, you're stuck in a cycle of saying yes to things that don't align with your priorities. Over time, this leads to frustration—you're busy, but not necessarily productive or fulfilled.

In the end, spreading yourself too thin doesn't just affect your workload—it affects your entire life. You lose focus, sacrifice quality, and drain yourself emotionally and physically. Learning to set boundaries, say no, and prioritize what's truly important is key to breaking free from this cycle. By doing less, you create space to focus on what really matters—and you do it well, with energy and intention. It's not about how much you can take on, but how well you manage what's most important.

Recognizing the Signs of Overcommitment and Burnout

Overcommitment and burnout don't just hit you like a sudden storm, they build up slowly, creeping in over time until one day you find yourself exhausted, uninspired, and struggling to keep up. The tricky part is that these signs often appear subtly, like background noise, until they grow too loud to ignore. Recognizing the early signs can save you from reaching that breaking point.

One of the first signs of overcommitment is a constant feeling of overwhelm. You wake up already thinking about the mountain of tasks ahead, and instead of feeling focused or motivated, you're weighed down by a sense of dread. It feels like you're perpetually behind, no matter how hard you work or how many hours you put in. The to-do list never seems to shrink, and there's never enough time in the day.

As the overwhelm builds, your productivity begins to suffer. Tasks that used to be simple now feel like an uphill battle. You might procrastinate, avoid certain tasks, or complete them half-heartedly because you lack the mental energy to give them your best effort. Your attention becomes scattered, making it hard to focus on any one thing for very long. The more commitments you take on, the more spread out your energy becomes, leaving little left for high-priority tasks that actually matter.

Then comes the emotional toll. You may feel irritable, impatient, or even resentful of things you once enjoyed. Small setbacks start to feel overwhelming, and your stress levels stay elevated. You might snap at colleagues, friends, or family members, not because they've done anything wrong, but because your emotional bandwidth is completely drained. When you're in a constant state of overcommitment, stress can easily transform into burnout—an emotional and physical exhaustion that leaves you disconnected from yourself and the world around you.

Burnout doesn't just affect your work—it seeps into every part of your life. You may withdraw from social activities or hobbies that once brought you joy because you're too tired to engage. Even when you're physically present, your mind is elsewhere, preoccupied with what still needs to get done. Physical symptoms often appear too: frequent headaches, muscle tension, disrupted sleep patterns, and a general sense of fatigue that lingers, no matter how much rest you get.

Another key sign of burnout is a loss of passion or purpose. What once excited you now feels like an obligation. You may find yourself asking, "Why am I even doing this?" Tasks that used to bring a sense of accomplishment now feel like meaningless chores. This is often when people start considering drastic changes—quitting a job, stepping away from commitments, or re-evaluating their entire approach to life.

But it doesn't have to get to that point. Recognizing these signs early allows you to make necessary changes before burnout takes over. If you're constantly feeling overwhelmed, emotionally drained, and physically exhausted, it's time to take a step back and assess your commitments. Are you saying yes to too many things that don't align with your goals or values? Are you overextending yourself in areas that drain your energy instead of fueling your passions?

The good news is, once you're aware of the signs, you can take proactive steps to reset. Start by setting clearer boundaries, prioritizing what truly matters, and giving yourself the space to rest and recharge. Remember, saying no isn't a weakness—it's a strength. It's a way to protect your time, energy, and well-being so you can continue to thrive in both your work and personal life. Recognizing overcommitment and burnout is the first step toward reclaiming balance and living with more intention.

Strategies for Saying No Gracefully

Saying no doesn't have to be uncomfortable or confrontational. In fact, when done thoughtfully, it can actually strengthen your relationships and build respect. It's all about learning how to say no gracefully—setting boundaries without burning bridges.

The first step is to recognize that you don't owe anyone a lengthy explanation. Often, we think we need to justify our decision with excuses or detailed reasons, but the truth is, a simple and polite response is enough. Something like, "I'm sorry, I can't commit to that right now," is clear and respectful without over-explaining. The key is to be direct yet kind. You're not shutting the door on the person—just on the request.

Another strategy is to offer an alternative when it feels appropriate. If you can't take on a particular task or commitment, suggesting another time, person, or solution can show that you're still supportive, even if you're unavailable. For instance, you could say, "I'm tied up with another project, but maybe we can revisit this in a couple of weeks," or "I can't handle this right now, but I'd be happy to help you connect with someone who might be able to." Offering a solution not only softens the no but also shows that you care about the person's needs, even if you're unable to fulfill them directly.

Timing also plays a big role in how gracefully you say no. If you know right away that something doesn't align with your priorities, it's better to say no promptly than to drag it out. The longer you wait, the more likely you'll feel pressured to say yes, or the other person will count on your involvement. A timely, polite response prevents misunderstandings and gives the other party time to adjust their plans. Something like, "I appreciate you thinking of me, but I won't be able to participate," is both efficient and respectful.

Another important aspect of saying no gracefully is managing your own emotions around it. Guilt often comes hand in hand with the word no, but remember that by setting boundaries, you're protecting your time, energy, and well-being. When you feel guilty about saying no, remind yourself why you're saying it. If your reasons align with your goals and priorities, then it's not only okay to say no—it's necessary. People who respect you will also respect your boundaries.

Lastly, it's important to stay firm in your decision once you've said no. Sometimes, people might try to convince you to change your mind, but being wishy-washy can lead to more stress down the line. Stand by your decision without being defensive. If someone pushes back after you've said no, simply reiterate your original response: "I understand this is important, but I really can't take it on right now." Staying calm and composed ensures you're communicating with respect while keeping your boundaries intact.

Saying no gracefully is a skill that takes practice, but it's one that can significantly improve your relationships and your ability to protect your time and energy. By being clear, kind, and firm, you'll find that saying no isn't as uncomfortable as you might have imagined. Instead, it becomes a powerful way to honor your own needs while still maintaining positive connections with others. And the more you practice, the more natural it becomes to say no in a way that feels authentic and respectful—both to yourself and to the person you're saying it to.

Effective Communication Techniques

Clear, thoughtful communication is one of the most powerful tools you have, both in business and in life. It's the foundation of strong relationships, productive collaborations, and mutual respect. But communicating effectively goes beyond getting your message across—it includes how you deliver it, how you listen, and how you navigate the conversation. Whether you're saying no to a new commitment or working through a challenging issue, mastering a few key communication techniques can make all the difference.

One of the most essential elements of effective communication is active listening—and it's a big one. We often get so focused on what we're going to say next that we miss what's actually being said by the person right in front of us. Active listening requires being fully present in the conversation—not just waiting for your turn to speak. You need to make eye contact, nod, and provide verbal affirmations like, "I see" or "That makes sense," to show you're engaged. Doing this not only shows the person you're talking with that you're listening, but it also trains you to stay involved, rather than just planning your next response. By focusing on understanding the other person's perspective, you create a space where they feel valued and heard. This can defuse tension, build trust, and make even difficult conversations more productive.

Another powerful communication technique is learning to be concise and direct. While it's tempting to over-explain or dance around uncomfortable topics, being clear and straightforward is often the most respectful approach. People appreciate honesty, especially when it's delivered with kindness. For example, if you're turning down a request, you don't need to give a laundry list of reasons. A simple "I'm unable to take this on right now" can be far more effective and respectful than a long-winded explanation. The key is to be direct, but with empathy for the other person's position.

Tone matters, too. The way you say something can be just as important as the words themselves. A warm, calm tone can soften a firm message, making it easier for the other person to accept. On the flip side, an aggressive or defensive tone can escalate a simple conversation into an argument. Your tone conveys emotion, so ensure it matches your intent. If you're delivering feedback or addressing a sensitive issue, choose your words and tone carefully to keep the conversation constructive and respectful.

Non-verbal communication is another crucial piece of the puzzle. Your body language, facial expressions, and posture all send strong signals about your engagement and attitude. Crossing your arms, avoiding eye contact, or appearing distracted can make the other person feel like you're not fully present, even if your words are polite. Conversely, open body language—such as maintaining eye contact, uncrossing your arms, and leaning in slightly—signals attentiveness and engagement.

In addition to listening and clarity, empathy plays a key role in effective communication. Showing empathy means understanding the other person's feelings and perspective, even if you don't necessarily agree. When you respond with empathy, you acknowledge the other person's experience, which helps ease tension and build rapport. Simple statements like, "I understand this is important to you," or "I can see why you'd feel that way," can make the other person feel understood and respected.

Timing is everything when it comes to communication. Knowing when to speak—and when to hold back—can make or break a conversation. For instance, trying to address a sensitive issue when someone is stressed or distracted is unlikely to result in a productive outcome. Choosing the right moment, when both parties are calm and able to focus, creates a better environment for meaningful dialogue. Similarly, if you're delivering difficult news, it's often best to be straightforward and get to the point, rather than dragging out the conversation and increasing tension.

Effective communication is a skill that takes practice, but it can transform the way you interact with others. By actively listening, being clear and concise, paying attention to your tone and body language, and showing empathy, you can create more meaningful connections, reduce misunderstandings, and navigate even the most challenging conversations with grace and confidence. When you communicate well, you build stronger relationships, and that's the foundation for success in any area of life.

The Power of a Polite, Assertive No

As we've discussed, saying no can be one of the hardest things to do, but there's a particular strength in delivering a polite, assertive no. It can protect your time, energy, and well-being while still maintaining positive relationships—a polite, assertive no respects both your boundaries and the needs of the other person.

This kind of no is rooted in clarity and self-respect. When you're clear about your priorities and what you're realistically able to take on, saying no becomes less about rejection and more about alignment. You're not saying no because you don't care or because you're unwilling to help; you're saying no because you understand that you can't do everything. And when you do say yes it should be to something you can give your full attention and effort to. Delivered correctly, a thoughtful no actually strengthens relationships—people come to respect your honesty and your boundaries.

The key to a powerful no is in its delivery. Assertiveness means being direct without being harsh. It's about standing your ground with confidence while remaining polite and considerate. For instance, if a colleague asks for help on a project but you're already swamped, you can say, "I really appreciate you thinking of me, but I'm unable to take that on right now." This response acknowledges their request without over-explaining or leaving the door open for negotiation. It's firm but kind, striking that balance of respect for both your own needs and theirs.

A polite, assertive no also prevents resentment from building up. When we say yes to things we don't really want to do, we often feel frustrated or overwhelmed. We may deliver on the task, but it's out of obligation, not genuine willingness. Over time, this can lead to burnout or even resentment toward the person or situation we've said yes to. By learning to say no politely and assertively, you protect your peace of mind and ensure that when you do say yes, it's for the right reasons.

And here's the magic of a polite, assertive no: it helps others see your value more clearly. When you constantly say yes, people may start to take your time and effort for granted. But when you say no thoughtfully, it signals that your time is valuable. It shows that you're in control of your commitments and that you don't overextend yourself just to please others. Paradoxically, this often leads to greater respect and appreciation because people understand that when you do say yes, you mean it—and you're fully committed.

Saying no, when done correctly, will help you create healthy boundaries that allow you to thrive and accomplish more. The power of a polite, assertive no is that it preserves your energy, maintains your focus, and keeps your relationships intact. It's not selfish; it's simply giving yourself the time to recharge. And when you're clear and kind in your delivery, saying no becomes a tool for success, not an act of rejection. You're simply making room for what truly matters, and that's something worth standing firm for.

Language and Phrases for Declining Requests Without Guilt

Learning how to say no without guilt starts with using language that's respectful, clear, and kind. The goal isn't to shut someone down, but rather to protect your time and energy in a way that's honest and compassionate. Saying no doesn't require excuses or apologies. In fact, the most effective way to decline a request is to be straightforward while maintaining a positive tone.

To recap and expand on this a bit, here are a few ways to decline requests gracefully, without guilt:

1. **The Direct but Polite No**: Sometimes, the best approach is simplicity. You don't need a long explanation—a respectful, straightforward no will suffice.

   - "Thank you for thinking of me, but I won't be able to take this on."

   - "I'm honored that you asked, but I'll have to pass this time."

2. **The "No with an Alternative" Approach**: If you'd like to offer help in some way but can't fully commit, suggest an alternative. This shows support while maintaining your boundaries.

   - "I can't take this on right now, but I'd be happy to help you find someone else who can."

   - "I'm unavailable at the moment, but how about we revisit this in a few weeks?"

3. **The Time-Blocker No**: Referring to your busy schedule is an easy way to decline while communicating that your time is already committed.

   - "I've got too many commitments right now to give this the attention it deserves."

   - "My schedule's full at the moment, so I can't add anything more."

4. **The Grateful but Firm No**: Expressing gratitude while being clear about your limits can help soften your no.

- "I appreciate the offer, but I need to prioritize my current projects."

- "I'm flattered you thought of me, but I can't take on any more responsibilities right now."

5. **The Self-Preservation No**: If you're feeling stretched too thin, this approach focuses on protecting your well-being while respecting the other person's request.

    - "To give my best effort to my current projects, I won't be able to commit to this."

    - "For my health and balance, I need to decline this request."

6. **The "Let Me Get Back to You" Approach**: If you're not ready to say no immediately, this buys you time to evaluate the request without committing right away. Be careful that this is not just a "stall" technique. If you know you're not going to be able to do this, say so up front. If you are really interested, but you really do need to see if it fits, this can be a good technique.

    - "Let me think it over, and I'll get back to you."

    - "I'd love to consider this, but I need to check my other commitments first."

Each of these responses allows you to say no with confidence while maintaining respect and goodwill. The key is to be firm without over-apologizing or feeling the need to justify your decision. Remember, there's no need to feel guilty for protecting your time and energy. Saying no is essential to maintaining balance and gives you the space to say yes to what truly matters in your life. By using language that's both kind and assertive, you establish healthy boundaries without guilt or discomfort.

Setting Clear Boundaries

Setting clear boundaries is one of the most powerful ways to protect your time, energy, and well-being. Whether in your personal or professional life, boundaries define what you're willing to accept and what you're not. They are essential for maintaining balance and ensuring that your commitments align with your values and goals. But it's not enough to simply know your boundaries—you need to communicate them effectively so others can respect them.

The first step in setting boundaries is getting clear on what they are. Ask yourself: What are my non-negotiables? In your personal life, this could mean protecting time for family, prioritizing your health, or ensuring you get enough rest. In your professional life, it might involve defining work hours, setting limits on your workload, being diligent about not taking projects back that you've delegated because it's easier than teaching them to do it—this will only set you up for taking projects back on a regular basis, which blows the benefits of delegating, or determining which projects deserve your attention. Once you have a clear understanding of what's important to you, you can create boundaries that safeguard those priorities.

Once your boundaries are established, the next challenge is learning how to communicate them. This can feel tricky, especially if you're used to saying yes to everything. However, when you communicate your boundaries respectfully and clearly, people are much more likely to honor them.

In your personal life, communicating boundaries may involve having candid conversations with family or friends about your availability. For example, if you're reserving weekends for family time, you could say, "I've decided to keep my weekends free for family, so I won't be able to join any events during that time." By being upfront about your boundaries, others can adjust their expectations accordingly.

Personally, I've chosen to rarely schedule evening or weekend events. My typical response is, "Have your people call my people (my wife), and we'll see if we can get something scheduled." This allows me to check in with my wife to make sure it's a good fit for both of us, confirm I'm not overcommitting, and ensure that what we say "yes" to aligns with our overall priorities.

In professional settings, boundaries are just as crucial—if not more so. Without clear boundaries, it's easy to fall into a pattern of overworking, which can lead to burnout and resentment. To set professional boundaries, it's important to communicate your limits early on, whether it's about workload, deadlines, or after-hours availability. For instance, you might say, "I'm happy to take on this project, but I'm unavailable after 6 p.m.," or "I can't take on more work at the moment, but I can revisit this in a few weeks." Setting expectations upfront helps prevent misunderstandings later.

Consistency is key when it comes to maintaining boundaries. It's not enough to set limits once—you need to enforce them regularly. This may involve reminding others of your boundaries if they forget or standing your ground if someone tries to push past them. For example, if a colleague continues to text you after hours despite your boundary, you might respond during work hours with, "Just a reminder, I'm unavailable outside of 9 to 5. I'll get back to you during my next working day." By consistently reinforcing your boundaries, you teach others to respect them while reinforcing your own commitment to maintaining balance.

Remember, boundaries aren't static—they can evolve as your life and priorities change. You may start with one boundary, like limiting your work hours, and later realize you need to set another, such as preserving your lunch break for rest or reflection. You may choose to do, as I have, and turn off notifications from email message, texts, and social media during specific hours. And, yes, you can set exclusions to the Do Not Disturb for certain people like family. The key is to stay attuned to your needs and adjust your boundaries as necessary.

Setting and communicating boundaries might feel uncomfortable at first, especially if it's new to you. But boundaries are essential for protecting your time, energy, and mental health. They allow you to focus on what's most important without being pulled in a million directions. While others may not always understand or agree with your boundaries, standing firm shows that you value yourself and your time. As you practice setting and communicating clear boundaries, you'll find that both your personal and professional life start to feel more balanced, intentional, and manageable.

Consistency in Maintaining Boundaries

Setting clear boundaries is the first step toward protecting your time and energy, but the real challenge lies in maintaining them consistently. Boundaries, like any habit, only work if you stick to them. Without consistency, even the most well-defined boundaries lose their effectiveness. By enforcing your boundaries regularly, you send a clear message—to yourself and others—that your time, energy, and well-being are valuable and non-negotiable.

At first, maintaining your boundaries might feel uncomfortable. You may worry about how others will react or feel guilty for saying no. But the truth is that people will follow your lead. If you're clear and consistent, others will learn to respect your boundaries. On the flip side, if you set a boundary but constantly make exceptions, you signal that those limits aren't firm. Over time, this erodes your ability to protect your time and energy, as people come to expect you to bend your rules.

Consistency builds trust—not just with others, but with yourself. When you consistently honor your boundaries, you reinforce the idea that you're in control of your life and are prioritizing what matters most. This leads to a greater sense of balance and empowerment. The more you practice consistency, the easier it becomes to uphold your boundaries without feeling guilty or second-guessing yourself.

That said, consistency doesn't mean rigidity. Life happens, and sometimes flexibility is necessary. The key is to ensure that flexibility doesn't become the norm. You want to be adaptable when truly needed, but not at the expense of your well-being. For example, if a work emergency arises and you need to work outside your set hours, it's okay to make that adjustment—just be sure to return to your established boundaries as soon as possible. This prevents occasional exceptions from becoming habits that erode your boundaries over time.

Communication plays a crucial role in maintaining consistency. If someone crosses your boundary, don't hesitate to gently remind them. For instance, if you've communicated that you're unavailable after 6 p.m. but receive a call or email during that time, respond politely the next day to reinforce your boundary: "I noticed you reached out last night, but as mentioned, I'm offline after 6 p.m. I'll respond during my working hours." Consistently communicating your boundaries reinforces them and teaches others to respect your time.

Maintaining consistency also requires holding yourself accountable. It's easy to let your boundaries slip when no one is watching. Maybe you've committed to turning off work notifications after hours, but you find yourself checking emails late at night. Or perhaps you promised to spend weekends with family but end up squeezing in work tasks. In these moments, it's important to remember that maintaining boundaries is as much about self-discipline as managing external expectations. Consistently respecting your own boundaries is just as crucial as getting others to respect them.

Consistency doesn't mean perfection. There will be times when you slip up—saying yes when you should have said no or letting someone encroach on your time. The key is to recognize those moments, learn from them, and recommit to your boundaries moving forward. The more consistent you are, the less likely you are to experience burnout, resentment, or overwhelm. Boundaries are an ongoing practice, and each time you reinforce them, you strengthen your ability to protect your time and energy.

In the end, consistency is what transforms boundaries from ideas into reality. It's the difference between a boundary that works and one that fades into the background. By consistently honoring your boundaries, you create a life where your priorities are respected, your well-being is safeguarded, and your energy is preserved for what truly matters. And the more consistent you are, the more natural it will feel to uphold those boundaries—without guilt, without apology, and with a deep sense of empowerment.

I'm reminded of the famous *Seinfeld* episode about the rental car reservation. Jerry confidently approaches the counter, assuming his reservation guarantees a car, only to learn the rental agency doesn't actually have one available. That's when Jerry delivers one of his classic lines: "You know how to *take* the reservation, you just don't know how to *hold* the reservation. And that's really the most important part, the holding. Anybody can just take them!"

It's a perfect metaphor for boundaries, isn't it? Setting boundaries is like making that reservation—it feels like a big step. But just like with Jerry's car, making the reservation is only half the battle. The real challenge is keeping it, holding that boundary, and ensuring it's respected. As Jerry points out, the most important part isn't just setting the boundary—it's maintaining it.

In the same way the rental company failed Jerry by not honoring his reservation, we fail ourselves if we don't uphold our boundaries. You might say no or set clear limits on your time, but if you consistently make exceptions, it's like showing up for a car that isn't there. Sure, you told people you weren't available after a certain time or that your weekends were off-limits, but if you cave to every request or let others push past those limits, you're not "holding" that boundary. And just like Jerry, you'll end up frustrated, wondering why the very thing you tried to protect has been run over by other people's needs.

So, think like Jerry suggests—don't just make the boundary, hold the boundary. After all, anybody can make a reservation.

Now that we've unpacked the art of saying no, it's time to put these strategies into practice. The truth is, the power to protect your time and energy is already in your hands—you just have to be willing to use it. Saying no might feel uncomfortable at first, especially if you're used to pleasing others or juggling multiple commitments. But remember, we're not trying to be difficult or selfish—the goal is set boundaries that allow you to live the life you envisioned.

By saying no when necessary, you're creating space for the things that matter most. Think about how much more focused and energized you'll feel when you're no longer spread too thin. Imagine the progress you'll make on the projects that truly excite you when you're not bogged down by obligations that don't serve your bigger picture. And envision the peace of mind that comes from knowing you're in control of your time, rather than letting others dictate how you spend it.

The strategies we've discussed aren't just theoretical—they're practical, proven methods that can help you reclaim your time, protect your energy, and stay aligned with your priorities. It's about taking charge of your life and realizing that saying no doesn't shut doors—it opens new ones by making room for the opportunities that are genuinely right for you.

So, here's your call to action: start small. This week, take note of one area where you feel overcommitted or drained. It might be a project you've taken on out of guilt or a social obligation that doesn't align with your goals. Practice saying no, and observe how it feels. Use the strategies we've discussed to be clear, respectful, and firm. You don't need to overhaul your life overnight—just take one step toward protecting your time and energy.

Call to Action

If you're serious about breaking free from overcommitment and burnout, it's time to take action. Visit and download the workbook that accompanies this book. Inside, you'll find exercises designed to help you pinpoint where your time is going and how to set boundaries that stick. The tools are here for you—now it's time to put them to work.

By taking this step, you're investing in your own well-being and your future. Don't wait until burnout takes over to make changes. Start now. Learn to say no when it matters most and watch how your life begins to shift toward greater focus, balance, and fulfillment. You've got this—now go make it happen.

Chapter Seven
Mindfulness and Meditation
Tools for Mental Clarity

IN TODAY'S WORLD, WHERE distractions are endless and constant, it can feel like your mind is always running in overdrive—juggling emails, notifications, meetings, and a never-ending to-do list. But imagine, even in the midst of this chaos, finding a way to create mental space, tap into a deeper sense of calm, and regain your focus. That's exactly what mindfulness and meditation offer.

In this chapter, we're diving into two powerful tools—mindfulness and meditation—that can transform how you approach your day, your work, and your life. What we're NOT going to talk about her; sitting in silence for hours or escaping to a retreat in the mountains (spoiler alert: meditation isn't about clearing your mind of all thoughts). What we ARE going to address is finding presence in the middle of everyday life. So, here's the deal... Mindfulness is going to help you stay grounded and fully engaged in whatever you're doing, while meditation offers a structured practice to train your mind in focus and calm.

Whether you're a seasoned meditator or someone who thinks they could never sit still for more than two minutes, this chapter will walk you through what mindfulness and meditation are, why they matter, and how you can easily integrate them into your daily routine—even if your life feels way too busy for it. These practices can help you gain mental clarity, reduce stress, improve decision-making, and create an overall sense of balance and well-being. And here's the best part: it doesn't take hours of practice to see the benefits; just a few moments of mindful attention can make a world of difference. Now, doesn't that sound like it could be worth your time?

Imagine starting your workday feeling mentally scattered, juggling meetings, emails, and tasks all at once. Now, picture that same morning with a few moments of mindfulness—giving you the clarity to prioritize your tasks and stay focused. That's the kind of shift these practices can bring.

We'll explore how mindfulness can help you stay present in both your work and personal life and how meditation can be a powerful tool for quieting your mind and reducing overwhelm. From simple, beginner-friendly techniques to deeper practices, we'll cover everything you need to get started—and keep growing.

By the end of this chapter, you'll have practical strategies that fit into even the busiest of schedules—whether you have two minutes or twenty—to bring more mindfulness into your day and start building a meditation practice that truly works for you. You're in the right place if you're ready to stop living in reaction mode and start creating space for clarity, calm, and focus.

Let's get started on this journey toward mental clarity and a calmer, more centered mind.

A Cautionary Tale

In a world where the demands on our time and energy seem endless, it's easy to fall into the trap of running on autopilot. We convince ourselves that we can juggle it all, but over time, the mental strain builds up, leaving us vulnerable to burnout and exhaustion. This is a lesson I learned through a close friend of mine, Chet, who found himself trapped in a cycle of relentless overcommitment—until an event that could have ended a near disaster, or a real disaster, opened his eyes to the dangers of never hitting pause.

Chet was the epitome of someone who seemed to be managing everything, though it came at a heavy cost. At the time, he was finishing his degree at a Bible college, which was enough to keep anyone busy. But Chet didn't stop there—he was also a key player on his college basketball team, balancing academic deadlines with intense training and games. If that wasn't enough, every Friday he would drive two hours to our small town to serve as the associate pastor at the church my dad pastored.

His weekends were far from restful. Between working with the youth, preaching occasionally, visiting hospital patients, and planning church events, Chet ended up with almost no downtime. Any moments of reprieve were spent with me in our basement playing late-night ping-pong matches, often pushing well into the early hours of the morning. By Sunday evening, he'd hop back in his car, drive the two hours back to school, and start it all over again Monday morning.

But it was on one of these Friday drives when the reality of his unsustainable pace hit hard. He showed up at my house with a story that was a bit more scary than most of the stories she showed up with upon arriving. At some point during the drive, completely zoned out from exhaustion, he realized he'd driven several miles without any memory of the road—through at least three major curves. He wasn't sure if he had fallen asleep or if his mind had simply gone blank from sheer fatigue, but the realization that he had been operating on autopilot was a bit scary for all of us.

Chet's brush with reality was a powerful reminder of what happens when we don't give our minds a chance to reset. He was so consumed with his responsibilities that he'd unknowingly started living in a mental fog. And the scary part? It happens to so many of us. We get caught up in the grind, thinking we can handle it all, until something forces us to face the fact that our mental clarity is slipping away.

That's where mindfulness and meditation come in. These practices offer us a way to break free from the cycle of overcommitment and autopilot living. They provide the tools to pause, breathe, and regain control of our mental state before it reaches a breaking point. Mindfulness is what helps us to become fully present in the moment, aware of our thoughts and surroundings. Meditation, too, is about creating space in the mental clutter so we can reconnect with our inner calm.

Chet's story could have ended very differently, but it serves as a stark reminder of the dangers of pushing ourselves to the limit without ever taking a moment to recharge. Mindfulness and meditation are not luxuries for the leisurely—they're essential practices for anyone who wants to maintain mental clarity and avoid burnout in a world that demands so much from us.

In the following sections, we'll explore practical ways you can incorporate these powerful tools into your life—no matter how busy your schedule. The goal isn't perfection or long, drawn-out practices. The goal is to create small moments of pause throughout your day, to stay sharp, focused, and present. Because when you give yourself the gift of mental clarity, you're not just surviving—you're truly living.

Where Are We Headed

In this chapter, we're diving into the powerful practices of mindfulness and meditation, two essential tools for achieving mental clarity and focus. I firmly believe that one of the main reasons people don't reach their goals or realize their dreams is because they skip this crucial step. I can assure you that as I look back on my less productive times, I can clearly remember that I was letting these things slip. Without incorporating mindfulness and meditation, it's far too easy to get swept away by the endless distractions that hit us daily.

Before we get started, let's clarify what mindfulness and meditation are. There's no need to be a Zen master or sit cross-legged for hours to experience their benefits. I want to dispel those myths right away. Instead, we'll focus on the real, tangible impact these practices can have—things like reducing stress, improving decision-making, and enhancing your overall well-being. So, even if you're skeptical or uncertain, I encourage you to give this chapter your full attention. These practices can make a significant difference in your life.

You'll learn how to begin incorporating mindfulness into your day-to-day routine, whether through simple, everyday actions or by setting aside dedicated time to practice. We'll also cover how to start a meditation routine, even if you've never tried it before. Along the way, we'll address common challenges, such as restlessness or trouble staying focused, and I'll offer tips on how to deepen your practice as you progress.

Mindfulness and meditation aren't just trendy buzzwords—they are practical, transformative techniques that can reshape how you approach both your work and personal life. By learning to slow down and focus on the present moment, you'll gain the mental clarity needed to make better decisions, remain calm under pressure, and cultivate a deeper sense of balance in your daily routine. This chapter will provide you with everything you need to start these life-changing practices and build a foundation of mental clarity that lasts.

Let's begin this journey together.

Don't Get Distracted

I want to pause for a moment and emphasize something critical here. When the topics of mindfulness and meditation come up, a lot of people tend to tune out. How do I know? I've seen it happen—whether in conversations with others or when I bring up these concepts myself. Maybe it feels too abstract, or maybe you're thinking, "I don't have time for this. My schedule's already packed." But hear me out—stick with me on this one. These two practices can be absolute game changers, not just for your mental clarity and well-being but for your entire journey toward reaching your goals and dreams.

I've seen firsthand how the simple act of being present and taking just a few moments each day to clear your mind can make the difference between falling short of your potential or unlocking it. Before you dismiss mindfulness and meditation as something that doesn't apply to you, I encourage you to dive in and explore these concepts with an open mind. What we're about to discuss might just be the missing key to finding the focus, balance, and energy you need to take your life and business to the next level.

Understanding Mindfulness and Meditation

Mindfulness has become one of those buzzwords that seems to be everywhere these days. You hear it in conversations, see it splashed across headlines, and it's even found its way into corporate boardrooms as a tool for productivity and stress reduction. But let's strip away the trendy veneer for a moment. At its core, mindfulness isn't just some apps on your phone or wellness crazes. It's a simple yet powerful practice that invites you to be fully present—right here, right now—no matter where you are or what you're doing.

Mindfulness is the art of paying attention to the present moment without judgment. It helps you to be aware of what's happening around you and inside you—your thoughts, emotions, and surroundings—without getting swept away by them. We've all experienced the opposite of mindfulness, haven't we? You're sitting at your desk, but mentally, you're already in tomorrow's meeting or agonizing over the unanswered emails stacking up. Or you're in a conversation, but instead of really listening, your mind is cycling through your never-ending to-do list. Or you're reading a report that you requested and believe it to be important, but you find you have to continue to go back and read what you just read again. Mindfulness helps break that autopilot mode by pulling you back into the present. It's like hitting the pause button on your mental noise and tuning back into what's happening right in front of you.

One of the biggest misconceptions about mindfulness is that it's about clearing your mind of thoughts. The truth is, it's quite the opposite. Mindfulness isn't about stopping your thoughts, but about noticing them as they come and go—without getting tangled up in them. You're not trying to turn off your brain; you're observing your thoughts and emotions without judgment or attachment. Picture yourself sitting by a river, and your thoughts are like leaves floating downstream. Mindfulness is like sitting beside a river, watching your thoughts float by like boats drifting downstream. Rather than feeling the need to jump in and steer each boat, you simply observe them pass, letting them come and go without getting swept away.

And here's the beauty of mindfulness: it's not confined to quiet, meditative moments. You can weave it into your everyday activities. You can practice mindfulness while drinking your morning coffee, truly savoring the taste, feeling the warmth of the cup in your hands, and taking in the aroma. You can practice it while walking, noticing the feeling of your feet touching the ground and the breeze against your skin. Mindfulness allows you to fully engage with life, rather than mindlessly rushing through one task after another without truly experiencing any of it.

Mindfulness helps break the cycle of overthinking, stress, and overwhelm by giving your mind the space to breathe. When practiced regularly, it allows you to step back from the chaos and find clarity. And the great thing is, anyone can do it. You don't need a meditation cushion or a peaceful retreat in the mountains—just a few moments of focused attention can bring calm and presence to your day.

So as we move forward in this chapter, remember that mindfulness is about cultivating awareness, staying present, and creating mental space for clarity. You do not have to be perfect at it, nor does it demand hours of practice. It's simply intentional moments of attention that, over time, can change the way you approach your work, relationships, and everyday life.

What is meditation?

Meditation often gets grouped with mindfulness, and while they're closely related, they aren't exactly the same thing. Think of mindfulness as the practice of staying present throughout your day, moment by moment, and meditation as a more structured way to cultivate that presence. If mindfulness is being aware while moving through your day, meditation is like setting aside dedicated time for a mental workout—training your mind to focus, calm down, and deal with life's challenges with more clarity and less stress.

At its core, meditation is simply the act of intentionally focusing your attention. This is often done by concentrating on something specific, like your breath, a mantra, or even the sounds around you. Contrary to popular belief, meditation isn't about emptying your mind of thoughts (an impossible feat, really). Instead, it's about noticing the thoughts that arise without getting caught up in them. Think of it as watching clouds pass through the sky—your thoughts are the clouds, and meditation teaches you to sit back and observe them without judgment or attachment.

There's a common misconception that meditation requires sitting cross-legged on the floor for hours, but that's far from the truth. Meditation can be as simple as sitting in a chair for five minutes, focusing on your breath as it flows in and out. And when (not if) your mind wanders, the practice is all about gently bringing your attention back to the present moment—again and again. This process of noticing when your mind drifts and refocusing strengthens your ability to stay calm, grounded, and present in daily life.

Another myth is that meditation is about achieving a blissful, transcendent state. Sure, that might happen on occasion, but for most of us, meditation is about learning to sit with whatever comes up—whether that's frustration, boredom, restlessness, or a racing mind. The real magic of meditation happens when you can calmly observe these distractions and still return to a place of focus.

Like mindfulness, meditation is a tool for mental clarity. It helps cut through the noise and mental clutter that build up during a busy day, giving you space to reset and refocus. It allows you to step back from the demands of life and reconnect with yourself. And over time, regular meditation can boost your concentration, reduce stress, and increase your capacity for compassion—both for yourself and for others.

The best part? You don't need hours each day to see the benefits. Even a few minutes of meditation can make a noticeable difference in how you handle stress and stay focused. It's less about how long you meditate and more about showing up consistently, even if it's just for a few moments in the middle of a hectic day.

Prayer

For many, prayer serves as a deeply personal form of meditation. Like traditional meditation, prayer is often about stillness, reflection, and connecting with something greater than ourselves. It offers a space to quiet the mind, express gratitude, seek guidance, or find comfort in moments of uncertainty. Just as meditation involves focusing the mind, prayer often centers on intentional thoughts, words, or even silence as a way to ground oneself spiritually.

In both practices, there's a conscious effort to step away from the noise of daily life and find inner peace, clarity, and a sense of purpose. Whether through reciting specific prayers or simply sitting in contemplative silence, prayer can serve as a powerful form of meditation, nurturing both the mind and spirit. It allows individuals to not only seek connection with a higher power but also to experience a deep sense of presence and focus, much like other meditative practices. For those who pray, it can become a valuable tool for finding calm, gaining perspective, and fostering a sense of centeredness amidst the busyness of life.

In this chapter, we'll explore how to start a meditation practice that works for you—no matter how busy your schedule is. Whether you're completely new to meditation or have tried it before and struggled to stick with it, we'll walk through techniques that will help you build a routine that fits into your life.

Key Differences Between Mindfulness and Meditation: How They Complement Each Other

Mindfulness and meditation are closely linked, but each has a distinct role, and they work beautifully when practiced together. Let's break it down further:

Mindfulness: A Way of Being

Mindfulness is all about staying fully present in whatever you're doing, moment by moment. It's less about carving out specific time for practice and more about infusing everyday activities with a heightened sense of awareness. Whether you're walking, eating, or having a conversation, mindfulness is the practice of tuning into the current moment and noticing what's happening around and within you without judgment. It helps you break free from autopilot mode, allowing you to be more engaged in the task at hand or the people around you. The beauty of mindfulness is that it can be woven into your day-to-day life anytime, anywhere.

Meditation: A Structured Practice

Meditation, on the other hand, is more formal. It's when you intentionally set aside time to train your mind—usually in a quiet space—focusing on something specific like your breath, a mantra, a verse, scripture, or just observing your thoughts. Unlike mindfulness, which is fluid and can be practiced in any situation, meditation creates a dedicated moment for stillness, deep concentration, and mental rest. It's like a workout for your mind, strengthening your ability to focus, reduce stress, and gain clarity. Meditation is typically done for a set amount of time and serves as a way to cultivate a deeper level of mental awareness.

How They Complement Each Other

When combined, mindfulness and meditation create a powerful synergy that can transform how you live and work. Here's how they complement each other:

- **Mindfulness as a Daily Companion**: Mindfulness is a portable practice you can carry with you throughout your day. It keeps you grounded, present, and less reactive in the moment, whether you're managing a stressful meeting or enjoying a peaceful walk.

- **Meditation as a Mental Reset**: Meditation is a dedicated time to train your mind to focus and calm down. It's the formal practice that sharpens your awareness and resilience, making it easier to carry that presence and focus into your everyday life.

- **Meditation Fuels Mindfulness**: The focus and calmness you cultivate during meditation naturally spill over into your everyday experiences. The more you meditate, the easier it becomes to maintain mindfulness in your daily activities. You'll find yourself more present, less distracted, and more able to handle stress with grace.

- **Mindfulness Extends the Benefits of Meditation**: While meditation is typically practiced for a set period, mindfulness is continuous. By practicing mindfulness, you extend the calm and clarity from your meditation sessions into the rest of your day, allowing you to maintain mental clarity even in busy or stressful moments.

In essence, **mindfulness** helps you stay present in the moment, while **meditation** deepens your mental clarity and focus. Together, they create a well-rounded approach to managing stress, improving focus, and fostering mental clarity in both your personal and professional life. Incorporating both practices into your routine can help you maintain a sense of calm, balance, and intention in everything you do.

Mindfulness in Everyday Life

Mindfulness is simply cultivating a heightened awareness of your present experiences, no matter how routine or mundane they may seem. It's not reserved for special occasions or quiet moments—it can be woven into the fabric of your everyday life, bringing clarity and intention to your thoughts, actions, and surroundings. Whether you're brushing your teeth, preparing a meal, or taking a walk, mindfulness will help you fully engage with the task at hand, noticing the sights, sounds, smells, and sensations without allowing your mind to wander off into distractions.

The true benefit of mindfulness is that it pulls you out of autopilot mode. How often do we go through the motions of our daily routines—answering emails, driving to work, or even talking to loved ones—without being fully present? We're physically there, but our minds are elsewhere, jumping from one task to the next or getting caught up in past events or future worries. Practicing mindfulness helps you break free from this mental fog, enabling you to be more intentional and present in each moment.

By being fully present, you make clearer, more thoughtful decisions, whether they're small everyday choices or bigger life decisions. Mindfulness also deepens your connection with the people around you—when you're fully engaged in conversations and interactions, others feel more valued and understood. And perhaps most importantly, mindfulness helps reduce stress by quieting the constant mental clutter that often builds up as we rush through the day. It encourages you to slow down, breathe, and find calm in the middle of your busy life.

Incorporating mindfulness into everyday activities can be as simple as paying attention to the feel of the water while washing dishes, noticing the rhythm of your breath during your morning commute, or savoring each bite of a meal. These small moments of mindful attention create space for mental clarity and calm, allowing you to engage more deeply with the present and feel more grounded, even during your busiest days.

In summary, mindfulness, particularly when applied to eating, can help people develop healthier eating patterns, reduce overeating, and ultimately support weight loss by fostering a more intentional and aware relationship with food.

Meditation as Mental Training

Meditation is like a workout for your brain. Just as you hit the gym to build physical strength, meditation trains your mind to develop mental muscles—such as focus, calm, and clarity. In meditation, you practice guiding your attention to a single point of focus, whether it's your breath, a mantra, or simply the present moment. The goal isn't to eliminate distractions, but rather to notice them and gently return your focus. This repeated process helps train your brain to settle, making it easier to let go of distractions both during meditation and in daily life.

Think of meditation as the foundation that supports mindfulness. The more you meditate, the better equipped you are to stay present and focused throughout the day. It's like sharpening a tool that you'll use in every aspect of life. Meditation builds your capacity for mindfulness by cultivating a steady, calm mind, allowing you to apply that same sense of centeredness to everyday tasks and interactions.

Where mindfulness is about bringing present-moment awareness into your daily life, meditation is the structured practice that strengthens that awareness. The two are deeply intertwined: mindfulness enriches your meditation practice by heightening your awareness during meditation, while meditation deepens your mindfulness by enhancing your ability to focus and maintain mental clarity in the midst of life's chaos. Together, they create a powerful combination that helps you navigate life with greater calm, focus, and intentionality.

Mindfulness: The "What" of Presence

Mindfulness is the "what" of staying present. It's about noticing what's happening around you and within you without being overwhelmed by it. Whether you're working, relaxing, or having a conversation, mindfulness invites you to engage fully with the moment. It's the practice of catching yourself when your mind starts to wander and gently guiding your focus back to the present. The beauty of mindfulness is that it can be practiced anywhere, at any time, offering a simple but powerful way to stay grounded and aware in the here and now.

Meditation: The "How" of Training the Mind

Meditation, on the other hand, is the "how" of training your mind to stay focused and calm. It's the dedicated practice you commit to—whether for five minutes or fifty—that equips you with the mental tools to stay grounded in the present. Meditation helps you repeatedly return to the moment, sharpening your focus, mental clarity, and emotional resilience.

In short, mindfulness is how we live our lives, moment by moment, while meditation is the structured practice that helps us do it more effectively. When you integrate both, you build a powerful foundation for mental clarity, emotional balance, and overall well-being. Think of meditation as the workout, strengthening your mental muscles, while mindfulness is how you apply that strength to your daily activities. Together, they enable you to navigate life's ups and downs with greater focus, resilience, and peace of mind.

The beauty of mindfulness and meditation is that they're accessible to everyone. You don't need hours of free time or a secluded retreat to reap their benefits. Just a few minutes of meditation each day can significantly enhance your ability to be mindful, and that mindfulness, in turn, can transform even the most routine moments into opportunities for clarity and calm. Whether you're sitting in meditation or simply paying attention to the present moment during a hectic day, you're equipping yourself with tools to reduce stress, stay focused, and approach life with a deeper sense of purpose and presence.

The Science Behind Mindfulness and Meditation

While mindfulness and meditation have ancient roots, they are far from outdated. In fact, modern science has delved deeply into these practices, uncovering compelling evidence that they have profound effects on both the mind and body. This isn't just about sitting in silence or achieving a "zen" state—there's substantial research showing that mindfulness and meditation can physically alter brain function and significantly enhance overall health.

Brain Power and Mental Clarity

Let's start with the brain. Research has shown that has shown that meditation can lead to measurable, positive changes in brain structure and function. Dr. Sara Lazar, a neuroscientist at Massachusetts General Hospital and Harvard Medical School, conducted groundbreaking research revealing how just eight weeks of mindfulness meditation can reshape the brain. Her study showed that areas of the brain associated with memory, emotional regulation, and self-awareness—such as the hippocampus and prefrontal cortex—experienced increases in gray matter density. Meanwhile, the amygdala, the part of the brain responsible for processing stress and anxiety, actually shrunk in size.

What does this mean for you? These findings suggest that meditation not only enhances your cognitive abilities—like focus, memory, and decision-making—but also reduces the intensity of your stress responses. Essentially, meditation acts as a form of mental training, rewiring your brain to be calmer, clearer, and more focused over time.

So, in simple terms, regular meditation has the potential to boost your brain power while simultaneously quieting the mental noise that leads to stress. It's not just a relaxation technique—it's a powerful tool for building mental clarity and emotional resilience, helping you tackle challenges with a sharp and calm mind.

Stress Reduction and Well-Being

Another key area where mindfulness and meditation have proven their power is in stress reduction. Mindfulness-Based Stress Reduction (MBSR), a widely researched program, has been shown to have profound effects on lowering stress levels. A landmark study from the University of Massachusetts found that participants who completed an 8-week mindfulness course reported a significant drop in stress and anxiety. Many also experienced improvements in their mood and an enhanced overall sense of well-being.

What's happening here? Mindfulness helps you break free from the endless cycle of overthinking and rumination, offering your mind a much-needed pause from the constant noise. By focusing on the present moment, mindfulness reduces the mental clutter that typically fuels stress and anxiety. This shift allows for better emotional regulation, meaning you can respond to stressors with more calm and clarity rather than reacting impulsively or feeling overwhelmed.

The result? Reduced stress, a greater sense of emotional balance, and an overall increase in mental well-being. Mindfulness doesn't just provide temporary relief—it builds resilience, helping you manage life's challenges with a clearer, more composed mindset.

Improved Focus and Attention

Let's face it—we live in a world that constantly competes for our attention, from buzzing phones to endless streams of information. Our ability to focus is under siege, but mindfulness and meditation offer a way to reclaim it. A study from the University of Washington demonstrated that meditation significantly improves attention and task focus, even with brief practice. Participants who meditated for just 20 minutes a day over five days showed marked improvements in their attention span and accuracy at work.

Like I've said, it's like training a muscle: the more you practice mindfulness and meditation, the stronger your ability to concentrate becomes. You're better equipped to stay on task and filter out distractions, which means higher productivity and fewer mistakes. This kind of mental training not only improves focus in the short term but also builds long-term resilience against the constant barrage of distractions in our everyday lives.

Boosting Emotional Resilience

Beyond the cognitive and attention benefits, mindfulness and meditation have also been shown to enhance emotional resilience. Research published in the journal *Emotion* found that individuals who meditate regularly are better equipped to manage difficult emotions, recovering more quickly from setbacks and challenges. The practice of mindfulness helps you observe your thoughts and feelings without becoming consumed by them, creating a space between stimulus and response. This gives you the ability to respond thoughtfully and calmly, rather than reacting impulsively.

Emotional resilience takes you beyond just "feeling good", helps you develop the mental tools to navigate life's inevitable stressors with clarity and grace. Regular meditation strengthens this ability, enabling you to face challenges with a level head and bounce back more easily, regardless of what life throws your way. Over time, this leads to greater emotional stability and an increased capacity to handle adversity without feeling overwhelmed.

Better Decision-Making and Creativity

One of the most exciting benefits emerging from research on mindfulness and meditation is their ability to enhance decision-making and creativity. A study from the University of Amsterdam found that meditation helps people make more rational, informed decisions by reducing emotional reactions. Instead of getting caught up in the immediate stress of a difficult choice, meditation allows you to step back, see the bigger picture, and make more thoughtful decisions. This sense of detachment doesn't make you indifferent—it just helps you approach situations with clarity rather than emotional bias.

Similarly, a study from the University of Groningen showed that mindfulness practices can boost creative thinking. By fostering a calm, focused mind, mindfulness helps you break free from conventional patterns of thought, leading to more innovative and out-of-the-box solutions. It's not about forcing creativity; it's about creating the mental space for ideas to flow more freely.

What do all these findings tell us? The science is clear: mindfulness and meditation aren't just beneficial—they're transformative. These practices improve brain function, reduce stress, boost emotional resilience, and even foster creative thinking. And the best part? You don't need hours of practice to see results. Just a few minutes of mindfulness or meditation each day can significantly impact how you approach your work, relationships, and overall life.

For entrepreneurs and busy professionals, this reinforces the immense value of integrating these practices into daily routines. By doing so, you'll better manage stress, improve decision-making, spark creativity, and set yourself up for long-term success.

Physical Benefits

Mindfulness and meditation are often praised for their mental and emotional benefits, but the physical effects are just as profound. These practices not only calm the mind but actively engage the body's natural healing processes, leading to tangible improvements in long-term health and well-being.

One of the most well-documented physical benefits of mindfulness and meditation is their ability to reduce stress hormones. When you're stressed, your body releases cortisol, the "stress hormone." Elevated levels of cortisol can have negative health effects, including high blood pressure, weight gain, a weakened immune response, and an increased risk of heart disease. Studies have shown that mindfulness practices can lower cortisol levels, helping the body return to a balanced state. For example, a study published in *Health Psychology* found that participants who engaged in regular mindfulness meditation experienced significant reductions in cortisol, demonstrating that these practices have a direct impact on how the body processes stress.

Mindfulness and meditation are also linked to improved sleep quality, which is essential for overall health. Many people struggle with sleep disturbances due to stress, anxiety, or an overactive mind. Meditation helps quiet the mental chatter that often keeps people awake at night, promoting relaxation and setting the stage for better rest. In one study published by *JAMA Internal Medicine*, participants who practiced mindfulness meditation experienced less insomnia, fatigue, and depression compared to those who used other methods to improve sleep. By calming both the mind and body, meditation enables deeper, more restorative sleep, which is key to maintaining physical and emotional well-being.

Beyond the immediate benefits, mindfulness and meditation offer significant long-term health advantages. Regular practice has been shown to lower blood pressure, reducing strain on the cardiovascular system. By promoting relaxation and reducing the body's stress response, meditation helps the heart work more efficiently, decreasing the risk of heart disease. A study by the American Heart Association found that participants who practiced meditation regularly experienced a significant reduction in heart attacks, strokes, and mortality rates related to cardiovascular issues.

Mindfulness practices also have a positive effect on immune function. Stress weakens the immune system, leaving the body more vulnerable to illness, but mindfulness and meditation counteract this by promoting overall relaxation and reducing stress. Research from UCLA found that individuals who practiced mindfulness had higher levels of antibodies—proteins that help fight infections—compared to those who didn't meditate. This suggests that mindfulness doesn't just relieve stress; it also builds a stronger, more resilient immune system.

In the long run, mindfulness and meditation may even slow aging at the cellular level. Studies have shown that meditation increases the activity of telomerase, an enzyme that helps maintain the length of telomeres, which protect chromosomes from deteriorating. Longer telomeres are associated with slower aging and reduced risk of age-related diseases, while shorter ones are linked to a faster aging process. This suggests that consistent meditation may help not just in feeling healthier, but in living longer, healthier lives.

Incorporating mindfulness and meditation into daily life can lead to a cascade of physical benefits, from reduced stress hormones to improved immune function and cardiovascular health. Over time, these practices help the body recover from the daily toll of stress, promote better sleep, and may even extend lifespan. It's clear that the benefits go far beyond mental clarity—they provide a full-body reset that nurtures physical health in ways that are both immediate and long-lasting.

Getting Started with Mindfulness

Starting a mindfulness practice doesn't require drastic changes to your routine or hours of dedicated time each day. As I've already said, mindfulness is simple way to bring awareness and presence into the moments you're already living. All it's really doing is helping you learn how to fully engage with what's happening right now—whether you're having a conversation, preparing a meal, or sitting quietly—without being carried away by the constant stream of thoughts that usually dominate your mind.

One of the simplest ways to begin practicing mindfulness is to focus on your breath. Breathing is something you do all day, every day, without thinking, but when you stop and consciously pay attention to it, it can become a powerful anchor to the present moment. Start by taking a few deep breaths, paying close attention to the sensation of air flowing in and out of your lungs. Feel the rise and fall of your chest or notice the coolness of the air as it enters your nostrils. When your mind inevitably starts to wander, gently bring your focus back to your breath. This simple exercise helps you develop awareness, gives your mind a much-needed break from its usual busyness, and only takes a minute or two.

Another mindfulness technique you can try is a body scan. This involves slowly directing your attention to different parts of your body, starting at your toes and moving up to your head. As you do this, notice any sensations, tension, or discomfort in each area. The body scan reconnects you with your physical body and helps pull you out of your mental whirlwind and into a calmer, more present state. It's especially useful for reducing stress and promoting relaxation.

You can also practice mindfulness through mindful eating. The next time you sit down to a meal, take a moment to truly appreciate what's in front of you. Observe the colors, textures, and smells of the food. As you eat, focus on the flavors and the act of chewing. By fully engaging in the experience of eating, you slow down, savor your food, and involve all your senses. This practice enhances the enjoyment of your meal while also making you more aware of your body's hunger and fullness cues.

On a side note, that I've found to be interesting to a lot of people are the studies that have shown that mindfulness, particularly mindful eating, can be a helpful tool for weight loss and maintaining a healthy relationship with food.

Several key benefits of mindful eating related to weight loss include:

1. **Reduced Overeating**: Mindful eating encourages individuals to eat more slowly, which gives the body time to signal when it's full. Studies show that people who eat mindfully are more likely to stop eating when they are satisfied, rather than overeating out of habit or distraction. This can naturally reduce calorie intake.

2. **Improved Portion Control**: By being more present during meals, people become more aware of the amount of food they are consuming. Mindful eating reduces the likelihood of mindless snacking or eating out of boredom or stress, helping individuals better control portion sizes and make healthier food choices.

3. **Reduced Emotional Eating**: Mindfulness practices can help individuals become more aware of emotional triggers that lead to overeating or unhealthy food choices. By recognizing when emotions such as stress, boredom, or anxiety are driving eating behavior, individuals can learn to address these emotions in healthier ways, rather than turning to food for comfort.

4. **Better Food Choices**: People who practice mindfulness around food often become more attuned to how certain foods make them feel. As a result, they may naturally gravitate toward healthier options that nourish the body and avoid

foods that cause discomfort or sluggishness.

5. **Increased Satisfaction**: Mindful eating can enhance the overall enjoyment of food, leading to greater satisfaction with smaller amounts. By savoring each bite and focusing on the flavors and textures, people often find that they need less food to feel satisfied.

Research has supported these benefits. For instance, a study published in *Obesity Reviews* found that mindfulness-based interventions were effective in reducing binge eating and emotional eating, both of which are significant contributors to weight gain. Another study in *Appetite* found that individuals who practiced mindful eating had a reduction in calorie intake, weight, and body mass index (BMI).

Okay, I hope that little side-bar was interesting!

Another simple yet powerful way to practice mindfulness is through mindful walking. Whether you're walking to your car or taking a stroll in nature, pay attention to the sensations of each step. Feel the ground beneath your feet, notice how your body moves, and take in your surroundings. Walking is something we do every day, but when done mindfully, it becomes a way to ground yourself in the present and clear away mental clutter.

The key to starting with mindfulness is to begin right where you are. Incorporate small, intentional moments of presence into your daily routine. You don't need to carve out extra time or create a complex schedule. Instead, focus on weaving mindfulness into the activities you're already doing. When you're washing dishes, for example, notice the feel of the water, the sound of the plates, or the rhythm of your movements. When driving, instead of mentally running through your to-do list, bring your attention to the road, the feel of the steering wheel, or the changing scenery outside.

What we're aiming for here is to develop an awareness of where, and when, our mind wanders and gently guide it back to the present moment, again and again. Over time, with consistent practice, these small moments add up, cultivating a deeper, lasting sense of calm, clarity, and focus. Mindfulness isn't a destination—it's an ongoing practice, a continual return to the present. We're training ourselves to simply "be here" in whatever we're doing, fully engaged in the moment. As we weave more presence into our daily lives, the benefits of mindfulness begin to naturally unfold, helping us navigate life's ups and downs with greater ease, awareness, and joy.

Simple Daily Practices to Incorporate Mindfulness Into Everyday Life

Incorporating mindfulness into your daily routine doesn't require a complete lifestyle overhaul. You just need to find small, intentional moments to bring your awareness back to the present. They don't need to take up much time. Even so, they can significantly impact how you approach your day, reduce stress, and cultivate a sense of calm and clarity. While I've touched on a few practices earlier, let's dive deeper and explore additional, yet simple, ways to integrate mindfulness seamlessly into your everyday life.

Mindful Morning Routine

Start your day with mindfulness, even before you get out of bed. Rather than immediately reaching for your phone or jumping into the mental to-do list, take a moment to pause and breathe. Notice the temperature in the room, how your body feels, and allow yourself to set a gentle intention for the day ahead. Just focusing on three deep, calming breaths can center you before you even step foot on the ground.

As you move through your morning routine, bring awareness to those everyday tasks that often slip by in autopilot mode. While brushing your teeth, tune in to the sensation of the toothbrush against your teeth and gums. When you're showering, notice the warmth of the water on your skin, the scent of the soap, or the sound of the water. By engaging your senses in these simple actions, you ground yourself in the present moment, turning an otherwise mundane routine into an opportunity for mindfulness. These mindful moments, small as they may seem, set a peaceful and intentional tone for the rest of your day.

Mindful Listening

Throughout your day, whether you're at work, chatting with a friend, or spending time with family, practice mindful listening. Often, we listen merely to respond, our minds are preoccupied with formulating what we're going to say next, rather than truly hearing what the other person is saying. Mindful listening shifts this focus and allows the speaker to feel your full, undivided attention. This means you will need to set aside distractions and judgments, being present, and genuinely engaging with what the other person is sharing.

By doing this, you create space for deeper understanding, which not only improves your relationships but also strengthens your connection with others. You'll notice that people feel heard and valued when you're fully present, and in turn, conversations become more meaningful.

Mindful Eating

I just addressed this one, so I won't go into detail here, but I wanted to bring it back up. But, whether it's a quick snack or a full meal, take the time to slow down and savor each bite. Notice the colors, textures, and smells of your food. Focus on the flavors, the sensation of chewing, and how your body reacts to the flavors and nourishment. And, there's the added benefits of improved digestion, recognizing satiation to help prevent overeating. This simple practice turns something we often rush through into a more enjoyable, nourishing, and mindful experience.

Mindful Breathing Throughout the Day

No matter how hectic your day becomes, your breath is always with you, making it one of the simplest ways to practice mindfulness. Whenever you feel overwhelmed or stressed, pause for a moment and focus on your breathing. Inhale deeply through your nose, letting your belly expand, and then slowly exhale through your mouth. You can do this anywhere—whether you're at your desk, in your car, or waiting in line. Just a few deep breaths can reset your nervous system, bringing a sense of calm and focus to help you navigate whatever challenges you're facing.

Mindful Walking

Whether it's a leisurely stroll around your neighborhood or simply walking from your car to the office, use walking as a moment to practice mindfulness. Instead of letting your mind race ahead to your to-do list, focus on the rhythm of each step. Feel the ground beneath your feet, notice how your body moves, and take in your surroundings—the breeze, the colors, the sounds. Mindful walking not only anchors you in the present but also cultivates a sense of gratitude for the simple, yet profound, act of movement.

Mindfulness in Transitions

In our busy lives, it's easy to rush from one task to the next without pausing, which can leave us feeling scattered and overwhelmed. One effective way to incorporate mindfulness is by making the most of transitions—those brief moments between activities—as opportunities to reset. Before starting a new task or walking into a meeting, take a moment to pause, breathe, and check in with yourself. Set a clear intention for the next part of your day. This short pause can help you refocus, allowing you to approach each new activity with clarity, purpose, and a calm sense of presence.

One of the routines I've developed to make these transitions intentional involves stepping away from my home office. I'll typically get up, walk to the kitchen to refresh my coffee/water, and exchange a few words with my wife to catch up on what's happening in each other's day. When I return to my desk, I do so with a fresh mind, ready to pick up where I left off, and that small transition allows me to hit the ground running with more focus and energy.

Evening Wind-Down

As your day comes to a close, mindfulness can help ease the transition from the busyness of the day into a restful night. Before bed, take a few moments to reflect on your day, acknowledging any challenges or victories without judgment. Consider doing a simple body scan, where you mentally check in with different parts of your body, releasing any tension and allowing yourself to fully relax. This mindful practice not only calms your mind but also prepares your body for better sleep.

Incorporating mindfulness into your daily life doesn't require big changes. It's about bringing attention and awareness to the small moments that already exist in your routine. Whether through mindful breathing, listening, walking, or an evening wind-down, these simple practices help you stay present, reduce stress, and cultivate a deeper sense of peace and well-being throughout your day. Over time, these moments of mindfulness will become second nature, allowing you to approach life with greater clarity, focus, and calm—even in the midst of a busy schedule.

Mindful Gratitude

At the end of each day, take a moment to reflect on what you're grateful for. It could be something big, like a personal achievement, or something small, like a kind word from a colleague. Practicing gratitude helps shift your focus from what's lacking to what's abundant in your life, fostering a positive mindset and increasing overall well-being. By consciously acknowledging the things that bring you joy or fulfillment, you're training your mind to focus on the positive aspects of life, which enhances your mental clarity and emotional resilience. Over time, this simple practice of mindful gratitude can create a lasting sense of contentment and perspective.

To ce clear, I'm not saying that you need to implement each and every one of these mindfulness practices, but as you get more adept at them, I suspect you'll naturally start to be more mindful in everything you do. I've included them here, and in the exercises that follow in the workbook, to help you to see all of the places that we go through life without being mindful of what we are doing, and what's going on around us. And to help you begin to practice more mindfulness throughout your day.

Mindfulness Exercises

Please go to www.RogerGBbest.com/workbooks to download these exercises.

Beginning a Meditation Practice

I have to admit, I've started meditating about a hundred times—literally. I'd start, then stop, and sometimes months (or even years) would pass before I'd try again. I could give you a list of reasons for why that happened, but I'll address them systematically as we move through this section. What I've come to realize is that meditation may not be the easiest habit to form, especially at first. Many of the struggles I faced were based on misconceptions I had about what meditation really is. It wasn't until I understood that meditation is deeply, personal, and flexible that it started to stick for me.

The first step is to create intentional moments of stillness where you can connect with something greater—whether that's your inner self, a higher power, God, or the universal consciousness—and build mental clarity, calm, and focus. Let's start by laying out the broad brushstrokes for how to get started with meditation.

Step 1: Start Simple

When you're beginning a meditation practice, the key is to start small. Many people get overwhelmed at the thought of sitting still for long periods. Don't worry about that. Start with just five to ten minutes. Gradually, as you get more comfortable, you can increase your time.

Find a quiet space where you won't be disturbed. It doesn't need to be a perfectly serene environment—just somewhere comfortable and relatively distraction-free. This could be a corner of your bedroom, your office during a break, or even a quiet spot outside.

I always start my day by taking 3-5 minutes to meditate while still in bed. This allows me to clear my head and begin to focus on the day ahead. Afterward, I get up and knock out a few quick morning routines before heading out to our balcony, which overlooks the Atlantic Ocean. It's there that I spend time with my gratitude journal, reflecting on what I'm thankful for. Once I've completed that, I dive back into meditation, taking a bit more time to center myself. I wrap up the morning with some planning, setting a clear direction for the day. This routine helps me start the day with clarity, calm, and a sense of purpose.

Step 2: Focus on Your Breath

One of the simplest ways to meditate is by focusing on your breath. Sit comfortably, whether cross-legged on the floor or in a chair with your feet grounded. Close your eyes and take a deep breath in through your nose, feeling your lungs expand. Slowly exhale through your mouth. Focus on the rhythm of your breath and the sensation of the air flowing in and out of your body.

Your mind will wander—it's inevitable. When it does, gently guide your attention back to your breath. This act of returning to the present moment is what meditation is all about. Don't judge yourself for getting distracted. The practice is in the return, not in achieving perfect focus.

Step 3: Try Guided Meditation

If sitting in silence feels daunting at first, try guided meditation. There are many apps and online platforms that offer guided sessions designed specifically for beginners. These meditations provide gentle instructions that can help you stay focused, whether you're concentrating on your breath, doing a body scan, or using visualization techniques.

Guided meditation can be as short as five minutes, which makes them an easy way to get started.

Popular apps like **Headspace**, **Calm**, and **Insight Timer** offer a variety of meditations on topics like stress relief, sleep, and focus.

Step 4: Consistency Over Perfection

When building a meditation habit, consistency is more important than length. Meditating for five minutes every day is more effective than doing an hour-long session once a month. Find a time that works best for you—whether it's first thing in the morning, during your lunch break, or before bed—and stick with it. The more consistently you practice, the more benefits you'll see over time.

It's important to remember that meditation is not about achieving a completely quiet mind. It's about cultivating awareness. Some days your mind will be busier than others, and that's okay. The goal to progress. Over time, you'll find meditation easier, and you'll notice benefits like reduced stress, improved focus, and greater emotional resilience in your daily life.

Step 5: Be Patient and Kind to Yourself

Meditation is a practice, not a performance. Be kind and patient with yourself as you develop this new habit. There's no "right" way to meditate, and it's normal for your mind to wander. When your mind wanders just keep bringing your attention back. Each time you do, you're strengthening your ability to stay present.

As you continue, you'll experience increased mental clarity, emotional calm, and a deeper sense of inner peace. Over time, you'll notice these benefits spilling over into other areas of your life, helping you manage challenges with greater awareness and ease.

Final Thoughts

Starting a meditation practice is one of the best gifts you can give yourself. It's a way to carve out moments of stillness in a busy world, to cultivate deeper awareness and connection with yourself. Take it one breath at a time, and before long, meditation will become a cherished part of your daily routine. You don't need to be perfect or rigid with your practice—just start, and let it grow naturally. You'll be amazed at the difference it makes. Oh, and BTW, I've added more info about types of mediation in the Workbook. You know where it's at. If you haven't already, go grab it at: .

Tips for Creating a Conducive Environment for Meditation

1. Minimize Distractions: Before you begin meditating, minimize potential distractions. Silence your phone, close any unnecessary apps, and let family members or housemates know you'll be meditating for a few minutes. Even a small interruption can disrupt your focus, so setting up a distraction-free environment can help you dive deeper into your practice.

2. Use Natural Lighting: If possible, meditate in a space that has natural light. Sunlight helps create a calm and uplifting atmosphere. If natural light isn't available, soft, warm lighting can also create a soothing ambiance.

3. Incorporate Relaxing Scents: Scents can play a powerful role in relaxation. Consider using essential oils or candles to enhance your space. Lavender, sandalwood, and chamomile are all great options for promoting relaxation and calm. However, make sure the scent isn't too overpowering, as that could become distracting.

4. Maintain Cleanliness: Clutter can distract your mind, making it harder to focus during meditation. Keeping your meditation space clean and organized helps create a sense of order and calm. It doesn't need to be minimalist, but a tidy space will help put your mind at ease.

Building a consistent meditation practice takes time, but the rewards are well worth it. By starting small, creating a peaceful environment, and remaining flexible in your approach, you'll find that meditation becomes not just a habit but a grounding practice that supports your mental, emotional, and even physical well-being. Embrace the process and remember that consistency is the key to unlocking the transformative benefits of meditation.

Overcoming Common Challenges

Meditation is a powerful tool for cultivating mental clarity and emotional balance, but like any new habit, it comes with challenges—especially when you're just starting out. The good news is that these obstacles are not only normal, they're also surmountable with the right mindset and strategies. Many people struggle with restlessness, a racing mind, or the frustration of not "doing it right," but the key is to remember that meditation is a journey, not a destination. Perfection is not the goal—in fact, it's the opposite. Meditation is about noticing when your mind wanders and gently bringing your focus back, all without judgment. Here's how to overcome some of the most common challenges and create a meditation practice that works for you.

Common Obstacles

When starting a meditation practice, you are likely to come across at least one of several obstacles that can make the process feel frustrating. Let's take a look at some of these challenges and explore strategies to overcome them, ensuring you can stick with your practice and reap its full benefits.

Restlessness and Fidgeting

Many beginners struggle with sitting still for extended periods, feeling restless, or having an urge to fidget. This is natural, especially in a world where constant activity is the norm. The solution? Start small. Rather than trying to sit for long sessions right away, begin with just a few minutes. Over time, your body will become accustomed to sitting, and the restlessness will diminish.

Racing Thoughts

One of the biggest misconceptions about meditation is that you're supposed to completely clear your mind. The truth is, having thoughts pop into your head is entirely normal. Rather than fighting them or getting frustrated, acknowledge the thoughts and gently guide your attention back to your breath or focal point. Meditation is about noticing your thoughts without getting attached to them, not eliminating them altogether.

Time Constraints

In our busy lives, finding time to meditate can feel like just another task on the to-do list. The trick is to integrate meditation into your day without feeling like it's a burden. Start by setting aside five minutes in the morning or evening, or even during a lunch break. You can gradually increase the time as it becomes a habit. You can also experiment with "micro-meditations," short moments of mindfulness throughout the day—like while waiting in line or during your commute.

Discomfort and Pain

Sitting still for long periods can cause physical discomfort, especially for those who aren't used to it. The key is to find a position that works for you. You don't have to sit cross-legged on the floor if that's uncomfortable—sitting in a chair with your feet on the ground or using cushions for support can help ease physical tension. If discomfort arises during meditation, acknowledge it and try to adjust your position or focus on your breath.

Boredom or Frustration

Many people find meditation boring or frustrating, especially when they're not immediately feeling the benefits. Understand that meditation is a practice—it takes time and patience. Like physical exercise, the benefits of meditation accumulate over time. Acknowledge that frustration, boredom, or impatience is part of the process, and remind yourself that even five minutes of mindfulness is progress.

Expecting Immediate Results

It's easy to get discouraged when you don't feel the immediate calming effects that meditation promises. Like any new skill, meditation takes time to master, and expecting instant results can lead to disappointment. Set aside your expectations and embrace the practice as a journey rather than a quick fix. The benefits—like reduced stress, improved focus, and emotional clarity—will come with consistency.

By acknowledging these challenges and approaching them with patience and curiosity, you'll be better equipped to navigate the journey of meditation. Remember, the goal isn't perfection—it's progress. Meditation is about creating a space for mental clarity, calm, and focus, even in the midst of life's distractions. Keep showing up for yourself, and over time, you'll find that the obstacles become easier to manage, and the benefits become more profound.

Maintaining Consistency

Making meditation a regular part of your life requires you to consciously prioritize your well-being. It's about acknowledging that meditation isn't a luxury or an indulgence—it's a vital practice for maintaining mental clarity, emotional balance, and physical health. When you begin to see meditation as an investment in your overall well-being, the act of showing up for your practice, even when you're busy, becomes much easier.

Each session, no matter how short, is an opportunity to recharge and reset. It's a break from the endless cycle of thoughts, tasks, and worries that dominate our minds. By committing to this practice regularly, you're giving yourself the tools to handle stress, make better decisions, and stay grounded amid life's challenges.

Consistency as a Choice and Mindset

Staying committed to meditation over the long haul is more than just having a routine—it's a conscious choice to prioritize your mental and emotional health. It may help to reframe how you think about meditation. Instead of seeing it as another "task" to complete, view it as an essential part of your self-care routine—just like brushing your teeth or getting enough sleep.

If you find yourself struggling to stay consistent, remind yourself of the bigger picture: meditation is not about immediate results; it's about long-term benefits. Each session builds on the last, helping you develop resilience, focus, and calm over time. The more you practice, the more these benefits compound.

The Mindset Shift

The mindset shift necessary for long-term commitment is rooted in the idea that meditation isn't about achieving perfection, nor is it about drastic changes. It's a practice that evolves with time, and each session, no matter how brief, contributes to your overall well-being.

When you view meditation as a regular, intentional investment in your mental and emotional health, you'll find that consistency becomes easier to maintain. You'll start to notice the ripple effects in other areas of your life—greater focus at work, more patience with loved ones, and an increased sense of inner peace. These are the lasting rewards that come from making meditation a priority, and they're well worth the dedication it takes to stay consistent.

In the end, it's about making a conscious choice to prioritize yourself. Meditation isn't just a practice—it's a commitment to showing up for yourself, time and time again, and that's something truly worth sticking with.

Reflection

As we've explored in this chapter, mindfulness and meditation are far more than relaxation techniques—they are gateways to greater mental clarity, emotional resilience, and a more focused, intentional life. These practices empower you to step back from the relentless chaos of daily life and return to the present moment, fully aware, calm, and grounded.

At the heart of both mindfulness and meditation is a simple but profound truth: the present moment is where life truly happens. By consciously choosing to be more present, you unlock a wealth of clarity and peace that can transform how you approach challenges, stress, and uncertainty, navigating them with grace and ease.

Whether you're just beginning or have been practicing for years, now is the perfect time to either commit or recommit to this journey. Even dedicating a few minutes a day can yield significant changes. Remember, mindfulness and meditation are not about achieving perfection but about making steady progress. Each breath, each moment of focus, is a step toward living a clearer, more centered life.

As you move forward, remind yourself that this practice is a gift of reconnecting with your true self, refocusing your energy, and recharging your mind and spirit. Picture the impact this can have on your relationships, your work, and your overall sense of purpose. Let this be your motivation: the rewards of consistency are profound, extending into every corner of your life. Take this opportunity to begin or deepen your practice and watch as it gradually transforms not only your daily experiences but your entire well-being.

Chapter Eight

Beyond Boundaries

Reinventing Limits as Life Evolves

WE'VE ALREADY SPENT TIME discussing the importance of boundaries in earlier chapters, touching on how they protect your time, energy, and well-being. You've learned how crucial they are for preventing burnout and maintaining focus. But here's the thing—boundaries are not a one-size-fits-all solution, nor are they static. As your life evolves, so must your boundaries. What worked for you when you started your journey might not serve you as effectively today, especially as your personal and professional worlds expand.

In this chapter, we're going to move beyond the foundational understanding of boundaries and explore how they can be adapted to meet the demands of a dynamic, ever-changing life. Whether you're navigating the growth of your business, new personal responsibilities, or an evolving sense of purpose, boundaries will be your compass, helping you maintain clarity and balance.

We'll focus on advanced strategies for integrating boundaries into both your personal and professional lives, so you can thrive in each without sacrificing the other. I'm going to take you beyond simply saying "no" more often or even just managing your time better. I plan to help you create a fluid framework that allows you to honor your values and maintain your well-being while still pursuing your bigger dreams.

Boundaries are an ongoing practice, not a one-time fix, and as you grow, they need to grow with you. This chapter will guide you through refining, evolving, and enforcing your boundaries in a way that aligns with your long-term vision for success and personal fulfillment. Let's dive in and discover how to take your boundary-setting skills to the next level, ensuring that they continue to support you as you build the life you truly want.

Revisiting Boundaries in Light of Changing Goals

Boundaries aren't meant to be rigid; they need to evolve as your life, goals, and responsibilities change. As an entrepreneur or professional, you'll inevitably experience moments when the boundaries you've set no longer serve you as they once did. Recognizing when it's time to adapt your boundaries is essential for sustaining a healthy balance.

Take Sarah, for example. When she started her tech startup, her boundaries were almost non-existent. She worked all hours of the day, took every client call, and never said no to an opportunity. As her business grew, so did her responsibilities—but she hadn't adjusted her boundaries to reflect the shift. Soon, Sarah found herself teetering on the edge of burnout, exhausted and feeling disconnected from her family.

It wasn't until Sarah stepped back and reevaluated her boundaries that things changed. She realized that what had worked when her business was smaller no longer applied. She set stricter limits on her work hours, started delegating more, and began protecting her weekends for family time. The transformation wasn't instant, but as Sarah stuck to her new boundaries, she noticed a profound shift—not just in her energy levels but in her ability to lead with clarity and focus.

The lesson here? Just because a boundary worked for you a year ago doesn't mean it will serve you now. Boundaries should evolve as you do.

So ask yourself: *Are your current boundaries helping or hindering you? Are they aligned with your current goals and priorities, or are they rooted in a past version of your life?* Don't be afraid to adapt them. Growth in business and life requires constant recalibration, and adjusting your boundaries is part of that process.

Remember, boundaries go beyond saying no; they're there to help you to say yes to what matters most right now. The more intentional you are with setting and adjusting them, the more space you create for what truly fuels your success and well-being.

Work-Life Integration vs. Work-Life Balance

In today's world, the concept of work-life balance often feels like an unattainable ideal. The idea that work and life should be perfectly compartmentalized, with equal time and attention given to each, can leave many feeling frustrated and as though they're constantly falling short. For entrepreneurs and professionals juggling multiple roles, achieving this kind of equilibrium is almost impossible. But what if we reframed the entire concept?

Rather than striving for balance, a more realistic and advanced approach is to focus on *work-life integration*. This isn't about striving for a perfect 50/50 split between work and personal life; it's about creating a harmonious relationship between the two, where work and life complement each other rather than compete. In work-life integration, the lines may blur, but the key is that they do so in a way that supports your overall well-being and goals—without causing burnout.

Practical Strategies for Work-Life Integration

Work-life integration starts with a shift in mindset. Instead of viewing work and personal life as two opposing forces constantly pulling you in different directions, think of them as parts of the same whole. The goal isn't to completely separate them but to weave them together sustainably.

1. Align Your Values Across Both Domains

The first step in work-life integration is ensuring that your work aligns with your personal values. If your professional life is pulling you in a direction that conflicts with what's most important to you personally, integration will always feel like a struggle. Take time to reflect on your values and see where they overlap between your work and personal life. When there's alignment, it's much easier to find harmony between the two.

2. Set Clear Priorities

Rather than trying to give equal weight to everything, focus on what's most important at any given moment. Sometimes, your work will need more attention, and other times, your personal life will take precedence. The key to work-life integration is flexibility—being able to adapt based on what's currently most important while making sure that both areas are getting the attention they deserve over the long term.

For example, if you have an important business deadline, your focus may need to shift toward work for a few days or weeks. But once that deadline is met, you can consciously reallocate time to your family, hobbies, or rest, making sure that personal life doesn't get perpetually sidelined.

3. Create Fluid Boundaries

In work-life balance, boundaries are often rigid, with strict separation between work time and personal time. While that works for some, work-life integration requires more fluid boundaries that can shift based on your current needs and circumstances. This might mean being available for a client call during personal time if it's urgent but then making sure you carve out extra personal time the next day. It's about give-and-take rather than strict division.

This doesn't mean letting work spill into every aspect of your life unchecked; instead, consciously decide when those boundaries can flex to serve your broader goals.

4. Build Intentional Transitions

One of the biggest challenges of work-life integration is avoiding the feeling of constantly being "on." By building intentional transitions between work and personal life, you can maintain a sense of presence in whatever you're doing. For example, if you've been working all morning, take a few minutes to decompress before switching to a personal activity, like spending time with family or exercising.

These intentional pauses give your mind the space it needs to reset, making it easier to be fully present in the next part of your day. This ties back to the mindfulness practices we discussed in Chapter 7. Mindfulness is a key factor in successful work-life integration because it teaches you to be fully engaged in whatever you're doing, whether it's a work task or a personal activity. The ability to stay present prevents work from bleeding into personal life and vice versa, helping you maintain mental clarity and emotional balance.

5. Embrace Flexibility and Fluidity

Work-life integration requires you to embrace flexibility and fluidity. Rather than adhering to rigid schedules, be open to adjusting your routine as needed. This might mean blending work and personal activities—such as taking a business call while on a walk or brainstorming while cooking dinner—but doing so in a way that feels harmonious rather than overwhelming.

Mindfulness: The Key to Making Integration Work

Mindfulness plays a crucial role in work-life integration because it allows you to be fully present in whatever part of your life you're engaged in at the moment. As discussed in Chapter 7, mindfulness is about paying attention to the present without judgment, and this skill is invaluable when navigating the blurring lines between work and personal life.

When you're at work, mindfulness helps you focus on the task at hand without being distracted by personal responsibilities. When you're at home or engaged in personal activities, mindfulness helps you be present with your loved ones or in your self-care practices without worrying about work tasks. This presence of mind ensures that you're not constantly trying to "balance" multiple things at once but instead are fully engaged in each aspect of your life as it arises.

Integration, Not Perfection

Ultimately, work-life integration leads you to a place where you reach harmony, not perfection. There will be times when work demands more of you, and times when personal life needs to take precedence. The key is finding a flow that allows both to coexist in a way that supports your overall well-being. By setting flexible boundaries, aligning your values, and using mindfulness to stay present, you can create a life where work and personal fulfillment don't compete but complement each other.

In the next section, we'll explore how to revisit and evolve your boundaries as your professional and personal responsibilities grow, ensuring that your integration strategy continues to serve you well over time.

The Personalization of Boundaries: Tailoring to Your Life

Boundaries aren't a one-size-fits-all solution. What works for someone else might not work for you, and the boundaries you set today may need to evolve as your life changes. The beauty of boundaries is their adaptability—they're deeply personal and can be shaped to reflect your values, lifestyle, and goals. Whether you're an entrepreneur scaling a business or a professional balancing work and family life, your boundaries should honor the unique circumstances of your life.

Think of boundaries like a living blueprint for your life. They aren't rigid rules set in stone; rather, they're dynamic guidelines that shift with you as your priorities and responsibilities evolve. What served you well during one phase of your journey might need to be reshaped as new challenges and opportunities arise. In this section, we'll explore how boundaries can and should look different for everyone, with examples of how to tailor them to your current needs. You'll also find exercises designed to help you reflect on where you are right now in life and adjust your boundaries accordingly.

As you move through different seasons, whether it's growing your business, starting a family, or even embarking on a new career—your boundaries should evolve alongside you. Setting boundaries that align with your personal and professional goals allows you to protect your energy, focus on what truly matters, and avoid burning out. By revisiting and reshaping your boundaries regularly, you ensure they continue to serve you, creating a life that feels balanced and fulfilling in every season.

How Boundaries Differ from Person to Person

Just as no two lives are identical, no two sets of boundaries will ever be the same. Your boundaries are a reflection of who you are—your values, the demands of your business, and the lifestyle you've chosen. Some people may need firm, structured boundaries to protect their time with family, while others might embrace more flexibility to navigate the shifting tides of a growing business.

Take the example of an entrepreneur with young children. Their priority may be to create a hard stop in the workday by 6 p.m. to ensure they're fully present for family dinners and bedtime routines. For them, boundaries might mean no checking emails after hours and setting strict limits on evening work commitments. In contrast, a solopreneur building a business might allow for late-night work sessions but set non-negotiable personal time on the weekends to recharge. Their boundaries flex to meet the demands of their business, but still protect what matters most—time for themselves.

The key takeaway is this: there is no "right" way to set boundaries—only the right way for you. Your boundaries should be as unique as your journey. What matters is that they honor your current priorities and create a balance that allows you to thrive, both personally and professionally. As life evolves, so too should your boundaries, ensuring that they continue to serve and protect what's most important to you.

Tailoring Boundaries to Your Values and Lifestyle

Setting boundaries all starts with clarity about your values. Ask yourself: *What truly matters most to me? What do I need to protect in my life to feel fulfilled, balanced, and energized?* Once you're clear on these priorities, you can set boundaries that safeguard them, ensuring that your life and actions align with what's most important to you.

Here are some ideas on how you can tailor your boundaries to fit your values:

- **Family-Centric Boundaries**: If your family is your top priority, your boundaries might involve strict work cut-offs. For example, you might set a "no work calls during dinner" policy or block off Sundays for family activities, fully dedicating that time to your loved ones. These boundaries ensure that your presence with family is undistracted and meaningful.

- **Growth-Focused Boundaries**: If you're in a phase of rapid business growth, flexibility might be key. You might allow work to occasionally spill into evenings, but balance this with boundaries for recovery—like scheduling downtime after a major project or setting aside quiet moments for personal reflection to avoid burnout. These boundaries protect your energy while still allowing for ambitious growth.

- **Health-Driven Boundaries**: If your health is a core value, boundaries might center on prioritizing time for exercise, rest, and self-care. You could reserve your mornings for a workout, commit to mindful eating without distraction, or ensure work doesn't interfere with getting quality sleep. These boundaries go beyond just about keeping fit—they're about making your well-being non-negotiable.

The beauty of boundaries is that they're not intended to restrict you—they help you keep your focus trained on honoring your priorities. Boundaries help you protect the things that matter most, allowing you to create a life that feels balanced, intentional, and aligned with your values. The more you design your boundaries around what's meaningful to you, the more empowered you'll feel to pursue both personal and professional success—on your terms.

Exercise: Reassessing Your Boundaries Based on Your Current Life Stage

Please go to www.rogergbest.com/workbook to get this exercise.

Reassessing and Evolving Your Boundaries

As you evolve, both personally and professionally, your boundaries need to evolve with you. Life is dynamic, and what worked for you at one stage may not serve you in the next. Regularly reassessing your boundaries ensures that they continue to support your growth, rather than holding you back. Ask yourself, *"Are my boundaries still protecting what matters most? Or are they in need of adjustment to fit the next chapter of my life?"*

For example:

- **Growing Your Business**: If you've transitioned from being a solo entrepreneur to managing a team, your boundaries may need to shift. Perhaps you'll need more flexibility in your work hours to accommodate team needs. At the same time, you might tighten your boundaries around personal time to protect yourself from burnout, ensuring you're fully recharged to lead effectively.

- **Shifting Priorities**: If you've just hit a major career milestone, you might find that your focus shifts. Instead of chasing growth, you may want to prioritize personal well-being, or even travel, if that's one of your big goals. This could mean adjusting boundaries to make more time for meditation, exercise, trave, or hobbies that nourish your energy and keep you grounded.

Think of boundaries as flexible guardrails, providing structure while allowing you the freedom to adapt to new circumstances. The road ahead will change—so should the boundaries guiding your journey. Make it a habit to check in with yourself regularly, perhaps at the end of each quarter or after major life or business changes. This practice ensures your boundaries are always aligned with your evolving goals and values, supporting you in every phase of your personal and professional growth.

The Power of Personalized Boundaries

The real power of boundaries lies in their ability to be uniquely yours—tailored to your life, your values, and your personal goals. Instead of trying to fit into someone else's expectations or adopting generic solutions, personalized boundaries give you the freedom to design a life that reflects who you are and where you're headed.

By regularly revisiting and adjusting your boundaries as your circumstances evolve, you ensure that these boundaries remain flexible, effective, and aligned with your priorities. This ongoing practice allows you to create harmony between your personal and professional life, protect your well-being, and continue driving toward success without sacrificing what matters most.

As you move forward, remember that the goal is not to set rigid, unbreakable boundaries. Instead, keep your eyes on creating boundaries that serve you in the here and now—boundaries that grow with you as you rise to new challenges and pursue new dreams. With personalized boundaries in place, you empower yourself to live and work in a way that feels authentic, balanced, and sustainable.

Advanced Boundary Techniques: Beyond Simply Saying "No"

Setting boundaries is often seen as the simple act of saying "no," but in reality, it's much more nuanced—especially when those boundaries are tested by clients, family, or friends. Maintaining your boundaries in the face of pushback requires not only confidence but also strategic techniques that help you stay firm without damaging important relationships. In this section, we'll explore advanced strategies for managing and adjusting boundaries in challenging situations and reinforcing them over time—even when they're repeatedly tested.

Handling Pushback from Clients, Family, or Friends

When someone pushes against your boundaries, it's easy to feel pressured to give in. But compromising your boundaries can lead to resentment, burnout, and even strained relationships. Instead, you can approach these situations with a combination of firmness and tact.

For instance, if a client repeatedly requests work beyond agreed hours, rather than just saying "no" outright, you might use an "I statement" to reinforce your boundary clearly and professionally: *"I understand the urgency of this task, but I've committed to set working hours to ensure the quality of my work remains high. Let's discuss how we can address this within our usual hours."*

Of course, there's always the. "Sure, I can do that but my rates for that is $X.XX", and make that number REALLY high, as in high enough that you're confident they will rethink whether it needs to be done in those hours you've chosen as "off hours". I'm not a big fan of that approach, but I have used it a few times with great success. If the price is high enough, they typically get the point and decide it will wait until your normal hours.

With family or friends, it can be more personal. If a family member constantly interrupts your personal time, you could express your need in a way that acknowledges their importance while holding firm: *"I value our time together, but I need an hour of quiet after work to recharge. After that, I'll be fully present with you."*

Using empathetic language allows you to maintain boundaries while showing respect for the other person's needs.

Reinforcing Boundaries Over Time

It's common for boundaries to be tested repeatedly, whether by the same individuals or in different circumstances. The key is to maintain consistency and be prepared to revisit and restate your boundaries when necessary.

One effective technique is **boundary role-playing**—rehearsing how you'll respond to common scenarios where your boundaries might be challenged. This helps you develop confidence in maintaining them. For example, if you know a client often asks for last-minute revisions, you can practice saying: *"I'd love to help, but as we agreed, all changes need to be finalized by the end of the business day. Let's plan ahead next time to make sure everything is completed within our timeline."*

When boundaries are pushed repeatedly, reinforce them calmly but assertively. You might say, *"As I mentioned before, my personal time is important for my well-being, so I won't be available after 6 p.m."* Over time, people will come to understand and respect your limits as long as you remain consistent. If both sides plan appropriately, working within your chosen hours can be dealt with easily. I've found that the vast majority of the time, when clients are demanding time after my chosen hours, it's because they have chosen to work those hours. Ask them to take your call at 5:00 a.m. and they will almost always back away.

The big key here is that flexibility should be something we strongly consider when we have certain situations, like a preset deadline is approaching, or it's one of those growth times. I simply do not show flexibility with my time when the client didn't plan ahead, or they just happen to be working at 11:00 p.m. one evening. I have a coffee cup that read; "Lack of planning on your part, does not necessarily constitute an emergency on my part." One time, I actually sent a picture of that cup to one of my clients. Granted, he was a friend, and I knew he would laugh and get the point. That's not a tactic I recommend as a general practice.

Adjusting Boundaries to Meet Evolving Needs

Boundaries aren't static; they need to evolve as your life and circumstances change. Reassessing them regularly ensures that they continue to serve you. If you find yourself feeling more overwhelmed or drained than supported by your current boundaries, it may be time to adjust them.

For example, if you've recently taken on more responsibilities at work, or you've taken on a new client that is going to be resource intensive for a while, your previous boundaries around personal time may no longer suffice. You might need to adjust your availability by setting new expectations with clients or coworkers, such as: *"I'll be available for meetings from 9 a.m. to 3 p.m., but I need the remainder of the day for project focus and personal time."* Or you may need to simply make a new, temporary contract with yourself that you are going to spend a little extra time, or hire someone, to make sure that this new client is given the service that you promised.

The power of these advanced techniques lies in your ability to adapt, maintain consistency, and communicate with clarity—even when circumstances change, or boundaries are tested repeatedly. By mastering these approaches, you'll protect your well-being, foster healthier relationships, and create a more balanced and fulfilling personal and professional life.

Specific Strategies

Strategy 1: The Art of Offering Alternatives

Saying "no" doesn't always have to feel like a hard stop. One of the most effective ways to maintain your boundaries while preserving relationships and professionalism is by offering thoughtful alternatives. This strategy shows that while you're committed to your own well-being and time management, you're also willing to collaborate and meet others' needs—just within mutually agreed-upon limits.

When a client requests something that falls outside your boundaries, such as a late-night meeting that disrupts your personal time, instead of declining outright, you can offer an alternative solution. For example, suggest a meeting during your working hours or propose providing a written update or summary if that works better for their schedule.

This approach does more than simply reinforce your boundaries—it demonstrates flexibility, problem-solving, and a commitment to delivering value on your terms.

For instance: *"Unfortunately, I won't be available for a meeting at that time, but I'd be happy to schedule a call for tomorrow morning, or I can prepare a detailed report before the end of today."*

By offering an alternative, you set a clear boundary while maintaining the relationship and showing your willingness to work together. This not only helps avoid confrontation but also reinforces the professionalism with which you handle your commitments, making it easier for others to respect your boundaries in the future.

Strategy 2: Setting Expectations Early

One of the most effective ways to avoid pushback on boundaries is by establishing clear expectations from the very beginning. When clients, colleagues, or family members understand your limits upfront, there's less room for confusion or resistance later on. Proactive communication eliminates the need for reactive boundary-setting, creating smoother interactions and fostering mutual respect.

Whether you're setting expectations around your availability, response times, or preferred methods of communication, being transparent from the start helps manage others' expectations while preserving your time and energy. Think of it as laying the groundwork for healthy, long-lasting professional or personal relationships.

For instance, when onboarding a new client, you might say: *"To ensure we work efficiently and effectively, I'm available for calls between 9 a.m. and 5 p.m. Monday through Friday. Any requests outside of these hours will be addressed the next business day."*

By stating these guidelines up front, you're not only setting a boundary but also positioning yourself as a professional who values structure, balance, and mutual understanding. This transparency allows others to work within your framework, reducing the likelihood of friction or disappointment down the road.

Setting expectations early isn't just about avoiding awkward boundary conversations later. When people know where the lines are, they're far more likely to respect them, and you're far less likely to face unnecessary challenges in maintaining your personal and professional balance.

Strategy 3: Using Empathy to Reinforce Boundaries

When others push back on your boundaries, it's often because they don't fully understand your perspective or needs. Responding with empathy can turn potential friction into collaboration, making it easier for them to accept your limits. By acknowledging their point of view first, you can create a sense of mutual respect, which increases the likelihood that your boundary will be respected.

Empathy allows you to connect with the other person while still holding firm on your limits. This technique is especially useful in professional settings where the relationship matters, or in personal situations where feelings are involved. The key is to validate their concerns while maintaining your stance in a way that feels respectful and non-combative.

For example, if a colleague or client pushes for urgent work outside your designated hours, you might respond with:

"I completely understand that this is a top priority for you, and I want to support you as best I can. At the same time, I need to honor my work hours so I can continue to deliver high-quality results and maintain my own balance. Let's schedule a time first thing tomorrow to tackle this together."

This approach conveys understanding while reinforcing your boundary. You're showing that you respect their urgency, but you're also ensuring they understand your need to protect your time. By leading with empathy, you're more likely to diffuse any tension and gain their cooperation moving forward.

Empathy doesn't mean you have to compromise your boundaries—but it does require expressing them in a way that helps the other person feel heard, making it easier for them to respect the limits you've set.

Strategy 4: Create "Boundary Rituals"

Rituals are powerful tools for reinforcing boundaries because they serve as physical and mental cues that help you transition between different areas of your life. By creating intentional habits that signal the end of your workday or the start of personal time, you can maintain a stronger separation between work and life—even when external pressures arise.

A boundary ritual is a specific routine you practice consistently, making it clear when you're shifting from work mode to personal time. This doesn't just help you; it also signals to others that your workday has ended. Whether it's closing your laptop, leaving your workspace, or engaging in a mindfulness exercise, these small habits create a symbolic—and practical—boundary between your work and personal life.

For instance, at the end of your workday, you might:

- Close your laptop, tidy up your workspace, and physically leave the area where you've been working.

- Take a short walk outside to clear your mind and decompress after a busy day.

- Engage in a brief meditation or breathing exercise to signal the shift from work to relaxation.

- Light a candle or play a calming playlist that marks the start of personal time.

These rituals don't need to be elaborate; the key is consistency. By practicing these habits daily, you train your mind to recognize when it's time to switch off from work, which helps prevent burnout and preserves your personal time. For example, if you take five minutes every day to sit quietly or meditate after work, your brain will begin to associate that ritual with the end of work stress and the beginning of personal relaxation.

Why This Works:

- **Mental Separation**: Boundary rituals give you a clear mental break between work and home life, helping you reset and be fully present outside of work.

- **Physical Cues**: These small actions signal to your body and brain that it's time to disengage from work, making it easier to relax and recharge.

- **Reinforces Boundaries for Others**: When practiced consistently, these rituals also inform those around you—whether it's family, friends, or colleagues—that your workday is done.

For example: After wrapping up your day, try stepping away from your desk, doing a short stretch or a walk, and then lighting a candle or playing soft music as you settle into personal time. This simple yet effective practice creates a clear and peaceful boundary between work and home, allowing you to recharge and reconnect with your non-work self.

Strategy 5: Use a Buffer System

When boundaries are consistently tested, it's easy to feel pressured into responding immediately to every request, which can lead to burnout and frustration. A buffer system is a powerful tool to create distance between yourself and the demands of others, giving you time and space to evaluate how best to respond without sacrificing your boundaries.

A buffer system can take many forms—delaying responses, having preset times for communication, or using an intermediary like a virtual assistant to manage requests. These strategies allow you to filter incoming demands, ensuring that your time and attention are spent on the highest-priority tasks, while maintaining the flexibility to say "no" when needed.

For example:

- Instead of answering every client call or email as it comes in, you could route inquiries through an assistant who organizes and prioritizes them based on your availability and importance.

- Alternatively, you might introduce a policy of responding to non-urgent requests within 24 hours, giving yourself breathing room to assess whether the request aligns with your current priorities.

Why This Works:
- **Protects Your Time**: A buffer helps you avoid the trap of constantly being on-call, allowing you to maintain your focus on high-value activities.

- **Adds a Layer of Protection**: With an assistant or gatekeeper, you're not the first point of contact for every issue, making it easier to uphold your boundaries without feeling guilty.

- **Reduces Pressure**: By implementing a delay in responses, you relieve yourself of the immediate pressure to react, giving you more control over how and when you engage with others.

Example in Practice: Imagine you're an entrepreneur juggling multiple projects, and clients frequently reach out for updates, often outside of your dedicated work hours. Instead of being on-call 24/7, you could have a virtual assistant handle client communication, forwarding only the most urgent matters to you during your designated response time. This allows you to maintain focus on your primary tasks and enjoy personal time without interruptions.

Or, if you're a professional receiving constant requests from colleagues, you might implement a policy where you only check and respond to emails during set times, such as once in the morning and once in the afternoon. This creates a buffer that helps you maintain productivity while still being accessible in a structured way.

Pro Tip: If hiring an assistant isn't feasible, use technology as your buffer. Automate your email responses with a message that lets people know when they can expect to hear back from you. For example: "I've received your message and will respond within 24 hours. If this is urgent, please call my office directly."

Strategy 6: Reinforce Boundaries with a "Yes, and..." Approach

When someone pushes back against your boundaries, it can be tempting to either give in or come across as overly rigid in your response. The "Yes, and..." technique offers a balanced middle ground. It allows you to acknowledge the other person's needs or concerns while still holding firm to your boundary, preserving both your relationships and your personal or professional limits.

This technique is particularly effective because it blends empathy with assertiveness, making it easier for others to accept your boundaries without feeling dismissed. By validating their urgency or request while still reinforcing your limit, you maintain a sense of cooperation without compromising your own needs.

For example:
- If a client requests a last-minute meeting outside of your work hours, you might say, "Yes, I understand that this feels urgent, and I'll be able to address it within the next two business days."

- If a friend asks for your help on a weekend when you've reserved time for family, you could respond, "Yes, I'd love to help, and I'm available on Monday to give it my full attention."

Why This Works:
- **Acknowledge, Don't Reject**: You're acknowledging the other person's needs or feelings without flat-out rejecting them, which makes them feel heard and understood.

- **Positive Framing**: By starting with "Yes," the response feels collaborative and positive, which helps soften the impact of the boundary.

- **Maintains Flexibility**: The "and" portion gives you room to uphold your boundary while offering a reasonable alternative, keeping the interaction flexible and professional.

Example in Practice: Imagine you're leading a small business and one of your key clients regularly calls after hours, expecting immediate attention. Instead of bluntly saying "No, I don't work outside of business hours," you could say: "Yes, I understand this is important, and I'll prioritize it first thing tomorrow when I'm back at work." This response shows you're taking the request seriously without compromising your personal time.

In a personal context, if a family member asks you for a favor that conflicts with a prior commitment, you could say: "Yes, I'm happy to help, and I'll be free after 5 p.m. today." This shows you're willing to contribute, but within the boundaries you've set.

Pro Tip: If you find that someone frequently tests your boundaries despite this approach, consider setting a firmer timeline or framework. For example, "Yes, I'm happy to address this, and going forward, let's plan to schedule requests like this during business hours to ensure I can give it the attention it deserves."

Reinforcing Boundaries Over Time

Setting boundaries is an important first step, but maintaining them—especially when repeatedly tested—requires ongoing commitment and vigilance. Over time, it's easy to fall into the trap of letting boundaries slide, whether it's due to a mounting workload or to keep the peace in personal relationships. However, strong boundaries are essential for your well-being and long-term success.

The key to reinforcing boundaries lies in consistency and adaptability. You need strategies that help you uphold your boundaries while allowing flexibility when life changes. Here's how to maintain your boundaries over the long term without compromising on what's important to you. Here are a few additional thoughts to move them back to the top of your mind and maybe give you a few more ideas.

1. **Consistency is Key**

The most effective way to ensure your boundaries are respected is to stick to them consistently. This doesn't mean being rigid or inflexible, but rather being clear and firm in how you communicate and uphold your limits. When others see that you take your boundaries seriously, they're more likely to respect them over time.

For example, if you've established work hours that protect your personal time, be diligent about maintaining them—even when it's tempting to "just take one more call." By consistently reinforcing your boundaries, you create a culture of respect around your time and energy, reducing the likelihood of overcommitment.

2. **Regularly Reassess and Adjust**

Your boundaries should evolve with you. As your career grows, your personal responsibilities change, or your life circumstances shift, it's important to reassess your boundaries to ensure they're still serving you. Take time every few months to reflect on whether your current boundaries are protecting your well-being or if they need adjustment.

For instance, as your business expands, you may find that your boundary around client communication needs to change. Maybe you need to delegate some client interactions to a team member or adjust your availability to accommodate new demands. The goal is to make sure your boundaries remain aligned with your evolving goals.

3. **Use Gentle Reminders**

When others forget or overstep your boundaries, it's helpful to offer gentle, non-confrontational reminders. This reinforces your limits without creating unnecessary conflict. For example, if a colleague or client starts pushing for after-hours communication despite your established boundaries, you can politely remind them:

"Just a quick reminder that I'm not available for work calls after 6 p.m. Let's reconnect first thing tomorrow morning to go over this."

This approach is firm but friendly, reinforcing your boundary while preserving the relationship.

4. Create Accountability

It's easy to let boundaries slip when no one is holding you accountable. To combat this, consider sharing your boundaries with someone who can help keep you on track—a business partner, a mentor, or even a close friend. Accountability doesn't mean someone policing your every move, but it can be a valuable way to stay aligned with your goals.

For example, if you're working to protect your weekends from work intrusions, tell a trusted colleague or friend about your plan. Ask them to check in periodically to ensure you're sticking to your commitment. This external support can help you maintain your boundaries more effectively over time.

5. Stay True to Your Priorities

Finally, remember that your boundaries are directly tied to your priorities and values. When the temptation arises to let them slip, revisit why you set those boundaries in the first place. Are you protecting time for family? Guarding your health? Prioritizing personal growth? Keeping these priorities in front of your mind will give you the motivation you need to reinforce your boundaries when they're tested. With these strategies in place, you can protect your time, energy, and focus over the long term, ensuring that your boundaries continue to serve you as your personal and professional life evolves.

Maintaining Flexibility Without Compromising Your Boundaries

In both your personal and professional life, there will be times when flexibility is necessary. Major life changes—like a new family member, a relocation, or expanding your business—might require you to adjust your boundaries to accommodate shifting priorities. The key to maintaining flexibility without compromising your boundaries is knowing when, how, and why to adjust. Flexibility is a strength, but it's important to ensure it doesn't turn into boundary erosion, where your limits become so blurred they're no longer effective.

Embracing Flexibility with Intention

Flexibility should be intentional and strategic, not reactive. This means making adjustments that serve your long-term well-being, rather than bending to every external pressure or immediate demand. When you choose to adjust a boundary, do it from a place of clarity and control, ensuring that the new boundary still protects your core values and needs.

For example:

- **In a growing business**: You may need to temporarily extend your availability during a product launch or busy season. However, you can still protect your well-being by setting a clear end date for the extended hours and scheduling personal time afterward to recharge.

- **In personal life**: When a loved one is going through a crisis, you may find yourself offering more time and support. It's okay to adjust your boundary in this case, but once the crisis subsides, return to your original boundaries to prevent burnout.

Practical Steps for Maintaining Flexibility

Reassess Before Adjusting: Before making any boundary shifts, reassess your current situation and the long-term impact of the change. Is this adjustment necessary to align with your goals and values? Or is it driven by a temporary pressure? Ensure that any flexibility serves a clear purpose.

Example: Let's say your business is growing and you're getting more requests for after-hours consultations. Rather than letting these requests permanently alter your work-life balance, you could temporarily accommodate a few after-hours sessions but set a rule that after the first 90 days, you'll return to your usual hours.

Set Clear Terms for Flexibility: If you need to adjust a boundary, set specific terms for how long or under what circumstances the adjustment will apply. This ensures the boundary remains intact overall, preventing any long-term erosion.

Example: You could say, "For the next two weeks, I'll be available until 7 p.m. to accommodate the project deadlines, but after that, my workday will end at 5 p.m. as usual."

Communicate Adjustments Clearly: When you decide to be flexible, make sure those affected understand that the change is temporary and clearly outline when the original boundary will be reinstated. This ensures that others don't take advantage of your flexibility or expect it to be the new norm.

Example: If you typically don't respond to work emails after hours, but a big project requires late-night coordination, you might say, "I'll be checking my email after 6 p.m. this week for the project wrap-up, but this will only be temporary. After Friday, I'll return to my regular communication hours."

Balancing Flexibility and Boundaries for Long-Term Success

Flexibility is a tool for navigating life's inevitable changes, but it should always be used with intention and within limits. By staying mindful of why and how you adjust your boundaries, you can maintain a sense of control and prevent the erosion that leads to burnout. Flexibility, when balanced properly, can actually strengthen your boundaries by making them adaptable to changing circumstances without losing their protective power.

The ultimate goal is to ensure that any flexibility serves your well-being and long-term goals, allowing you to thrive both personally and professionally.

Real-World Examples of Boundary Evolution

Boundaries evolve... they grow, change, and adapt as your personal life, business, and circumstances evolve. Refining your boundaries is sometimes necessary to get to where you want to go. In this section, we'll dive into some examples that demonstrate how boundary evolution plays out in the lives of professionals and entrepreneurs—offering actionable insights into how redefined limits can help you thrive.

Example 1: Reestablishing Boundaries After Business Growth

Susan, a marketing consultant, reached a breaking point when her business rapidly expanded, thanks to several high-profile clients. Initially, she accommodated every last-minute request, often working weekends to meet demands. While this built her reputation, the constant availability began to drain her energy and blur her work-life boundaries.

Realizing this approach was unsustainable, Susan redefined her boundaries, limiting her availability to standard business hours and setting a 48-hour response time for non-urgent matters. Although some clients hesitated at first, Susan remained firm, knowing these adjustments were essential for her well-being.

As a result, Susan maintained her client relationships while enhancing her focus and creativity. By aligning her boundaries with her business growth, she struck a balance that allowed her to thrive both professionally and personally.

Example 2: Navigating Unexpected Life Challenges

Jenna, owner of a thriving e-commerce business, was thrown a curveball when she was diagnosed with a chronic illness. Her high-energy, nonstop work routine was no longer sustainable, and she faced the reality that her health had to come first. At first, she struggled with stepping back, feeling torn between her drive to push through and her physical limitations.

Determined to find a balance, Jenna shifted her focus from time management to energy management, reserving mornings for rest and implementing flexible work hours. She began delegating more tasks to her team and set clear communication guidelines so her availability was understood. Initially, she worried about losing control, but soon saw her team rise to the challenge, taking on more ownership.

By prioritizing her well-being, Jenna found that her creativity and strategic focus improved, allowing for sustainable growth. This experience showed her that a business could thrive without sacrificing her health.

Example 3: Refining Boundaries for Professional Growth and New Passions

Tom, a serial entrepreneur, decided to build a consultancy that allowed flexibility for travel, personal projects, and family time. However, old habits crept back in, and he found himself overworking and taking on too many clients, risking the burnout he'd once escaped. Recognizing this, Tom set firmer boundaries: he capped his client load and blocked off time for personal passions, ensuring his work supported his life goals.

He also brought in team members to share responsibilities, allowing for steady business growth without stretching himself thin. This refined approach gave Tom the freedom and fulfillment he'd sought, aligning his business with the balanced life he wanted.

The Key Takeaway: Boundaries and Your Approach Evolve with You

These real-world examples underscore a fundamental truth: neither boundaries, nor our approach to business, have to be static—they evolve alongside you. Whether you're navigating business growth, personal milestones, or unforeseen challenges, your approach and boundaries should be as dynamic as the circumstances of your life. The entrepreneurs and professionals in these stories illustrate that when boundaries are allowed to adapt, they become tools for continued success, helping them thrive professionally while safeguarding their personal well-being.

The key is to regularly reassess, ensuring everything serves your current stage of life. Just as you would adjust a business strategy in response to market shifts, you need to remain flexible, protecting your core values while adapting to the inevitable changes life brings. The ability to fine-tune these boundaries over time is not a sign of compromise but of intentional growth.

These real-world examples demonstrate that evolving and changing as needed is critical for long-term success and personal fulfillment. Whether you're growing a business, adapting to life changes, or realigning your priorities, the key is to regularly revisit and refine your boundaries to stay aligned with both your professional and personal goals. This ongoing adjustment helps ensure that your boundaries continue to support your well-being and productivity, allowing you to thrive in all areas of life.

Work-Life Integration Strategies for Entrepreneurs

Achieving a perfect work-life balance often feels impossible, especially for entrepreneurs constantly facing changing demands. Rather than striving for a rigid separation between work and personal life, a more fluid approach—one that integrates work and life based on current needs and priorities—can be more effective. This mindset shift allows you to manage the ebbs and flows of both worlds, ensuring that neither overwhelms the other while giving you the flexibility to adapt as your circumstances evolve.

Shifting Focus: Integration Over Balance

The traditional idea of work-life balance suggests an equal split between work and personal life. However, for entrepreneurs and professionals, this model often feels unrealistic. Instead of striving for a perfect 50/50 balance, consider adopting the concept of *work-life integration*. The key is to adjust your boundaries in response to what is most important in the moment, without guilt over temporary shifts in focus.

Integration allows for flexibility and adaptation. This mindset shift not only removes the pressure to maintain a rigid balance but also gives you the freedom to navigate dynamic environments without feeling constantly stretched too thin.

Example: Imagine you're preparing for a product launch, which requires long hours and intense focus. During this period, your personal time might take a backseat, and that's okay—if you recognize it as temporary. After the launch, you can shift your focus back to family time, vacations, or personal hobbies, knowing that you gave your business what it needed in its crucial moment without permanently sacrificing your personal life.

This fluid approach to integration ensures that you're always adapting to what matters most at any given time, making it easier to move between business demands and personal needs without burnout.

Strategies for Dynamic Work-Life Integration

One of the most effective ways to manage work-life integration is by establishing flexible boundaries. Unlike rigid lines that divide work and life into strict compartments, flexible boundaries allow you to respond to the ebb and flow of your business and personal life without feeling overwhelmed. This approach acknowledges that sometimes life gets messy, and that's okay—it's about adjusting without guilt and ensuring your well-being remains a priority.

Let's look at an example. Imagine you've just entered a particularly busy season in your business. You're juggling multiple projects, and the demands seem endless. It's easy to let personal commitments slip, but this is where dynamic work-life integration shines. Instead of feeling like you're failing at balance, you can adjust your boundaries to match the moment. You might choose to expand your work hours for a few weeks, but maintain non-negotiable personal time to recharge, like keeping your weekend family hikes or morning meditation. This adaptability ensures that you don't burn out, even when the workload is heavy.

At the heart of this approach are your **core non-negotiables**—those personal commitments that remain sacred, no matter what. These might include family dinners, regular exercise, or simply carving out 30 minutes each day for yourself. For some, it might be about putting the phone down and being fully present with loved ones after 7 p.m., no matter how busy the day has been. These core boundaries act as anchors that ground you, ensuring that even during chaotic periods, you're not sacrificing what matters most to you.

Consider time-blocking as an example. Traditionally, it's seen as a structured tool to maximize productivity, but it doesn't have to be rigid. Time-blocking can actually be fluid and responsive, adapting to different seasons in life. During quieter periods, you might block out extra time for personal projects or leisure, while in busier seasons, the balance shifts—yet there's still room for short personal breaks or wellness activities that keep you energized. It's about intentionally putting what matters most on your calendar to maintain 'top of mind awareness' (TOMA) so that when things get busy, your priorities don't slip.

For example, a busy entrepreneur may set aside afternoons for client meetings while ensuring there's a walk with family or a quiet coffee break on the porch built into the day. Allowing your schedule to flex like this means you're not just chasing balance, you're embracing integration.

Maintaining Long-Term Well-Being Through Integration

Work-life integration is not just about scheduling—it's about nurturing your long-term mental and emotional health. By creating flexible boundaries that shift with your needs, you reduce the stress and guilt that often come with trying to maintain rigid lines between work and personal life. Integration allows you to flow more easily between both worlds, ensuring that you stay grounded even in the busiest seasons.

Take Jason, a tech entrepreneur, as an example. During the early stages of his startup, he found himself struggling to maintain a strict work-life balance. His business demanded long hours, but he also wanted to spend quality time with his family. Instead of forcing a rigid split, Jason adopted a work-life integration strategy. He redefined his boundaries by making his non-negotiables clear—he would always have dinner with his family, but after his kids went to bed, he allowed himself an extra two hours of focused work during intense periods. When business slowed down, he shifted that time back to personal pursuits, making sure he was present for weekend outings and school events.

By adjusting his schedule based on current priorities, Jason found he could still push his business forward without sacrificing his relationships. This flexible approach helped him avoid burnout while ensuring both personal and professional growth.

Work-life integration is a dynamic process. It's about tuning into your current priorities and allowing space for both business growth and personal fulfillment. By adopting flexible boundaries and an adaptable time-blocking approach, like Jason did, you'll find that it's possible to thrive in both areas—without burning out. The key is recognizing that balance doesn't mean equal division; it's about shifting your focus where it's needed most at the time, keeping your well-being intact along the way.

Creating Long-Term Success with Flexible Boundaries

As we've explored throughout this chapter, boundaries are not rigid structures—they are flexible tools that evolve as you do. The key to creating long-term success, both personally and professionally, lies in your ability to adjust and adapt these boundaries to meet the changing demands of your life.

The most successful entrepreneurs and professionals understand that boundaries aren't about achieving a perfect, unchanging balance. Instead, they reflect the fluid nature of life itself. Whether you're experiencing a period of intense business growth, navigating personal challenges, or simply shifting your priorities, the ability to reassess and redefine your boundaries will help you maintain clarity, focus, and well-being.

Take time to revisit your boundaries regularly. Reflect on whether they still align with your values and goals, and don't hesitate to make adjustments as you grow. Your boundaries should serve you—not restrict you. As your business, personal life, and circumstances evolve, your boundaries should evolve with them, ensuring you stay grounded, fulfilled, and capable of thriving in all areas of your life.

The goal isn't perfection—it's sustainability. By allowing your boundaries to be flexible, you create a foundation that supports long-term success, one that honors both your professional ambitions and your personal well-being. Keep revisiting, reflecting, and refining, and you'll find that boundaries are not just a tool for balance but a powerful guide to lasting growth, fulfillment, and peace of mind.

Now is the time to embrace that flexibility, trust in your ability to adapt, and take action to ensure that both your personal life and career thrive—on your terms.

> *"Daring to set boundaries is about having the courage to love ourselves, even when we risk disappointing others." Brene Brown*

Download the Exercises

If you're ready to dive deeper and put these exercises into action, I've got you covered! You can download a complete set of exercises from my website. Head over to to access the workbook designed to guide you through each step.

Remember, taking the time to work through these exercises is a powerful investment in yourself. You'll be able to define your values, set meaningful boundaries, and align your goals more clearly than ever before. Go ahead, download the workbook, and take that crucial step toward creating the balanced, purpose-driven life you deserve. You've got this!

Chapter Nine
Continuous Improvement

Ever feel like the pressure to constantly 'improve' is more draining than empowering? You're not alone. I remember a time in my own business journey when I was caught up in the constant hustle, striving to move forward without ever taking a moment to assess where I was heading. It wasn't until I learned to focus on small, consistent changes that I found not just success but also began to enjoy the process.

In this chapter, we're going to dive into the art of continuous improvement—but not in the way you might think. This isn't about pushing yourself to the brink with never-ending goals. Instead, we'll explore how to make steady, manageable progress while keeping your well-being (what I've often referred to as "sanity") at the forefront. Think of it as finding your rhythm: a pace that allows for growth without burning out.

We'll break down what continuous improvement really means and how it can be integrated into your balanced life. Along the way, we'll explore strategies for setting goals that inspire you rather than overwhelm you, and the power of using feedback—not as criticism but as a tool for growth. We'll also uncover how to stay consistent while adapting to the changes life inevitably throws your way.

By the end of this chapter, you'll have a roadmap for improvement that aligns with your values and supports a lifestyle of ongoing growth—one that's both achievable and deeply rewarding. So, let's get started on this journey toward a life of balanced, continuous progress. Trust me, it's a game-changer.

In the early 1990s, a Japanese car manufacturer, Toyota, found itself competing fiercely with automakers worldwide. Instead of striving to overhaul their entire production system all at once, they embraced the principle of "Kaizen," a Japanese term meaning "continuous improvement." Employees at every level were encouraged to make small, incremental changes to their work processes. No suggestion was too small—everything from adjusting the layout of a workstation to streamlining communication between departments was welcomed. Over time, these small improvements added up, significantly boosting productivity and quality. Today, Toyota is often cited as a prime example of how continuous, steady improvement can lead to world-class success.

The lesson here? Continuous improvement is about taking small, consistent steps that accumulate over time. Just like Toyota, you don't need to overhaul everything at once. By embracing small changes regularly, you can make a huge impact in both your business and personal life.

In this chapter, we're diving into the idea of continuous improvement but with a twist. We'll explore how to grow and enhance your personal and professional life without falling into the trap of perpetual hustle (you know how I hate the Hamster Wheel). Continuous improvement doesn't require you to push yourself to exhaustion. All that's required is for you to make small, steady changes that support your goals and core values.

We'll start by understanding what continuous improvement really means and why it's essential for achieving lasting success. Then, we'll look at advanced strategies for setting manageable, achievable goals and how to use feedback as a powerful tool for growth. You'll learn how to develop an "improvement rhythm" that keeps you moving forward while avoiding burnout.

We'll also introduce interactive tools like goal-setting exercises and journaling prompts to help you identify areas for growth. The chapter will wrap up with techniques for maintaining consistency, handling setbacks, and adapting your approach as needed. By the end, you'll see how balanced, continuous improvement can lead to a more enjoyable life in both business and personal areas. So, let's explore how to make improvement a part of your journey—not just a destination.

Understanding Continuous Improvement

Continuous improvement isn't just a business concept; it's a mindset that revolves around making steady, incremental changes over time. It's about focusing on progress rather than striving for perfection immediately. I'll admit that I push for perfection, but always pushing for perfection can be, and often is, the reason people don't accomplish what they set out to achieve. Try to do all things as good as you can but don't let the search for achievement keep you getting anything finished. I've heard, and often quoted the saying that "Done, is better than perfect!" The search for perfection has stopped many entrepreneurs in their tracks and led to frustration and complete failure. But when you adopt the mindset of Continuous Improvement, success transforms into a journey marked by regular, manageable steps forward.

What makes continuous improvement powerful is its simplicity. By consistently assessing what's working and what could be refined, you give yourself the flexibility to adapt to new challenges and opportunities. It keeps you on track toward your goals while allowing for the natural ebbs and flows of life. This approach applies just as much to your daily routines as it does to your long-term business strategies.

Embracing this mindset can lead to and ongoing sense of accomplishment. It's not a sprint to achieve rapid change; it's about nurturing a lifestyle of learning, refining, and steadily growing. Whether you're tweaking your morning routine or introducing small innovations in your business, each step, however small, brings you closer to the life you envision.

Defining Continuous Improvement

Continuous improvement involves making consistent, small changes that gradually build into something bigger over time. Think of it like planting seeds in a garden—you nurture them with small, regular actions until they grow into something substantial. Unlike relentless striving, which demands immediate, often exhausting effort, continuous improvement focuses on steady progress. It's the difference between sprinting toward a finish line and taking a mindful, manageable pace through a marathon.

What sets continuous improvement apart is its flexibility. Relentless striving frequently leads to burnout because it pushes you to your limits and leaves no room for mistakes. Continuous improvement, however, allows for reflection, adaptation, and growth. It's a more forgiving approach, recognizing that setbacks aren't failures but are actually opportunities to adjust and move forward. For instance, a business owner might start by making small tweaks to daily operations, like adjusting a workflow or changing how meetings are run. Over time, these small adjustments compound into noticeable improvements in efficiency and team morale.

In your personal life, this could mean altering a morning routine bit by bit—introducing a few minutes of meditation, a healthier breakfast, or simply setting a realistic wake-up time. The focus isn't on making everything perfect immediately but on integrating small, meaningful changes that support your long-term well-being. Each small step forward, no matter how minor it seems, contributes to a larger picture of growth.

Gradual Improvement Brings Long-Term Success

As we work toward continuous improvement, let's choose progress over perfection. It's manageable and sustainable, allowing you to embrace growth without the pressure to get everything right on the first try. By committing to these small, thoughtful changes, you build a foundation for lasting success and fulfillment.

Gradual, ongoing improvement is like laying down one small brick at a time to build something solid and enduring. By focusing on incremental changes, you create a path toward long-term success that feels achievable and rewarding. It's not about overhauling your life or business in one grand sweep. Instead, it's the little tweaks you make—day in and day out—that add up to significant progress over time.

The beauty of this approach is that it builds confidence. By setting small, achievable goals, you begin to trust your ability to tackle even bigger challenges. Remember when you learned to ride a bike? You didn't just hop on and race down the block. You started with training wheels, got the hang of balance, and then, piece by piece, built up to full-speed confidence. Continuous improvement is just like that. Each small success brings a sense of accomplishment and fuels your motivation to keep moving forward.

So, *what's one small change you can make today?*

In your personal life, small adjustments can lead to greater fulfillment. For example, carving out ten minutes each day for a walk or a moment of mindfulness can create a ripple effect. Soon, you find yourself feeling more energized and present. The same principle applies to work. Gradual improvements in your daily routines, such as dedicating the first hour of the day to deep-focus tasks, lead to better productivity and reduced stress over time.

Integrating Improvement into a Balanced Life

Integrating improvements into your balanced life means finding ways to enhance what you're already doing, not adding more to an already packed schedule. Just make small, meaningful adjustments that fit naturally into your daily rhythm. Think of it as fine-tuning a guitar string; a slight turn can change the entire sound without needing to replace the instrument itself.

Let me share a quick story. A few years back, I found myself overwhelmed, always on the go, juggling tasks with hardly any downtime. One evening, instead of adding something new to my routine, I simply turned off my phone notifications during dinner. That small change transformed my evenings. Suddenly, dinner wasn't just a meal; it became a peaceful, uninterrupted moment to connect with my family. That small shift had a ripple effect, improving my mood and focus for the rest of the night. It wasn't about doing more but enhancing what was already there. I've taken it to the next step at this point. My phone goes on "Do Not Disturb" at 8:30 in the P.M. every night. Only my kids and wife (who's always with me in the evenings) can get through.

Continuous improvement flows best when it aligns with your current lifestyle. For example, if you've already established a morning routine that works, think about adding a quick gratitude practice or a couple of minutes for deep breathing. Not a major overhaul, just a small step to get your morning off to a better start. Or, if you've set aside time for an afternoon walk, why not take that opportunity to listen to an inspiring podcast or music that energizes you? What we're talking about is integrating little enhancements into the routines that you already do.

Let's be honest—when we hear "self-improvement," we often think it means "adding more." But here's a truth worth embracing; you don't have to do more to get to where you want to be, sometimes you can just make your "right now" work better for you. By focusing on small, thoughtful adjustments, you can make your routines more meaningful without tipping the scales against yourself.

Ask yourself: what could I gain by something as easy as dedicating the first few minutes of your workday to prioritizing tasks rather than jumping straight into emails. I can assure you, that one simple change can make a world of difference. Or perhaps it's turning your evening coffee into a mini-mindfulness practice, savoring each sip instead of rushing through it. These changes don't demand extra time; they only require intention.

By making these manageable adjustments, you invite growth into your life in a way that feels natural and sustainable. Improvement then becomes a source of joy rather than pressure, enriching the balance you've already achieved.

Think of improvement as a tool that works for you, they're to make your routines more effective, your goals more attainable, and your free time more enjoyable. The moment you feel that your efforts toward self-improvement are compromising your peace of mind or well-being take that as a signal to step back and refocus. Pursuing growth should always amplify your sense of ease and accomplishment, not overshadow it. Ultimately, the best improvements are those that seamlessly integrate into your life, leaving you feeling energized, more present, and in harmony with your priorities.

Advanced Strategies for Continuous Improvement: Setting Achievable Goals

Setting achievable goals is essential for continuous improvement. When faced with a large, ambitious vision, it's easy to feel overwhelmed or unsure of where to start. That's why breaking down those big aspirations into smaller, more manageable steps can make all the difference. For instance, if your goal is to launch a new product, you might begin with market research, then move on to product development, and finish with testing. Each step becomes a mini win, boosting your confidence and building momentum as you progress toward the larger goal.

The key here is balance. Achievable doesn't mean it's "easy", it just helps you get it to a place where you can believe it can be done. Your goals should push you just enough to promote growth but not so far that they feel impossible. By setting realistic milestones, you create a roadmap that guides your efforts, transforming the daunting task of reaching a major goal into a series of smaller, more tangible actions. This way, improvement supports your overall well-being instead of adding to your stress.

When you break that goal into smaller targets, it becomes more approachable, and each completed step brings a surge of satisfaction. This forward motion helps you build confidence, making the journey feel rewarding rather than exhausting. By focusing on small, consistent progress, you turn the path of continuous improvement into a source of motivation rather than pressure.

Building on Incremental Growth

Think of this process like building a brick wall. Each small, realistic goal is a single brick. Laying each one carefully, one at a time, eventually creates a solid structure. Incremental goals allow you to experience consistent, bite-sized wins that keep you motivated without the stress of tackling a huge task all at once.

For example, imagine your goal is to write a book. Rather than setting your sights immediately on completing chapters, start smaller. Storyboard your ideas, create a book outline, then create the chapter outlines. Finally, when you get to the right point, decide on how much time you have to spend writing. Maybe it's just 200 words a day, maybe more. Just make sure you plan for what you can accomplish. Unless you're a full-time writer, you probably can't make the decision to write for 8 hours per day. Even if it's just those 200 words per day, they add up, and before long, you've made significant progress—all while maintaining balance and ending up stepping away without making it past the first few pages.

Tracking and Reflection: The Guiding Compass

Getting to where you want to be requires regular tracking and reflection. Ask yourself, "Are these incremental changes positively impacting my well-being and productivity?" Taking a moment to assess your progress helps you adjust your approach as needed. This reflection can reveal whether you're truly benefiting from your efforts or if you need to recalibrate.

I remember implementing this strategy myself. My goals have always been big and early on the big mistake I made was looking at the goal and beginning to run toward it with all my passion. That often left me feeling overwhelmed by my long to-do list, especially since most of those items on my list were huge all by themselves. I started breaking those big goals into smaller tasks and then scheduling the tasks into 15-minute increments, making the steps so small they seemed almost trivial. But day by day, I noticed how much more I was accomplishing. This sense of small, steady progress didn't just lighten my workload; it made me feel more in control and balanced.

By focusing on gradual, realistic steps, you allow improvement to become a natural part of your life. You're not adding more to your plate; you're enhancing what's already there, one small step at a time, and you're seeing daily progress. The journey to improvement really can be made with small, steady, and manageable growth.

So, let's get practical: What's one small change you can make today to bring you closer to your goals? Take a moment to identify a small, incremental step you can take right now. By doing so, you're setting yourself up for success, one brick at a time, building a life and career that aligns with your values and long-term aspirations. The key is to embrace these small changes as part of your everyday routine. Over time, they will compound into something remarkable, helping you achieve not just your goals but a balanced, fulfilling life.

The Role of Feedback

Feedback is an essential part of the continuous improvement journey. Think of it as a mirror, offering a reflection of how your efforts are playing out in reality. Without feedback, it's like driving through a fog—you may be moving forward, but you have no clear sense of direction. The beauty of feedback lies in its ability to act as a guide, helping you refine your strategies and ensure that your progress aligns with your ultimate goals. You can get this feedback from others, like from a Mastermind Group (which we offer), or by creating a feedback loop in any number of ways.

Understanding Feedback Loops

A feedback loop is the ongoing process of collecting information, reflecting on it, and making adjustments. It's a cycle that repeats, ensuring you're not just moving, but moving *purposefully*. This loop can come from different sources: your own observations, input from colleagues, or the outcomes of your actions.

Imagine you're trying to improve your time management skills by implementing time-blocking. At the end of the week, you review how things went. Maybe you notice that your energy dipped every afternoon, making it harder to stay focused during the blocks you scheduled. That's the feedback! By identifying this pattern, you can adjust your routine—perhaps by scheduling breaks or moving high-priority tasks to the morning. This is how a feedback loop works; it's a consistent check-in that helps you fine-tune your approach.

Both Successes and Failures are Learning Opportunities

Learning from both successes and failures is fundamental to continuous improvement. Celebrating victories feels natural, while setbacks often leave us uneasy. However, true growth stems from examining both. Successes illuminate what's working, providing a clear path forward, while failures often contain critical insights that can transform your approach to lasting progress.

Learning from Success

Success is more than a result—it's a source of valuable information. Reflect on the specific actions and strategies that led to that success. For instance, my productivity noticeably increased when I began implementing a morning routine. It wasn't merely about starting the day early; I'd always done that; it was about the sense of structure and clarity that shaped how I approached each task. By pinpointing these elements, you create a blueprint for future success. It's like extracting the "recipe" for what works so you can replicate it in different areas of your life.

Facing Failures Head-On

Failures can be some of our best teachers if we let them. I remember launching a project with full confidence, only to see it underperform. Initially, I was frustrated, but when I dug deeper, I realized the marketing strategy was off, and the target audience wasn't defined clearly. That so-called "failure" turned into a masterclass in refining my approach for future launches. Facing setbacks this way transforms them into opportunities rather than obstacles. It's about adopting a mindset where each failure is a "data point" guiding you toward a better strategy.

Creating Your Feedback Loop

Both successes and failures fuel your personal feedback loop. To maximize this, establish a regular reflection practice. I've made a habit of a Sunday evening check-in where I ask myself, "What went well this week? What didn't go well? And, why?" This simple exercise has had a profound impact. For example, I once noticed a pattern of feeling overwhelmed mid-week. By reflecting, I realized I was prioritizing too many low-impact tasks. The following week, I shifted focus to high-impact activities, and my productivity surged. This practice isn't just about looking back; it's about using insights to refine your actions moving forward.

Maintaining Motivation Through Reflection

Acknowledging your wins is crucial. Even small victories serve as fuel for your motivation, reinforcing the idea that you're on the right path. On the other hand, reframing failures as lessons changes their impact. A mentor once told me, "Failure is feedback; it's a compass pointing you in the right direction." This shift in perspective transforms obstacles into steppingstones. They become part of the journey, not the end.

So, here's your call to action: Create your feedback loop. Set a specific time each week to reflect on both your successes and setbacks. How can you build on what worked? Where do you need to pivot? Ask yourself, "What did I learn this week that can shape next week?" This process helps you make steady, thoughtful improvements which will help align your goals and values. Every reflection is a step toward your long-term vision, so embrace the journey of learning and growth.

By viewing feedback as a continual loop, you empower yourself to refine, adapt, and grow, creating a sustainable approach to improvement. This not only keeps you on track with your goals but also ensures that your journey is one of learning, growth, and evolution.

Incorporating Time to Recharge into Your Rhythm

Let's consider a real-world example: imagine an entrepreneur who neglected her personal well-being in pursuit of business growth. She constantly rushed from task to task, feeling overwhelmed and on the verge of burnout. She decided to incorporate small, daily habits—like taking a few minutes to breathe between meetings, setting boundaries around work hours, and allowing herself slow mornings. Over time, these small changes created a rhythm that allowed her to maintain energy, make clearer decisions, and ultimately achieve greater business success.

Caring for your well-being is not a one-time fix; it's an ongoing practice that must be woven into your daily rhythm. By incorporating these strategies, you're not just maintaining your health—you're actively supporting the slow and steady growth you're aiming for. It's easy to dismiss personal well-being as something you'll get to "when you have time," but the truth is, it's what creates the time, energy, and mental clarity you need to stay consistent.

Moving Forward

In the next section, we'll address one of the biggest threats to maintaining your rhythm: distractions. You'll learn how to identify and eliminate these time-stealers, making room for the well-being practices and focused work that genuinely drive success. But before we dive in, here's a quick action step: jot down one well-being practice you can integrate into your daily rhythm starting today. How will you make it a consistent part of your routine?

Success Stories

Let's revisit some earlier entrepreneurs and how they handled these issues.

Sarah, the Marketing Consultant Who Reclaimed Her Time

Sarah was a successful marketing consultant with a rapidly growing client base. For years, she operated under the belief that more work meant more success. This mindset led her to work 12-hour days, skip meals, and sacrifice weekends. Eventually, she hit a wall. The quality of her work declined, and she found herself too burnt out to think creatively.

Recognizing the unsustainable nature of her hustle, Sarah made a bold decision: she started to prioritize balance. She began by setting firm work hours—ending her workday at 5 p.m. and protecting her weekends. She introduced small daily practices into her routine, starting with a 10-minute morning mindfulness session to set a positive tone for the day. She also took regular breaks every hour to stretch and breathe.

By establishing these boundaries and micro-moments of rest, Sarah found she could maintain her energy levels throughout the day. Not only did her productivity and creativity improve, but she also felt more present in her personal life. As she focused on quality over quantity, her clients noticed a positive shift in her work, leading to more referrals. By prioritizing balance, Sarah grew her business steadily without sacrificing her well-being.

James, the Startup Founder Who Learned to Say No

James was the founder of a tech startup that had taken off faster than he had anticipated. Like many new entrepreneurs, he believed that every opportunity was worth pursuing, leading him to say yes to every meeting, project, and partnership that came his way. His calendar became packed with endless commitments, leaving him exhausted and overwhelmed.

After a particularly grueling week, James realized he was spending more time managing distractions than focusing on what truly mattered. He decided to take a different approach, starting with a morning routine that included exercise, a nutritious breakfast, and a moment of quiet reflection to identify his top priorities for the day.

Next, he embraced the concept of setting boundaries by implementing "focus blocks" in his schedule—periods during which he would turn off notifications, close his email, and dedicate time to deep, meaningful work. He also learned to say no to requests that didn't align with his business goals, recognizing that saying no was actually a way to protect his energy and focus.

Over time, James noticed a profound shift. By managing distractions and prioritizing his energy, he was able to concentrate on fewer projects with higher impact. His startup grew sustainably, and he experienced a renewed sense of control over his time, allowing him to enjoy both his work and personal life more fully.

Maria, the Boutique Owner Who Stopped Chasing Perfection

Maria owned a thriving boutique, but she constantly felt like she was running on a treadmill. She believed that success meant being available to her customers at all times, obsessing over every minor detail, and filling every free moment with work. Despite her dedication, she found herself increasingly stressed and unhappy, wondering if her hard work was even worth it.

After a particularly stressful holiday season, Maria decided she needed a change. She started small, reserving her mornings for activities that recharged her, such as yoga, a leisurely breakfast, and a few minutes of journaling. She also stopped striving for perfection in every aspect of her business, instead adopting a "good enough" mindset for less critical tasks.

To further prioritize balance, Maria began delegating more responsibilities to her team, recognizing that she didn't need to do everything herself. She also limited her store hours to ensure she had evenings free for family and relaxation. As she shifted her mindset and made these changes, Maria discovered that her boutique thrived even more. Customers appreciated the curated experience and positive energy she brought to her work, resulting in increased sales and loyalty. By letting go of the hustle mentality, Maria not only found fulfillment but also saw her business grow steadily in a way that aligned with her values.

Raj, the Consultant Who Adopted the "Less Is More" Approach

Raj was a management consultant known for his meticulous work ethic. He was always the first one in the office and the last to leave, convinced that the only path to success was to outwork everyone else. However, this relentless approach began to take a toll on his health and personal life, leading to frequent illness and feelings of burnout.

After a health scare, Raj decided to reassess his approach. He adopted a "less is more" mentality, focusing on building a sustainable rhythm. His first step was to integrate regular practices for well-being: he started taking short midday walks, eating nutritious meals, and carving out time for hobbies he enjoyed. He also began to set weekly goals that were challenging yet achievable, allowing him to track his progress, and avoid overwhelming himself.

Raj then tackled distractions by implementing a "power hour" each morning, where he would work on his most important tasks without interruption. He also practiced saying no to clients that demanded unreasonable timelines, understanding that maintaining balance was key to delivering quality work.

The result was transformative. By prioritizing his well-being and reducing distractions, Raj found he was more focused and productive. His work quality improved, leading to higher client satisfaction and repeat business. More importantly, he felt a renewed sense of joy in both his professional and personal life. His career continued to grow steadily, proving that prioritizing balance was not just beneficial but essential for long-term success.

Lessons Learned: How You Can Apply These Strategies to Your Life

While everyone's path to balance is unique, the experiences of others can offer valuable insights and shortcuts. By learning from Sarah, James, Maria, and Raj, you can take their lessons and weave them into your own journey toward growth and fulfillment.

1. Establish Boundaries and Protect Your Time

One of the most significant takeaways from Sarah and James's stories is the importance of setting clear boundaries around your time. Sarah learned to protect her evenings and weekends, while James set "focus blocks" and practiced saying no to tasks that didn't align with his priorities. These boundaries were their way of reclaiming control over their schedules and, in turn, their energy.

How You Can Apply This: Reflect on your current work boundaries—or the lack thereof. Are you allowing work to spill over into all hours of your day, and night? Identify one area where you can set a boundary, such as establishing a firm end to your workday or designating certain days as "off-limits" for meetings. Protecting your time in this way can help you find a more sustainable work rhythm and create space for rest and personal well-being.

Reflective Prompt: What one area of your life can you set a boundary around this week?

2. Make Recharging Non-Negotiable

Each of these individuals made their well-being a priority, recognizing it as the foundation for their ability to maintain steady improvement. For Sarah, it was a daily mindfulness practice. For Maria, it was reclaiming her mornings. Raj focused on taking short breaks and making time for hobbies he enjoyed. This shift in mindset—from seeing well-being practices as a luxury to viewing them as a necessary part of their routine—allowed them to maintain their energy and stay focused.

How You Can Apply This: Try incorporating one small habit into your daily routine that helps you recharge. This could be a five-minute mindfulness break, a morning stretching session, or even a short walk outside. Remember, you don't need to find hours of free time; even five minutes can make a significant impact over time. The key is to make this habit a non-negotiable part of your rhythm rather than something you squeeze in "if there's time."

Reflective Prompt: What small habit can you introduce into your daily routine to recharge, and how will you ensure it becomes a consistent part of your day?

3. Embrace Flexibility and Adaptation

James and Maria's experiences teach us that flexibility is crucial in finding your rhythm. When James began using focus blocks, he had to adapt his work to fit within these time constraints, which sometimes meant saying no to opportunities. Maria shifted from striving for perfection to embracing a "good enough" mindset, allowing her to delegate tasks and free up time.

How You Can Apply This: Experiment with introducing flexibility into your routines. Re-evaluate your current goals and identify where you might be overly rigid. Is there room to simplify or delegate specific tasks? By adopting a more adaptable approach, you can adjust to life's ebbs and flows without losing momentum.

Reflective Prompt: Where can you introduce flexibility in your work routine this week? What tasks can you delegate or simplify?

4. Use Setbacks as Learning Opportunities

Raj's journey highlights the importance of viewing setbacks as opportunities for growth. He faced burnout but used it as a wake-up call to reassess his priorities and adopt the "less is more" mentality. He learned to incorporate habits that restored his energy, not just as a recovery tool but as an ongoing strategy to prevent future burnout.

How You Can Apply This: When you encounter setbacks—whether it's feeling overwhelmed or missing a goal—pause to reflect on what the experience is teaching you. Try to reframe setbacks as valuable feedback, asking yourself: "What can I change in my approach to maintain a healthier rhythm moving forward?" By treating setbacks as learning moments, you build resilience and move forward with greater clarity and intention.

Reflective Prompt: The next time you face a setback, ask yourself: What is this teaching me about my current rhythm, and how can I adjust moving forward?

5. Celebrate Small Wins and Progress

A common thread in these stories is the emphasis on acknowledging small victories. Maria learned to celebrate moments of progress, even when things weren't perfect. This practice of recognizing small wins fueled their motivation and provided positive reinforcement to continue their balanced approach.

How You Can Apply This: Start a daily or weekly practice of reflecting on your achievements, no matter how small. Did you take your scheduled breaks today? Complete a key task during your focus block? These moments are worth celebrating! Acknowledging your progress keeps you motivated and reinforces the value of prioritizing balance over constant hustle.

Reflective Prompt: What small win can you celebrate today that reflects your commitment to a balanced, steady rhythm?

Your Next Steps: A Call to Action

Now, it's time to begin your own journey of balanced improvement. Start by systematically addressing the concepts we've discussed here. Take a close look at your current routines and strategies and identify areas for refinement. Remember, this is an ongoing process that evolves as you grow.

For some reflection questions go to: www.RogerGBest.com/workbooks

Moving Forward with Intention

Every small step will bring you closer to a more balanced. Consistently assessing and adjusting your strategies, will help you find joy and satisfaction in the process of growth itself. The power to change your path lies in the choices you make each day. Your journey starts now.

Chapter Ten

Sustaining Freedom

Long-Term Strategies for a Fulfilling Life

You've worked hard to achieve the freedom you've always dreamed of—whether it's personal, financial, or professional—but staying free is an entirely different challenge. What if your freedom wasn't just a fleeting victory but a permanent part of your life, something you could nurture and sustain every day?

Many people think that once they've "made it," they can relax, but the truth is, maintaining freedom requires the same dedication, balance, and intention that got you there in the first place—maybe even more. The good news is that this effort doesn't have to be overwhelming. By making small, intentional adjustments and learning how to maintain a steady rhythm, you can ensure that your freedom continues to grow and make life better.

In this chapter, we'll explore what it means to sustain freedom in a way that brings you long-term fulfillment. You've already broken free from the hamster wheel and started to redefine what success means to you. Now, it's about protecting that freedom and building a life where growth doesn't come at the expense of your well-being. We'll focus on balancing consistency with adaptability, learning how to adjust your goals as you grow, and ensuring that your actions align with your evolving vision of "The Good Life".

You'll also learn how to keep distractions in check and create a personal rhythm that supports both your work and personal time. We'll explore strategies to nurture your physical and mental well-being, maintain strong relationships, and continue pursuing your passions—all while staying connected to what truly matters to you.

By the end of this chapter, you'll have the tools to not just protect what you've built but to thrive, finding fulfillment and balance in both your work and personal life. True freedom isn't about coasting after you've achieved success—it's about feeling present, empowered, and excited for the future you're creating every day.

Let's dive in and discover how you can sustain freedom for the long haul, while living a life that feels deeply fulfilling, balanced, and truly yours.

> "Freedom is not the absence of commitments, but the ability to choose—and commit myself to—what is best for me."
> – Paulo Coelho

Rediscovering Freedom: The Power of Letting Go AGAIN

I've been running businesses for as long as I can remember—literally. I started my first business as a child and continued that path throughout my adulthood. In the early days, I knew all too well what the hamster wheel felt like. I was constantly pushing, hustling, and working hard without feeling like I was moving forward in a meaningful way. But over time, through trial and error, I began to find my rhythm. I made plenty of mistakes along the way, but I learned from them, gradually gaining more and more freedom.

A few years ago, that journey culminated in our decision to move to Puerto Rico. The freedom I felt was exhilarating. The businesses were growing, things were running smoothly, and I had the space to enjoy life in ways I hadn't before. I explored the island, entertained friends, and really embraced the life I'd worked so hard to create.

But as life does, it started creeping back in. Business concerns began slipping into the moments of freedom I thought I had secured. Even though I still had the flexibility to enjoy life, I found myself increasingly worried about whether things were getting done and whether they were being done the way I wanted. That worry started to weigh on me. I began focusing on who was or wasn't meeting my expectations, and before I knew it, the stress I thought I had left behind was creeping back into my life.

I realized I was falling back into old habits—the instinct to take control, to get more involved. But deep down, I knew that wasn't in line with my goals or the freedom I had worked so hard to achieve. It hit me hard: if I didn't do something, I could lose ground in what I had gained.

So, I took a step back and revisited everything I had learned through my experiences—and everything I've shared in this book. Instead of taking over, I leaned into delegation. I began focusing on what my team was doing well and encouraged them to keep going. Most importantly, I shifted my mindset back to gratitude, letting it shape my outlook instead of the stress.

It didn't take long before I found my rhythm again. That experience reminded me that sustaining freedom requires just as much intention as achieving it. It's about consistently making the right adjustments and remembering that freedom is something you nurture, day by day.

You've achieved the freedom you've been working toward—but how do you protect it over the long haul? In this chapter, we'll explore the key strategies needed to sustain your freedom and maintain balance in both your work and personal life. From managing distractions and nurturing your well-being to staying adaptable in a changing world, you'll discover how to keep your freedom intact. You'll also learn how a growth mindset and strong relationships can support you in continuing to thrive, without slipping back into old habits. By the end of this chapter, you'll have the tools to not only preserve your freedom but to truly enjoy the long-term fulfillment it offers.

Understanding Sustained Freedom

Sustained freedom starts once you've reached the point where you not only have some live the "good days", or you reach a point where you can take a break without worry. But, if you get there and let it slip away, you really haven't gained much. When it really makes a difference is when you've built a life where you regularly feel in control of your time, energy, and decisions, both personally and professionally. It's the kind of freedom that endures, not just something that comes and goes based on circumstances.

In your personal life, sustained freedom means having the space to pursue what you love, nurture meaningful relationships, and spend time on what aligns with your values. It's the ability to live on your terms, free from the constant pull of "doing more" or "being more." Instead, you can focus on what truly matters—whether it's your family, health, hobbies, or personal growth—without the overwhelming pressure to keep up with everything.

In your professional life, sustained freedom means running your business or career with clarity and intention. It's about putting systems in place that allow you to delegate and trust others, freeing you to focus on the bigger picture rather than getting caught up in the daily grind. It's about knowing your work is aligned with your long-term goals, not just a series of tasks that keep you busy.

From Achieving to Sustaining Freedom: Building a Life of Lasting Control

Achieving freedom is a pivotal first step in escaping the hamster wheel—a breakthrough that brings control over your time, energy, and choices. This moment often comes with a powerful sense of relief, a feeling of finally stepping off the relentless grind. However, true freedom requires more than this initial breakthrough; it demands ongoing commitment and conscious choices that withstand life's challenges.

Sustained freedom isn't a fleeting break from the grind but a stable reality where you feel consistently in control, both personally and professionally. In your personal life, this freedom means creating space for relationships, passions, and self-care, allowing you to invest in what aligns with your values without feeling stretched too thin. In your professional world, sustained freedom moves beyond simply avoiding burnout—it's about delegating effectively, trusting your team, and focusing on meaningful goals rather than endless tasks.

But maintaining freedom requires continual attention. Without mindful practices, the initial sense of control can quickly fade as old patterns and new demands threaten to pull you back into the grind. Sustained freedom is about protecting your time, energy, and mental space, making conscious choices daily to live in alignment with what matters most.

This kind of freedom is not just an achievement; it's a lifestyle that aligns with your deepest values, allowing you to pursue both personal satisfaction and professional fulfillment over the long term. Remember, stay off the Hamster Wheel!

Moving Forward

Sustained freedom requires the same intention that it took to achieve it. It's not something that happens by accident; it's something you must nurture daily. In the next sections, we'll explore how to balance consistency with adaptability, manage distractions, and protect your mental and physical well-being. By applying these strategies, you'll ensure that the freedom you've gained continues to grow and bring you lasting fulfillment.

The key isn't just to hold onto freedom but to keep it thriving, even as life changes around you.

The Role of Balance in Sustained Freedom

Balance is the cornerstone of sustained freedom. It's not enough to achieve success in just one area of life—whether that's work, health, or relationships. True freedom comes from harmonizing these key aspects, ensuring that no single area dominates at the expense of the others. Without balance, even the freedom you've worked hard to achieve can slip away, replaced by stress, overwhelm, or burnout.

In your professional life, balance means setting boundaries and knowing when to step away. It's about delegating effectively so that your work doesn't consume every waking hour. While your career or business is important, sustaining freedom requires that you make time for the other parts of your life that enrich your well-being. This could be as simple as carving out time for personal interests, spending evenings with family, going for a hike, or setting aside weekends for rest and rejuvenation.

When it comes to health, balance dictates that you take care of both your body and mind. You can't maintain freedom if you're running on empty—both physically and mentally. Regular exercise, proper sleep, and stress management aren't luxuries; they're necessities for sustaining energy, focus, and clarity over the long haul. When your health is neglected, your ability to fully enjoy your freedom diminishes.

In relationships, balance means being present for those who matter most. It's easy to get caught up in professional obligations or personal goals and forget about nurturing the people around you. Sustained freedom allows you the flexibility to prioritize relationships without sacrificing progress in other areas. When relationships are healthy and supportive, they provide a solid foundation that enhances your overall well-being, helping you stay grounded and connected.

Avoiding Burnout Through Balanced Growth

Achieving balance isn't just a nice-to-have—it's essential for avoiding burnout. When one area of life starts to dominate—whether it's work, health, or relationships—you may begin to feel overwhelmed, stressed, or even guilty as other parts of your life start to suffer.

This imbalance can make the freedom you've worked so hard to achieve feel more like a burden than a gift.

Balanced growth means progressing at a sustainable pace, where work, health, and relationships can all thrive. You might need to adjust your work schedule to carve out time for a hobby you've neglected, or create manageable fitness goals that fit into your daily routine. By regularly checking in with yourself and making small adjustments as needed, you can maintain the equilibrium that supports long-term well-being. This balance is key to ensuring that the freedom you've earned continues to enrich your life, not just in the short term but for years to come.

Reflection Prompt: Take a moment to reflect on your life right now. Is there an area—work, health, or relationships—that could use more attention to restore balance? What small changes can you make today to support sustained freedom across all aspects of your life?

Maintaining a Growth Mindset: Resilience and Adaptability

Life is unpredictable; no matter how well you prepare, challenges and setbacks will inevitably arise. Building resilience helps you navigate life's ups and downs while staying focused on your long-term goals. Resilience is about developing the inner strength to keep going and growing, even when circumstances shift unexpectedly. It's not simply about enduring tough times but about learning and adapting through them.

Building Resilience for Long-Term Success

Resilience involves responding to challenges in a way that fosters growth, not frustration. When approached with the right mindset, each setback becomes a steppingstone. For example, imagine an entrepreneur who encounters an unexpected market shift. Instead of viewing the situation as a failure, they see it as an opportunity to innovate, pivot, and find a new strategy. Their ability to adapt in the face of adversity turns the challenge into an advantage.

Resilience helps you lean into difficulties with confidence, knowing you have the strength to adapt and the mindset to see obstacles as opportunities for progress. This approach allows you to keep moving forward, even when life doesn't go according to plan.

Embracing Flexibility Without Losing Focus

Flexibility is essential in maintaining a growth mindset, but it doesn't mean you should lose sight of your goals. Being flexible allows you to adjust your approach without sacrificing your vision. When life takes unexpected turns, the ability to adapt helps you stay grounded and continue moving forward, even if the path changes.

One way to maintain flexibility without losing focus is to manage distractions effectively. By creating routines that allow for adaptability—like setting time blocks for focused work while also building in space for breaks—you create a structured environment that fosters both flexibility and productivity. This helps you stay focused on your long-term goals while remaining open to necessary adjustments along the way.

Managing Distractions for Sustainable Growth

Managing distractions is key to staying adaptable and focused in the long term. Whether it's constant notifications, social media, or interruptions, distractions can easily throw you off course. However, by putting systems in place—such as a daily distraction audit or setting clear boundaries—you protect your focus while allowing room for flexibility when life demands it.

The goal isn't to eliminate every distraction but to create a rhythm that balances structure and adaptability. When distractions are managed effectively, you maintain the mental space needed to embrace change without losing momentum.

Moving Forward with Resilience and Adaptability

Resilience and adaptability are essential in maintaining a growth mindset. Together, they help you navigate challenges, stay flexible, and keep growing, no matter what life throws your way. By building resilience, you gain the strength to move through tough times, and by embracing flexibility, you stay open to new opportunities and changes. This combination helps you stay on course for long-term success.

Reflection Prompt: Think about a recent challenge you faced. How did you handle it? What strategies could you use to build more resilience and adaptability in similar situations?

As life evolves, so do our priorities, and with that comes the need to adapt our goals to align with personal growth and life changes. Imagine an entrepreneur who set out with a bold goal: to scale their business rapidly over five years. In the beginning, the excitement of pursuing expansion fueled their long hours and relentless work ethic. But over time, the demands of constant growth began to take a toll. The long hours started to edge out time for family, personal interests, and even personal well-being. What once felt exhilarating became exhausting. Recognizing this, they decided to adjust their goals. Instead of focusing on aggressive expansion, they shifted toward a more sustainable, steady growth strategy—one that allowed them to regain balance. While it initially felt like stepping back, the reality was that this change opened up a path to personal fulfillment without sacrificing professional success.

Now consider the story of a professional who had always believed that working 60-hour weeks was the only way to advance their business. For years, they pushed themselves to the limit, equating more hours with more success. But after a bout of burnout, they began to see things differently. They realized that maintaining their well-being was just as important as advancing their business. So, they made a shift. They reduced their hours, set boundaries, and focused on working smarter, not harder. The result? Not only did their productivity improve, but they also found joy again—in both their career and personal life. The relief of finding balance was undeniable.

Family life also brings shifts in priorities. A business owner who once dreamed of opening multiple locations across the country suddenly found their goals changing after starting a family. What once felt like an exciting challenge now seemed overwhelming when it meant less time with their loved ones. So, they adapted. Instead of expanding, they focused on building a stronger, more profitable single location. This change allowed them to remain engaged in their business while being more present at home. They realized that success didn't have to mean constant expansion—it could also mean depth and quality in both work and family life.

Financial goals often undergo changes as well. Take the individual who set a clear-cut goal to retire by 45 with significant wealth. The pursuit of this goal led them to make sacrifices—long hours, missed experiences, and a constant focus on accumulating wealth. But as time passed, they realized that financial success didn't have to come at the cost of present happiness. They adjusted their goals, focusing on a balance between saving for the future and enjoying the present. By prioritizing meaningful experiences and relationships, they created a life that felt richer—both financially and emotionally.

Even leadership goals evolve with personal growth. A manager, once laser-focused on climbing the corporate ladder, realized that their true passion was in mentoring others. Instead of solely pursuing personal advancement, they began investing in their team's growth. They adapted their goals to focus less on individual success and more on fostering a thriving, collaborative environment. This shift in priorities not only enhanced their leadership skills but also brought them a deeper sense of fulfillment.

These stories remind us that goals aren't meant to be rigid. As we grow and change, so do the things we value most. Adapting your goals isn't a sign of giving up; it's a reflection of growth, wisdom, and the courage to align your life with what truly matters. When you allow your goals to evolve with you, you create a path that is not only successful but deeply fulfilling.

Financial Independence and Management: Achieving and Maintaining Financial Freedom

Financial freedom is far more than simply covering your expenses—it's reaching a place where money no longer dictates your decisions. When you reach financial independence, you gain the flexibility to prioritize what matters most to you, whether that's spending time with family, pursuing a passion, or scaling back on work to focus on personal growth. Achieving financial freedom is an important milestone, but maintaining it requires continuous effort and careful planning.

The foundation of financial freedom lies in understanding and managing your money effectively. This means having a clear grasp of your income, expenses, savings, and long-term goals. It's less about how much you earn and more about how you manage what you have. By creating a budget, tracking your spending, and setting clear financial objectives, you put yourself in control, ensuring financial stability for the long term.

Basics of Financial Planning and Management

Very few people like to address this topic, and those are the people who seldom get ahead of the financial hamster wheel; yes, there's one of those, too. Enough said about that but keep it in mind as we move forward. So, at the heart of financial management is clarity—knowing exactly where your money is going each month. Start by breaking down your expenses into categories: essentials like housing and food, discretionary spending like entertainment, and future investments such as savings or retirement funds. Taking control of your cash flow gives you the power to make intentional decisions about where your money goes rather than feeling like it's slipping through your fingers.

Please don't think of budgeting as limiting your life—it simply gives you the freedom to prioritize what's truly important. By setting aside a portion of your income for savings, investments, and an emergency fund, you build a safety net that allows you to focus on your bigger goals without financial stress weighing you down.

Investments and Saving Strategies

Once you've established a solid financial foundation, it's time to think about the future. Investments and saving strategies are key to growing your wealth over time. Investments, whether in stocks, bonds, mutual funds, or real estate, allow your money to work for you. By choosing investments that align with your long-term financial goals, you can build wealth steadily.

A diversified portfolio is one of the most effective ways to minimize risk while maximizing potential returns. Spreading your investments across different asset classes protects you from major losses if one area underperforms. If you're new to investing, start small and expand as your understanding grows.

Consistent saving is crucial in addition to investments. Whether through a traditional savings account, a retirement fund, or other long-term savings vehicles, regularly setting aside a portion of your income builds security. Compound interest can turn even modest savings into significant amounts over time, reinforcing the importance of starting early and staying consistent.

> *"My wealth has come from a combination of living in America, some lucky genes, and compound interest." Warren Buffett*

Passive Income Sources

Another strategy for achieving financial freedom is building passive income streams—sources of revenue that require little to no effort after the initial setup. Examples include rental properties, dividend-paying stocks, royalties from creative work, or even online ventures like affiliate marketing. The advantage of passive income is that it frees you from the constant need to exchange time for money.

For instance, owning rental properties can generate consistent income while the property appreciates in value. Dividend stocks allow you to benefit from a company's growth without selling your shares. By cultivating multiple passive income streams, you reduce your reliance on any one source of income, creating greater financial security and flexibility.

Achieving Long-Term Financial Freedom

Maintaining financial freedom is an ongoing process that requires focus and discipline. Start with a clear financial plan that reflects your long-term goals and be intentional about saving and investing. Explore passive income opportunities that align with your skills and interests, giving yourself even more flexibility and financial stability.

Each step you take—whether it's setting a budget, investing in the stock market, or establishing a passive income stream—brings you closer to true financial independence. It's not about how much you make; it's about how effectively you manage your money and build toward a future where you have the freedom to live on your terms.

Reflection Prompt: Consider your current financial habits. Are they aligned with your long-term goals for financial independence?

Living Below Your Means: The Importance of a Sustainable Lifestyle.

I know, I'm meddling again but this is worth covering, take it or leave it. Financial freedom can be addressed by more than just earning more. It's often just as easy to make some intentional decisions with what you already have. Living below your means allows you to build a life where money becomes a tool for achieving your long-term goals rather than a source of stress. Imagine someone who, after years of upgrading their lifestyle with every additional dollar that comes in—buying a bigger home, a nicer car, more gadgets—realizes they are still living paycheck to paycheck. It's not until they shift their focus to saving and investing that they finally feel a sense of financial control. Living below their means didn't feel like a sacrifice; instead, it gave them peace of mind and the freedom to make decisions based on what truly mattered.

By adopting this mindset, you can create a buffer that helps you prepare for the unexpected, invest in future opportunities, and reduce financial anxiety. Living below your means empowers you to build a sustainable lifestyle where financial security isn't based on how much you earn, but on how wisely you manage your resources.

Tips for Minimizing Expenses and Maximizing Savings

1. **Track Your Spending:** Understanding where your money goes is the first step toward financial control. It's often surprising to see how small expenses can add up over time. By tracking every dollar, you can identify unnecessary purchases and shift that money toward savings or investments that help secure your future. Most bank accounts and credit cards allow you to automatically associate charges to the appropriate account for tracking purposes. Even those that don't automatically hit the correct account can easily be manually set in a matter of seconds.

2. **Automate Savings:** One of the easiest ways to build wealth is by automating your savings. Set up automatic transfers from your checking account to your savings or investment accounts so that saving becomes effortless. You'll be growing your financial safety net without even thinking about it. There's a LOT less resistance to investing when you never see the money than it is to manually transfer it.

3. **Avoid Lifestyle Creep:** As your income grows, it's tempting to upgrade your lifestyle—bigger house, better car, more luxuries. But resisting the urge to inflate your lifestyle is crucial for financial independence. Instead of increasing your spending with every raise, commit to saving more. This way, you can build wealth while keeping your expenses steady. For instance, my wife and I have a car that we bought new when we moved to Puerto Rico. While I don't have to borrow money for things like cars, I typically do. While I like to keep cash reserves for investment opportunities, I also don't like to pay a lot of money in interest so I never take a loan out for more than three years on things like cars. We recently paid off the car we bought when we moved to Puerto Rico, so my wife suggested that we buy another car. I don't honestly have a big issue with that but the one we bought only has 16,000 miles on it (it's a small island) and a

TON of warranty left. The only money we've spent on it is oil changes. I told here that another car was unnecessary. She didn't have an issue with that but she had the same thought that a lot of others do when things change.

4. **Embrace a Minimalist Mindset:** Shifting your focus from accumulating things to investing in experiences or long-term goals can help reduce impulse purchases. By adopting a "less is more" mentality, you'll find that you spend less on material goods and more on what truly adds value to your life. Again, in our lives, we travel a lot and love to see new, exotic places. We could have another car in the garage that is seldom driven, or we could do something that will change our worldview forever. We choose the ladder.

5. **Negotiate Expenses:** From utility bills to insurance, many costs are negotiable. Don't hesitate to shop around for better deals or contact service providers directly to ask for lower rates. Small reductions in these recurring expenses can add up significantly over time. Again, back to the car; I could have easily take a loan from the dealership, but contacting a banker that I know, always saves me money.

6. **Use the 50/30/20 Rule:** Follow a simple framework to ensure balanced spending: allocate 50% of your income to needs, 30% to wants, and 20% to savings and investments. This rule helps you prioritize your financial future while still enjoying life today.

A Sustainable Lifestyle for Financial Freedom

Living below your means doesn't mean deprivation is the norm—it's just about making intentional choices that align with your long-term goals. By minimizing unnecessary expenses and maximizing your savings, you build a lifestyle that offers not only financial security but also peace of mind. This approach creates flexibility, allowing you to pursue opportunities, handle life's unexpected events, and focus on what truly matters.

By living sustainably, you ensure that your money works for you, helping you create a future where financial freedom isn't just a goal—it's your reality.

Nurturing Physical and Mental Well-Being

Achieving financial freedom and professional success is rewarding, but without good physical and mental health, it's difficult to fully enjoy that freedom. Your body and mind are the foundation of everything you do, and taking care of them is essential for long-term success and fulfillment. Nurturing your well-being isn't a luxury—it's a necessity that allows you to thrive in all aspects of your life.

Physical Health: The Foundation for a Balanced Life

Your physical health is the foundation for a life filled with energy and vitality. Regular exercise, balanced nutrition, and adequate sleep aren't just healthy habits; they directly impact how well you function, both personally and professionally. Take, for instance, someone who struggled with feeling drained due to poor sleep and a sedentary lifestyle. By committing to daily walks and prioritizing rest, they quickly noticed improved energy, reduced stress, and greater productivity. Simple changes like these can lead to transformative results, enabling you to easily manage life's demands.

Mental Health: Equally Important for Long-Term Success

Just as physical health is vital, your mind needs attention to handle life's demands. Without tending to your mental well-being, stress and overwhelm can quickly build. Managing stress, taking breaks, and nurturing supportive relationships are key to building mental resilience. Consider someone who pushes themselves at work without taking breaks or prioritizing their mental health. Eventually, burnout sets in. By integrating mindfulness and regular pauses into their day, they regain mental clarity and reconnect with their sense of balance, improving both their productivity and overall happiness.

Managing Stress: Stress is inevitable, but how you handle it makes all the difference. Practices like mindfulness, meditation, a gratitude journal, and deep breathing exercises can help lower stress levels and clear your mind. Whether it's taking a few minutes to breathe deeply or spending quiet time reflecting, these habits give you the mental space to recharge and refocus.

Prioritizing Your Health for Lasting Freedom

Caring for your physical and mental well-being allows you to fully experience the life you've worked so hard to create. By prioritizing exercise, a balanced diet, restful sleep, and routine health check-ups, you're setting yourself up for long-term vitality. At the same time, nurturing your mental health through stress management, mental breaks, and strong relationships ensures you can handle life's challenges with clarity and strength.

Take a moment to reflect on your current habits. Are you making time for regular exercise, eating well, and getting enough sleep? Are you taking care of your mental health by managing stress and staying connected with supportive people? Commit to making small changes today that will have a lasting impact on your well-being tomorrow.

Nurturing Relationships: Importance of Nurturing Personal and Professional Relationships

Success in both business and life is rarely a solo journey. Our relationships—personal and professional—are foundational to our well-being and contribute deeply to the fulfillment we gain from our achievements. Nurturing these connections requires effort, empathy, and clear communication. By investing in relationships, you build trust, create lasting bonds, and cultivate a network that enhances your personal and professional life.

Strong personal relationships offer emotional support, a sense of belonging, and stability. Whether with family, friends, or a partner, these connections provide a grounding foundation, offering encouragement in times of triumph and resilience in times of challenge. When you intentionally nurture these relationships, you not only build support for yourself but also ensure that your successes are shared and your difficulties are met with empathy and understanding.

In your professional life, cultivating relationships is equally essential. Building strong professional connections promotes collaboration, opens doors to new opportunities, and fuels growth. Trust and respect are cornerstones of a positive work environment, and when you invest in professional relationships, you develop a support network that amplifies both personal and collective achievements. By prioritizing both realms, you create a balanced support system that propels you toward resilience, growth, and a truly rewarding journey.

Effective Communication as a Relationship Tool

At the heart of any strong relationship lies communication. Whether personal or professional, clear and open communication creates understanding and ensures that all parties feel heard and valued. When you take the time to communicate effectively, you reduce misunderstandings, solve conflicts quickly, and build trust.

1. **Active Listening:** Communication is a two-way street. It's not just about what you say but also how well you listen. Active listening involves fully concentrating on what the other person is saying, understanding their message, and responding thoughtfully. This helps the other person feel respected and valued, fostering a stronger connection.

2. **Clarity and Transparency:** Whether discussing personal matters or professional goals, being clear and honest in your communication ensures that both parties are on the same page. When there is transparency in your conversations, trust grows, and mutual respect deepens.

3. **Constructive Feedback:** In both personal and professional settings, providing constructive feedback is key to growth. However, it's important to offer feedback in a way that encourages improvement rather than creating defensiveness. Balancing honesty with empathy ensures that your message is received in the spirit of growth and collaboration.

Empathy: The Foundation of Meaningful Relationships

Empathy—the ability to understand and share the feelings of another person—is a powerful tool in both personal and professional relationships. When you practice empathy, you demonstrate that you care not only about the outcome but about the person involved. It's a way of showing that you value the relationship beyond the transaction or immediate goal.

1. **Personal Relationships:** In personal settings, empathy helps you connect on a deeper level. By putting yourself in someone else's shoes, you can better understand their emotions and respond with care and compassion. Whether it's a

partner, friend, or family member, empathy strengthens the emotional bonds that make these relationships meaningful.

2. **Professional Relationships:** In professional environments, empathy builds trust and fosters collaboration. Understanding your colleagues' perspectives, especially during times of conflict or stress, helps you find common ground and work toward solutions. Empathy creates a more supportive and productive work environment where team members feel understood and valued.

The Long-Term Benefits of Nurturing Relationships

Investing in relationships yields long-term benefits. In personal life, these relationships become a source of joy, support, and personal growth. They offer balance and perspective, helping you stay grounded in the face of challenges. In professional life, strong relationships open doors to new opportunities, drive collaboration, and foster a positive work environment that leads to long-term success.

By nurturing your personal and professional connections, and leveraging effective communication and empathy, you create a network of support that enriches your life in countless ways. These relationships form the backbone of your success, ensuring that your journey is shared, supported, and celebrated by those around you.

Revisiting Time Management and Balance

Time management isn't just about checking off tasks—it's about building a life where you're in control of your time, energy, and priorities. Earlier in this book, we explored the techniques that help you do just that—prioritizing tasks, using tools like time blocking, and creating a balance between work, personal development, and leisure. These strategies are the foundation for sustained success, but they only work when applied consistently.

Take the story of a business owner I once worked with. At first, she prided herself on being a multitasker, constantly juggling emails, meetings, and projects. But over time, the stress of switching between tasks left her feeling exhausted and scattered. It wasn't until she implemented time blocking and set clearer boundaries that things started to shift. She began dedicating focused blocks of time to deep work, meetings, and personal activities—and suddenly, she found herself not only more productive but also more present and fulfilled. By intentionally managing her time, she created more space for what truly mattered—her business, her family, and herself.

Call to Action: Apply What You've Learned

As you reflect on the time management techniques we've covered, ask yourself: Are you using your time in ways that serve your long-term goals and well-being? If you haven't implemented these strategies yet, now is the time to start. Pick one approach, whether it's time blocking, task prioritization, or simply setting clearer boundaries, and experiment with how it impacts your daily life.

Think about the potential ripple effect—more focus at work can lead to less stress at home. More personal time can recharge your energy and creativity. The goal is to create a rhythm that supports your success without sacrificing the things that bring you joy.

Time as Your Greatest Asset

Ultimately, time is your most valuable asset. It's not about squeezing more tasks into your day—it's about creating a life where you're in control of your schedule, your energy, and your priorities. By applying the strategies we've discussed, you can build a life where work and personal fulfillment coexist, and success doesn't come at the cost of your well-being.

Take control of your time, and you take control of your life. The power lies in the small, intentional changes you make today.

Creating a Rhythm for Productivity

Productivity requires more than just pushing through a to-do list. You have to find the flow that works best for you. Everyone operates differently and creating a routine that maximizes your focus while allowing time to rest is key to long-term success. To build a sustainable rhythm, you need to manage distractions, take regular breaks, and set boundaries around your time and energy.

Managing Distractions and Setting Boundaries

One of the biggest obstacles to staying productive is the constant barrage of distractions. Whether it's emails, social media, or interruptions from colleagues or family members, these distractions break your focus and throw off your rhythm. To counter this, it's essential to create **distraction-free zones** during your most productive hours.

Start by identifying the times of day when you feel most focused and energized. These "power hours" are when you should be tackling your most important work. During this time, eliminate as many distractions as possible—turn off notifications, close unnecessary tabs, and let others know you're unavailable. Setting boundaries like this ensures that your most valuable time is protected.

Incorporating Time Blocks

Time blocking is a powerful tool for building rhythm. By setting specific periods of time for deep work, meetings, and personal tasks, you create a structure that keeps you moving forward without feeling overwhelmed. Each block of time should be treated as sacred—dedicated solely to the task at hand. This helps you stay focused and avoid the mental fatigue that comes from constantly switching gears.

For example, you might dedicate your mornings to high-focus tasks that require deep thinking. For me, that's very early in the morning before most people are out of bed and I start my meetings closer to the time the rest of the world is starting to circulate. Others might find that using afternoons for meetings, or collaborative work, is best for them. After that, set aside time for personal activities or downtime. By consistently following this structure, you create a natural flow to your day that helps you be more productive without burning out.

Taking Regular Breaks

No one can maintain focus indefinitely. To keep your energy and creativity high, it's important to take regular breaks. Short breaks throughout the day allow your brain to reset and help you stay sharp for longer periods of time. This can be as simple as stepping away for five minutes after an hour of focused work or going for a walk during lunch.

These breaks aren't just a luxury—they are essential for maintaining your rhythm. Over time, you'll find that regular breaks enhance your ability to stay on task when it matters most.

Finding Your Personal Rhythm

Everyone's ideal rhythm looks different, and it's up to you to discover what works best. Pay attention to when you feel most productive, when distractions hit hardest, and how you feel after taking breaks. One entrepreneur I worked with found her rhythm by experimenting with time blocks and breaks. Initially, she struggled with long stretches of work and constant distractions. But when she began structuring her day with focused morning work sessions and intentional breaks, her productivity soared. Mornings became her "power hours," and by setting boundaries around that time, she achieved more while creating space for family and relaxation.

Finding your rhythm is more about being in sync with your energy levels and needs. In doing so, work becomes more enjoyable, and you find more time for the things that bring you joy. This isn't a one-size-fits-all solution; it's a journey of self-discovery that will evolve as you grow.

Your Rhythm, Your Productivity

Ultimately, creating a rhythm for productivity is simply working smarter, not harder. By managing distractions, setting boundaries, and allowing space for breaks, you build a routine that helps you stay productive without sacrificing your well-being. Remember, your rhythm will evolve over time as you adapt to new challenges and priorities. Trust yourself to find what works and give yourself permission to adjust as needed. In doing so, you'll create not just a more productive life, but one that brings you fulfillment and balance.

Finding and Pursuing Passion

Passion is the driving force that makes life feel meaningful and fulfilling. When you're connected to what lights you up, everything feels more aligned, and the energy you put into your work and personal life becomes more purposeful. Finding your passion is one of the most powerful steps you can take to build a life that reflects who you truly are, and once you've identified it, the next challenge is to ensure it becomes a core part of your daily life and long-term goals.

Finding Your Passion

The journey to finding your passion starts with curiosity and self-reflection. It's not always obvious at first—sometimes it takes time to rediscover what excites you, especially if you've been caught up in the daily grind for a while. Ask yourself, what are the activities that energize you? What do you look forward to, lose track of time doing, or feel most fulfilled by?

For some, passion might be tied to a creative pursuit like writing, art, or music. For others, it could be a sense of purpose in helping others, solving complex problems, or even exploring new ideas. The key is to tune in to what makes you feel alive.

But finding your passion isn't just about a one-time discovery—it's about understanding that passions can evolve. What excited you five years ago might not be what excites you today. Your interests will grow and shift as you do, and that's something to embrace, not resist.

Aligning Your Passion with Daily Activities and Long-Term Goals

Once you've identified your passion, the next step is figuring out how to integrate it into your daily life. Your passion shouldn't be something you only visit on weekends or after work—it should become part of the way you live, guiding how you approach your time and energy each day.

Look at your current schedule. How much of your day is dedicated to things that excite you or align with your long-term goals? If the answer is "not enough," it's time to make adjustments. Aligning your passions with your daily activities doesn't always mean you need to overhaul your life overnight. Start by carving out small pockets of time for what excites you. Whether it's dedicating an hour each morning to a creative project, taking time to learn a new skill related to your passion, or finding ways to bring your passion into your existing work, the goal is to make it a consistent part of your routine.

For example, someone passionate about photography might find small ways to incorporate their love of capturing moments into their workday, perhaps by documenting company events or sharing their creative vision on social media. Over time, these small efforts grow, allowing them to align their passion with their long-term goals—such as turning photography into a business or a fulfilling side project.

Pursuing and Protecting Your Passion

Finding your passion is just the first step. The challenge lies in safeguarding it from the distractions and demands of everyday life. It's easy to let passions take a back seat when other priorities pile up, but protecting time for what fulfills you is crucial.

Setting Boundaries: Boundaries help protect your passion from getting lost in the shuffle. This means setting aside dedicated time and learning to say no to activities that don't align with your goals. Whether it's blocking off a few hours each week or creating non-negotiable "me time," these boundaries allow you to focus on what truly fuels you.

Avoiding Burnout: Passions should energize you, not exhaust you. It's important to balance your pursuit of passion with time to rest and recharge. By making sure your passion remains a source of joy rather than pressure, you create a sustainable rhythm that keeps you motivated.

Integrating Passion into Your Life: Rather than separating your passion from the rest of your life, find ways to weave it into your daily routine. Whether that means applying your passion for wellness to how you care for yourself or bringing creativity into your professional work, the more integrated your passion is, the easier it becomes to pursue it consistently.

Strategies for Protecting Time for Your Passion

In our busy lives, it's easy to let passions fall by the wayside. But passion is what fuels fulfillment, and without it, life can feel hollow, even if you're achieving other successes. Protecting time for your passion is really about **being intentional**. This means scheduling time for what excites you the same way you would schedule meetings or deadlines. Treat your passion as a priority—it's not "extra" or "optional."

One way to protect this time is by creating systems of accountability. Share your passion projects with someone who can help keep you on track or join a community of like-minded individuals who encourage each other to pursue their passions. We address this in mastermind groups. Sometimes, knowing that others are rooting for your success makes it easier to commit.

Another strategy is to **celebrate the small wins**. Each step you take toward pursuing your passion—whether it's setting aside an hour to practice or completing a project—is a victory. By recognizing these achievements, you reinforce the importance of your passion and stay motivated to continue integrating it into your life.

Living a Life Aligned with Your Passions

Ultimately, pursuing your passion is about living a life that feels aligned with how you really are. It's not just about what you accomplish—it's about creating a lifestyle that makes you excited to get out of bed in the morning. When you make space for your passions, you create a ripple effect of fulfillment that touches every part of your life.

So, take the time to find what fuels you. Build it into your daily life, protect it fiercely, and let it guide you toward a life filled with meaning, joy, and purpose.

Creating a Legacy

As we journey through life, one of the most meaningful goals we can pursue is the creation of a legacy—something that will endure long after we're gone. We're not just talking about your personal achievements; we more talking about the impact you leave on others, the values you live by, and the influence you have on the world. It's a reflection of who you are and the difference you make in the lives of others.

Defining Your Legacy

Defining your legacy starts with reflection. Imagine you're looking back on your life—what do you want to be remembered for? What contributions do you want to have made, and what values do you want to pass on? For one entrepreneur I know, his legacy isn't just about the successful business he built. It was about the mentorship he provided along the way. His ability to help others succeed became just as significant as his business achievements. That's what a legacy is: the long-term impact you create, both in your work and in the lives of those around you.

Your legacy might be tied to your relationships, the way you lift up your community, or the values you pass down to future generations. It doesn't have to be grand; sometimes the smallest, most consistent actions leave the deepest marks.

Consistency in Legacy Building

Building a legacy isn't a one-time achievement. It's a steady process that unfolds over the years, woven into your daily actions and decisions. Those occasional big gestures won't go far toward creating a lasting legacy. The things that move the needle are all of the small, purposeful actions you take every day that align with your values. THAT's where legacy is built!

Think about the habits and practices you engage in regularly. Are they contributing to the legacy you want to leave behind? One person might consistently show kindness in their interactions with others, creating a legacy of compassion. Another might mentor younger colleagues, building a legacy of guidance and support. These steady, thoughtful actions, taken over time, create a far-reaching impact.

Balance and Steady Actions

Creating a legacy is also about balance. It's not just about hard work or relentless pursuit—it's about harmonizing personal growth, relationships, and contributions. Balance ensures that you're nurturing every aspect of your life without burning out. Steady, balanced actions—showing up for your family, giving back to your community, and continuing to learn and grow—build a legacy that reflects a well-rounded, thoughtful approach to life.

For example, one might build a thriving business while also maintaining strong relationships with loved ones. Consistently showing up in both areas creates a legacy that reflects not just success, but balance, care, and intentionality.

Reflecting on Your Legacy

Take a moment to reflect on how your daily habits contribute to your long-term legacy. Are your actions today aligned with the impact you want to leave behind? What values do you consistently demonstrate in your work and relationships? By fostering a growth mindset and committing to steady progress, you can ensure your legacy reflects purpose, resilience, and meaning.

Call to Action: Building Your Legacy Every Day

Your legacy isn't something that happens in the distant future—it's something you build every day. Start by taking small, intentional steps toward creating the legacy you want. This might mean journaling about the values you want to live by or setting aside time to mentor others. Reflect on how your daily actions align with the person you want to become and make adjustments where needed.

As you move forward, remember that legacy is about more than success. It's about leaving behind something meaningful—something that continues to inspire and uplift others long after you're gone. Build your legacy with care, consistency, and a sense of purpose.

Encouragement for the Journey Ahead

As you stand on the edge of everything you've learned in this book, it's important to pause and reflect on just how far you've come. You've explored the idea of freedom—not just as a fleeting moment, but as a sustainable, lifelong pursuit. You've considered what it takes to maintain balance, to grow without burning out, to find your rhythm, pursue your passions, and build a lasting legacy. Every chapter has been another step in preparing you to take control of your life and make it your own.

The journey to sustaining freedom isn't a one-time event—it's a continuous process, one that evolves as you do. But remember, you have all the tools you need. You've already done the hardest part by committing to making changes, by recognizing the hamster wheel you were on and choosing a different path. Now, it's about staying the course, trusting yourself, and applying what you've learned, bit by bit.

It may not always be easy. There will be distractions, challenges, and moments when you'll feel tempted to revert to old habits. But remember, sustaining freedom is about consistency, balance, and the small, intentional steps you take each day. You have the power to create the life you want—a life where your time, energy, and passions are aligned with your goals.

Think back to the strategies we've discussed: finding your personal rhythm, managing distractions, prioritizing your passions, and building your legacy through steady, purposeful actions. These are more than just tactics—they are the foundation of a life that brings you fulfillment and purpose. Now is the time to put them into practice.

You've already made the decision to pursue freedom; now trust that you can sustain it. You have everything within you to create the life you want—one filled with balance, growth, and meaning. The journey ahead is yours to shape. Take it one step at a time, and watch how your consistent efforts transform your life, bringing you closer to the freedom you've been striving for.

This is your time. You've got this.

Reminder: Download Your Workbook

If you haven't already downloaded the accompanying workbook, now is the perfect time to do so. The workbook is designed to help you implement the strategies we've discussed in this chapter with practical exercises that will guide you step by step. Head over to and get started on the final exercises for this chapter. These exercises will help you solidify your legacy-building practices, align your passions with your daily life, and fine-tune your personal rhythm for long-term success.

Chapter Eleven
Embracing the Journey
Celebrating Small Wins

LET ME TELL YOU a story about someone we all know—maybe it's you, maybe it's a friend, or maybe it's someone you've worked with. This person had big dreams, ambitious goals, and a clear vision for their future. They poured themselves into their work, building something they were proud of, nurturing relationships, and striving for a life filled with purpose. But somewhere along the way, they began to feel stuck. The goals that once excited them now seemed distant, and the sense of accomplishment they craved felt out of reach.

Then something shifted. At first, it wasn't obvious what had changed—you might have simply noticed a new spark in their approach, a renewed energy they brought to their business. It seemed as if the weight they'd been carrying had lifted. What they likely realized was that they had been waiting for the "big win" to feel successful—the major milestones, the final goalposts. But what they hadn't been doing was recognizing the small wins along the way. When they started to celebrate those small victories—a new client, a finished project, even the smallest bit of progress—they felt a renewed sense of purpose. Their energy and focus returned. They were no longer overwhelmed by how far they had to go but empowered by how far they had already come.

This is what I want for you. I want you to realize that your journey is not just about the end goal. Every small win is a step forward, a marker of progress, and it deserves to be celebrated. These moments don't just boost your confidence—they sharpen your focus, increase your productivity, and remind you of why you're on this path in the first place. Celebrating small wins is more than just a feel-good moment; it's a strategy for staying motivated, productive, and in control of your journey.

Chapter Overview

In this final chapter, we're going to dive into the power of small wins and how recognizing your progress—no matter how small—will help you sustain the freedom and success you've worked so hard to build. It's easy to focus on the big goals, but real, lasting success is built on consistency and forward momentum. Every small win you acknowledge strengthens your motivation, reinforces your commitment, and makes it easier to keep going.

We've discussed finding your rhythm, nurturing your passions, and building your legacy. Now, we're bringing it all together by focusing on celebrating the journey itself. Celebrating small wins helps you stay balanced, prevents burnout, and keeps you aligned with your long-term goals. Keep in mind that reaching the destination may feel good but if you haven't embraced the journey, and learned to enjoy the process, you've missed the point of building a life you enjoy living.

As we wrap up this book, I encourage you to take a moment to reflect on how far you've come—both in this book and in your life. You have the tools, the mindset, and the ability to create the life you want. By consistently celebrating your small wins, you'll ensure that every step of your journey is fulfilling, productive, and aligned with your true purpose.

Now, it's time to take action. Start celebrating your wins—big or small—and watch how your journey transforms.

The Significance of Celebrating Small Wins: The Importance of Acknowledgement

Recognizing and celebrating small wins might seem like a small gesture, but it's one of the most powerful ways to sustain motivation and build long-term success. In a world that constantly pushes us to aim higher and do more, it's easy to focus only on the big milestones. But true success rarely happens through one grand achievement—it's a collection of many small victories along the way. These wins form the foundation of your progress, even when the destination still feels distant.

Acknowledging those small wins in the moment provides a necessary boost of confidence and encouragement. Every time you pause to recognize progress, you're reinforcing the idea that you're on the right track. It reminds you that success isn't built on one huge breakthrough, but on the daily, consistent efforts that move you forward. Over time, this practice becomes a habit—a habit that strengthens resilience, maintains a positive mindset, and keeps you energized for the long haul.

How Small Wins Tie Into Balance, Passion, and Legacy

Celebrating small wins does more than just offer a momentary lift; it has lasting effects that reach into the very core of what keeps us moving forward. In earlier chapters, we explored the themes of balance, passion, and legacy, and acknowledging small wins plays a key role in each of these areas.

When it comes to **balance**, celebrating small wins is essential to maintaining your equilibrium. In the pursuit of success, it's easy to get caught up in the constant push to achieve, which can lead to burnout. Recognizing those moments of progress allows you to pause and reflect on what you've accomplished. It's a reminder that balance isn't just about the time you allocate, but about appreciating the journey as much as the destination. By celebrating small wins, you create space to breathe and to enjoy the process, ensuring that you stay grounded and energized along the way.

Celebrating small wins also has a powerful connection to **passion**. Passion is not something that remains constant on its own—it requires nurturing and fuel. When you take the time to celebrate the smaller victories, you reignite that passion. These moments remind you why you started this journey in the first place, bringing you back to the core purpose behind your efforts. Every small win is like a spark, lighting the fire that propels you forward, and keeping your passion alive even during more challenging times.

Lastly, celebrating small wins is crucial for **building a legacy**. While it may not seem obvious in the moment, every small victory contributes to the larger picture of the impact you leave behind. Your legacy isn't built on one monumental achievement; it's made up of the daily wins, the incremental progress, and the challenges you've overcome. By honoring these small milestones, you are actively writing the story of your perseverance, your growth, and your commitment. Over time, these small wins build the foundation for the lasting impact you will leave behind.

Psychological and Emotional Benefits

Celebrating small wins isn't just a fleeting feel-good moment; it's an essential practice for supporting your mental and emotional well-being. In the grind of daily life, especially as an entrepreneur or busy professional, it's easy to get caught up in the stress of constant work and long-term goals. But when you pause to acknowledge your progress—however small—it acts as a reset button for your mind, giving you space to recharge, refocus, and regain your sense of purpose.

One of the key psychological benefits of celebrating small wins is the boost in **confidence** it provides. When you recognize the progress you've made, no matter how minor, it reinforces the belief that you're moving in the right direction. It affirms that your efforts are paying off, which builds momentum and keeps you motivated. Each small victory strengthens your belief in your ability to achieve larger goals. Over time, these moments of acknowledgment create a pattern of self-assurance, reminding you that you are capable of growth, even when the bigger milestones seem far off.

On an **emotional level**, celebrating small wins helps prevent burnout. Burnout often creeps in when we push ourselves too hard without pausing to reflect or appreciate the progress we've made. By taking a moment to celebrate, you allow yourself to experience joy and satisfaction, which fuels your emotional resilience. This emotional lift can be the difference between staying motivated and feeling overwhelmed.

In earlier chapters, we discussed the importance of maintaining **rhythm** and practicing **mindfulness** in daily life. Celebrating small wins aligns perfectly with these concepts. When you celebrate, you're consciously stepping out of the relentless pursuit of "what's next" and choosing to be present in the moment. It's a form of mindfulness that brings you back to the here and now, reminding you that the journey is just as important as the destination. Celebrating small wins also helps you maintain your personal rhythm, ensuring that your pace is sustainable and aligned with your long-term well-being.

In essence, celebrating small wins provides a mental reset and an emotional boost, keeping you confident, energized, and connected to your journey. These celebrations don't just mark progress; they nurture your emotional strength and prevent you from feeling drained or discouraged along the way.

Techniques for Recognizing Small Wins

Recognizing small wins requires intention, especially in the busyness of everyday life. We often focus so much on big goals that the smaller achievements pass by unnoticed. But it's these small victories that fuel our journey, providing bursts of motivation and moments of reflection. Learning to spot and celebrate them can shift your entire perspective on progress.

Identifying Accomplishments

Spotting small wins can be transformative. I remember working with an entrepreneur who was constantly chasing the next major milestone. They felt like they were always behind, always pushing toward a goal that seemed just out of reach. There was never time to pause and acknowledge what they had already accomplished. But when they started reflecting on their daily and weekly wins—whether it was onboarding a new client or simply completing a difficult task—their mindset changed. Each small celebration reignited their energy and confidence. They began to see that their progress wasn't stalled; it was happening in small, powerful steps.

This shift in perspective can work for anyone. Instead of waiting for the big win, take a moment to reflect on what you've accomplished today or this week. Did you complete a task that moved you closer to your goal? Did you make progress on a project or overcome a small challenge? These wins, no matter how minor they may seem, are the building blocks of long-term success.

To make it easier to celebrate these moments, set short-term, manageable goals. Breaking your larger objectives into smaller, actionable steps gives you more opportunities to celebrate progress. For example, if you're working on a complex project, create daily or weekly milestones. When you hit each one, take a moment to reflect on how far you've come. This practice creates a steady rhythm of progress, where each step forward is acknowledged and appreciated. By focusing on these smaller goals, you'll feel more motivated and less overwhelmed, and each win will fuel your drive for the next.

Role of Gratitude and Positive Reinforcement

Gratitude plays a powerful role in recognizing progress. In earlier chapters, we explored the importance of gratitude in shaping your mindset, and it's just as crucial here. When you pause to express gratitude for the small wins, you reinforce the idea that progress is being made, even when it's not immediately visible. Gratitude shifts your focus from what hasn't been done to what you've already achieved. It's a mindset that keeps you grounded in the present and allows you to appreciate the steps you've taken, rather than feeling anxious about the steps ahead.

Imagine you're working on a personal project that's been challenging. You may not be finished, but you've made significant headway. Instead of stressing over how much work remains, practicing gratitude helps you acknowledge the work you've already put in. This shift in perspective can boost your motivation and lighten the emotional load, reminding you to enjoy the journey as much as the outcome.

Positive reinforcement is another key to maintaining motivation and morale. When you celebrate a small win—whether with a simple moment of reflection, a reward, or sharing your success with others—you create a positive feedback loop. This reinforces the behaviors that led to the win, making it more likely that you'll continue moving forward. For instance, if you've set a goal to exercise more regularly, don't wait until you've hit your long-term fitness goal to celebrate. Each time you complete a workout or make a healthy choice, acknowledge it. These small rewards build momentum, making it easier to stay committed over time.

By incorporating gratitude and positive reinforcement into your routine, you'll find it easier to maintain your energy and focus. These practices help you stay connected to the progress you're making, no matter how incremental it may seem. Over time, celebrating small wins ensures that you remain motivated, resilient, and prepared to tackle larger challenges with confidence.

Stories of Celebrating the Journey

Learning to celebrate small wins transforms the journey into something more meaningful and fulfilling. For those who embrace this practice, the focus shifts from simply reaching a final goal to enjoying the daily progress that brings them closer to their vision. These stories highlight the power of small celebrations and how they lead to sustained motivation, balance, and success.

Real-Life Examples

John, a business owner, spent years solely focused on growing his company. His eyes were always set on the next big revenue milestone, and he often felt frustrated and exhausted when those goals seemed far away. As the pressure mounted, John realized that he was missing the opportunity to celebrate the progress he had made along the way. He decided to make a change, he began recognizing each new client, each successful project, and even the smaller wins, like when his team solved a tough problem. Something shifted. John's energy and enthusiasm returned, and his stress levels decreased. He no longer felt burdened by the long road ahead. By celebrating his daily wins, John found himself enjoying the process of building his business rather than constantly chasing an elusive future. His company began to grow steadily, and his renewed sense of joy became infectious, improving team morale and overall productivity.

What about you? How could celebrating small wins like John did help reduce stress and reignite your passion for the work you do?

Practical Exercises: Download Your Workbook

Before we dive into the practical exercises, I want to remind you—if you haven't already—now is the perfect time to download the workbook that accompanies this book. It's filled with exercises designed to help you apply everything we've discussed, including celebrating small wins and aligning your daily actions with your long-term goals. Head over to   to download it now and start putting these ideas into practice.

These exercises are your opportunity to take action, reflect, and celebrate your progress, so don't miss out. The journey of growth, freedom, and balance continues—let's make sure you're equipped to keep moving forward!

Enforcing and Maintaining the Habit

Celebrating small wins is not just a one-time action, it's a habit that needs to be reinforced consistently. Like any habit, the more you practice it, the more natural and beneficial it becomes. Consistency in celebration is what keeps the rhythm of progress alive, maintaining balance in both personal and professional life. It's easy to get caught up in the big picture, focusing only on the ultimate goal, but consistently celebrating small wins ensures that you remain grounded in the progress you're making every day.

Consistency in Celebration

We've already talked about how creating a rhythm for productivity is key to maintaining balance. Celebrating small wins is an integral part of that rhythm. By recognizing progress consistently, you keep yourself motivated, even during the inevitable ups and downs that come with any long-term pursuit. It's not just about the end result, it's about acknowledging that every step forward, no matter how small, is part of the larger journey.

Consistency in this celebration practice helps keep motivation alive. Think of those days when everything seems like a struggle when progress feels slow or nonexistent. It's in these moments that celebrating small wins becomes especially important. It gives you a reason to keep going, a reminder that you *are* moving forward. Consistent celebration shifts your focus from what remains undone to what you've already achieved, reinforcing a positive mindset and preventing burnout.

Consider a professional I once worked with named Greg, who was in the middle of a major career transition. For months, he felt like he was spinning his wheels, unsure if he was making any real progress. After all, his new business was still in its early stages, and success seemed a long way off. But when Greg began to consistently celebrate his small wins—completing a marketing plan, securing his first client, refining his services—he noticed a significant shift. He stopped feeling like he was treading water and started feeling energized by his progress. Each small win reminded him that success wasn't a distant goal but something he was actively building every day. Consistency in celebration kept Greg motivated, even when the big wins felt far away.

Handling Resistance

While celebrating small wins sounds simple enough, many people face resistance, both internally and externally. Internal resistance often stems from self-doubt or perfectionism—the belief that only big achievements are worth celebrating. This mindset can cause people to downplay their progress, leading to frustration and discouragement. On the other hand, external resistance might come from work cultures that prioritize constant productivity and major milestones, leaving little room for recognizing the smaller victories along the way.

Overcoming internal resistance requires a shift in mindset. Many individuals, especially high achievers, struggle to acknowledge small wins because they feel like they haven't done "enough" yet. But the truth is, small wins are the building blocks of larger success. Take the story of Emily, a perfectionist and project manager, who struggled to acknowledge her own progress. She would brush off small accomplishments, feeling like they didn't matter in the grand scheme of things. This led to chronic stress and burnout. It wasn't until she reframed her thinking—seeing each small win as part of her growth—that she began to feel more balanced and positive about her work. Emily learned that celebrating small wins didn't take away from her ambition; instead, it fueled her drive in a healthier, more sustainable way.

External resistance often arises in work environments that undervalue progress and prioritize only the big milestones. In these settings, it can be difficult to introduce the idea of celebrating small wins. However, small changes can make a big impact. If you work in a culture that's resistant to this practice, start by introducing it on a smaller scale. For instance, during team meetings, encourage colleagues to share small wins or milestones they've reached during the week. Over time, these moments of recognition can create a shift in the team's dynamic, fostering a more supportive and positive atmosphere.

Overcoming resistance—whether it's internal or external—takes time, but it's worth the effort. Consistently celebrating small wins doesn't just motivate individuals; it can transform entire teams and work cultures, creating environments where progress is valued and burnout is avoided.

Benefits of Embracing and Enjoying the Journey

When you make it a habit to celebrate small wins, the rewards go far beyond just feeling good in the moment. Over time, these celebrations have a profound impact on your mental health, motivation, and overall well-being. They create a sense of sustained progress, reminding you that success isn't just a destination, it's a journey filled with opportunities for fulfillment and growth every step of the way.

Long-Term Benefits

The long-term impact of celebrating small wins can be transformative. Over time, consistently acknowledging your progress strengthens a lasting cycle of positive reinforcement. Each small win provides a reminder that your efforts are adding up, even if the larger goals are still on the horizon. This steady recognition builds a reserve of energy and motivation that can help you push through the inevitable challenges along the way.

Celebrating these wins also nurtures mental resilience. When you shift your focus from what's left to accomplish to what you've already achieved, it helps ease feelings of stress and overwhelm. This mindful appreciation of progress has a calming effect, reducing anxiety and fostering a greater sense of control over your life and work. Bit by bit, this shift becomes a habit, reinforcing a more balanced perspective and strengthening your ability to stay grounded and motivated in the face of challenges.

Work-Life Balance and Fulfillment

Celebrating small wins doesn't just improve your mental health and motivation—it's also a critical tool for achieving **work-life balance**. By taking the time to celebrate your progress, you allow yourself to pause, reflect, and appreciate the balance between your personal and professional life. It's a moment of recognition that keeps you grounded in both worlds, preventing work from overshadowing personal growth and vice versa.

The practice of celebrating small wins ties directly into the themes of **passion** and **legacy**. When you celebrate progress in your work, you stay connected to your passion, reminding yourself why you started in the first place. This reignites your drive and enthusiasm. Celebrating personal achievements—whether in your relationships, health, or hobbies—helps you stay connected to the legacy you're building, the life you want to live beyond professional success.

If you're looking for practical ways to start celebrating small wins in your own life, try setting aside a few minutes each day to reflect on what you've achieved. Write it down, share it with a friend or colleague, or take a moment to appreciate it quietly. These celebrations will keep you motivated and balanced whether at work or home.

The long-term impact of embracing small wins is clear: they don't just lead to a more fulfilling professional journey; they also nurture personal growth and balance. By celebrating every step, you create a life that honors both work and well-being, ensuring that you experience success daily, not just at the finish line.

As we wrap up this chapter, it's important to remember the key takeaways about the power of celebrating small wins. We've explored how consistent recognition of your progress helps foster long-term freedom, balance, and fulfillment. Celebrating these smaller milestones isn't just about feeling good in the moment; it's about creating a sustainable rhythm of growth that will carry you through challenges and setbacks. It reinforces the idea that success is not just found in the big accomplishments but in the steady, daily progress you make toward your goals.

By acknowledging your small wins, you nurture motivation, boost your mental well-being, and maintain the balance necessary to avoid burnout. It's a simple yet powerful habit that can transform both your personal and professional life. Whether you're aiming to build a legacy, fuel your passions, or create a work-life balance, celebrating small wins is the key to keeping you grounded and connected to your journey.

Encouragement to Take Action

Now that you understand the importance of celebrating small wins, it's time to take action. Don't wait for the next big milestone to feel proud of your progress. Start today—reflect on the small victories you've achieved, no matter how insignificant they may seem. These wins are the foundation of your long-term success, and consistently acknowledging them will keep you motivated and fulfilled.

Make it a habit to celebrate every step forward, even the ones that feel small. The more you practice this, the more you'll find joy in the journey itself rather than just the destination. Whether it's taking five minutes to reflect on your day or sharing your success with a friend or colleague, start integrating these celebrations into your routine. The benefits will multiply over time, leading to a more balanced, fulfilling life.

The strategies you've learned in this chapter aren't meant to be left behind when you close the book. Use them as a guide, not just now but throughout your entire journey. Keep celebrating your wins and let those moments of recognition fuel your ongoing growth and success.

Chapter Twelve
About the Author

Roger Best is a seasoned entrepreneur who's navigated the wild ride of building multiple successful businesses. With years of battle scars and triumphs, he knows firsthand the relentless grind of entrepreneurship—those long hours, high-stakes decisions, and the relentless chase for success that can sometimes steal the joy out of life.

But Roger isn't just a survivor; he's a thriver. After his own transformation from a business owner burning the candle at both ends to a man who's mastered the balance of work and play, he's on a mission to help others break free from the chains of the endless hustle. In this book, he lays out practical, no-nonsense strategies to reclaim your time, achieve financial freedom, and craft a life packed with purpose, adventure, and a healthy dose of leisure.

When Roger's not in the trenches with one of his ventures, writing, or mentoring fellow entrepreneurs, you'll find him living life on his terms—spending quality time with family and friends, exploring new terrain, or just kicking back and enjoying the satisfaction that comes from running a successful business that doesn't dominate every moment.

Roger's been married to his soulmate for just over 45 years, a proud dad to two grown kids, and a devoted grandfather to two little princesses. In 2021, he and his wife decided to turn their island dream into reality, moving to Puerto Rico, where they now run their businesses while soaking up the hammock life.

Roger's mission is straightforward: to inspire and empower entrepreneurs to build thriving businesses without sacrificing their happiness, health, or freedom.